GANGLAND
BOSSES

Also by James Morton

GANGLAND
GANGLAND Volume II
GANGLAND INTERNATIONAL
MAD FRANK (co-author with Frankie Fraser)
MAD FRANK AND FRIENDS (co-author with Frankie Fraser)
A CALENDAR OF KILLING
NIPPER (co-author with Leonard Read)
BENT COPPERS
SUPERGRASSES AND INFORMERS
THE BARMAID'S TALE
SEX, CRIMES AND MISDEMEANOURS
EAST END GANGLAND
GANGLAND TODAY
FIGHTERS

GANGLAND BOSSES

The Lives of Jack Spot and Billy Hill

James Morton
and Gerry Parker

A *Time Warner* Book

First published in Great Britain in 2004
by Time Warner Book Group

Copyright © Gerry Parker and James Morton 2004

The moral right of the author has been asserted.

A CIP catalogue record for this book
is available from the British Library.

ISBN 0 316 85991 5

Typeset by Palimpsest Book Production Ltd,
Polmont, Stirlingshire
Printed and bound in Great Britain by
Mackays of Chatham plc, Chatham, Kent

Time Warner Book Group UK
Brettenham House
Lancaster Place
London
WC2E 7EN

www.twbg.co.uk

Contents

Introduction   1

1.   Young Jack Spot   5
2.   Young Billy Hill   12
3.   The Sabinis   20
4.   The Battle That Never Was   54
5.   The Fortunes of War   68
6.   Whitewash   87
7.   Hill and Spot Triumphant   96
8.   The Airport Disaster   108
9.   On the Up   118
10. Sliding   130
11. Smuggling   137
12. Hill's Angels   155
13. The Fight That Never Was   164
14. Perjury and the Vicar   187
15. The Slashing That Was   203
16. The Slashing That Never Was   221
17. The End of a Barrister   244
18. Aftermath   258
19. Graveyards   273

Bibliography   293
Index   297

Introduction

Towards lunchtime on the morning of 11 August 1954, at a time when there were plenty of shoppers and passers-by, a thick-set dark man fought with a taller, slimmer, fairer one on the corner of Frith Street and Old Compton Street, Soho. At least one had a knife and the fight rolled into a greengrocery where the proprietor's wife hit the men – or at least pushed them apart – with a set of brass scales. The men split away from each other and staggered into the street. One was collected by a friend and whisked away. The second managed to get himself to a barber's shop – ironically frequented by the other man – and collapsed. Both were taken to separate hospitals and for a time it was thought that at least one might die. However, within a matter of days each discharged himself and both were arrested and charged with causing grievous bodily harm and affray. For a variety of reasons the incident came to be known as 'The Fight That Never Was'.

One of the non-combatants was Albert Dimeo or Dimes or Italian Albert, a leading member of the Italian faction which had at one time controlled the allocation of bookmakers' pitches on racecourses and at the point-to-points, and whose members wanted to do so again.

He had been involved in one celebrated murder trial already which had resulted in the hanging of his friend, Babe Mancini, and was widely regarded as having killed another man, Chick Lawrence, an East End hardman, shortly before the war. The other non-combatant was John Comer, or John or Jacob Colmore, or Comacho, known throughout the Underworld as Jack Spot either because when wanted he was always on the spot, or more prosaically and more likely because he had a prominent mole on his face. He was the man from whom the Italians wished to wrest control of the racecourse pitches.

The fight was a crucial turning point in the career of Spot, that of his one-time friend Billy Hill and, indeed, in the battle for control of London's Underworld. In fact it could be said to be the catalyst which changed things permanently and led to the inexorable rise of the Kray Twins.

This is Jack Spot's story of the rise and fall of a man who regarded himself as the King of the Underworld and paid the penalty for his presumption. It is also the story of Billy Hill who, probably rightly, regarded himself as Boss of Britain's Underworld. It is the tale of the racecourse wars, illegal gaming and drinking clubs, protection rackets, robberies, prostitution, GBH, arrogance, pride, loyalty, betrayal and all the other things which, as was said in the musical *Irma La Douce*, go to make life in the Underworld so worthwhile.

We are talking about events which occurred up to eighty years ago in an industry in which truthfulness never gained full marks. As a result, many of the stories in the book cannot be substantiated. They have been honed by constant repetition and elaboration. In particular, many of Spot's tales of his prowess can now be proved to be demonstrably false. Over the years, for self-preservation or to defeat the libel laws, names and places were changed; memories genuinely faded; old scores were settled. Now, as the years have passed, there is for example no one left who can remember Tiger Lil (said to be one of Spot's girl-friends) who plays a prominent part in his memoirs – if indeed she ever existed outside *Peter Pan*. I have tried, wherever possible, to document those incidents which can be dated.

Those who think that the current interest in criminals is anything new should look back through the old papers of the 1950s and see just how much newsprint was devoted to Billy Hill and Jack Spot, the acknowledged London gangleaders of that era. They were also known outside the pages of the Sunday papers. Warming up the middle-class audience for the 1955 Royal Variety Performance, the comedian Tommy Trinder guyed Spot. As befitted Hill's superior status, he was teased in the film *Carlton Browne of the F.O.*. In the scene where Ian Bannen as the king of a Ruritanian country takes a girl to a nightclub, he is not wearing a black tie. The manager wants him thrown out but the waiter points out that he is Royalty. 'I don't care if he's Billy Hill,' replies the manager. 'Don't take a cheque.'[1] Even after his heyday, Spot in particular remained a household name to be used as a yardstick by which acceptable conduct was measured. It was reported, for example, that Meston Batchelor, a headmaster seeking to sell his prep school, said he would prefer to hand it over to Jack Spot rather than some of the applicants.[2]

Over the years there have been a number of accounts of the lives of both Hill and Spot. With the help of the reporter Duncan Webb and the pulp writer Hank Janson respectively, each published more or less self-serving memoirs. In both cases pseudonyms were used for the supporting casts. Subsequent accounts of their careers, particularly that of Spot, have relied on his version as gospel. For far too long there has been a tendency, in the words of *The Man Who Shot Liberty Valance*, to print the legend. It is time to print something much nearer the truth. I have also tried to unravel the identities of those who were given names such as Timber George and Teddy Odd Legs.

My thanks are particularly due to Gerry Parker, who suggested that I should write the story of Jack Spot. Parker came from the same part of the East End as Spot and boxed professionally after the war in which, unlike some of the other characters in the book, he served with some

---

[1] The previous year the journalist Claude Cockburn had written a three-page satirical article about him, 'Du Côté de Chez Hill', in *Punch*, 6 October 1954.
[2] *The Times*, 4 December 1982.

distinction. He met Spot at Jack Solomons' gymnasium in Great Windmill Street near Piccadilly Circus, and worked for him in clubs and at racecourses for some years. Many of the stories of Spot come from him. In strictly alphabetical order my thanks also go to the late Mickey Bailey, Dock Bateson, J.P. Bean, Barbara Daniels, Ronnie Diamond, Frank Fraser, Albert Hattersley, Jean Maund, 'Nipper' Read and John Rigbey, as well as the staff of the National Archives, the British Library, the British Newspaper Library at Colindale and those in the local history section of the Tower Hamlets Library at Bancroft Road.

1

Young Jack Spot

Myrdle Street, Whitechapel, was never the best address in the East End and times were hard for the immigrant Jewish and Irish communities in the early days of the twentieth century. 'It was dirt poor. You didn't earn enough to pay the six shillings a week rent.'[1] It was however Myrdle Street and its neighbours which were the homes of a number of people who over the years made reputations in their own fields; the boxers Ted 'Kid' Lewis and Jack 'Kid' Berg, the impresarios Lew and Leslie Grade and Nat Cohen, the film producer, were some. John Comer, born Jacob Comacho on 12 April 1913, was another.

His parents, Alexander and Rifka, were Polish Jews who had met and married in the East End. Comer was the youngest of four children; there were two older brothers called Piza and Irving and a sister, Rebecca. Spot went to Myrdle Street School where, 'I was called Spotty because I had a big black mole on my left cheek. I'd resented the nickname at first, but at eight years of age you don't resent anything too long.' At other times he would say he had his nickname because of his ability to be on the spot when wanted.[2]

[1] Gerry Parker in conversation with the author.
[2] Hank Janson, *Man of A Thousand Cuts*, pp. 27–8.

In his fictionalised memoirs Spot, without giving his age, says that his first two successful ventures into theft were with friends. One, Moishe Goldstein, was known as Moishe Blueball because of the colour of one of his testicles. In what passed as polite society, however, he was known as Blueboy. Spot names him as Smokey, because of the boy's habit of picking up cigarette ends and taking the remaining tobacco. His other friend, Bernard Schack, he calls Codger.[3] He dresses up the thefts as acts of a Robin Hood, claiming that Codger's sister was very ill and only chicken would mend her, something her parents could not afford. Spot and his friends stole lead from the local scrap dealer and sold it back to him for half a crown. The girl got her chicken and the boys did it again, this time receiving two shillings. Although the weight was exactly the same, they did not dare point this out to the scrap dealer. On the third expedition Codger, whose father was in prison, was caught and sent to an approved school. Spot says that he and Smokey dared not leave their home for several days but Codger remained staunch. It is impossible to say whether the story is true. What is certainly correct is that it was quite possible for a boy on a first offence to be sent away from home.

At the age of fourteen Spot joined with his father and his brother Irving in a tailoring business supplying garments for C. & A., earning fifteen shillings a week. He did not last long. His job was to take the clothes from the factory in New Road to the company's premises at Marble Arch but, so he would say, he watched an overseer humiliate his father and as a result he hit him. Either that or the bullying overseer threw a bundle of jackets at Spot who promptly hit him. His next job was with Piza in a barber's shop where at least he learned how to handle a razor. But he had ideas above his lowly station and in later years would boast how he had stuffed the lather brush in the mouth of a customer whom he considered to be obnoxious and then walked out.

[3] Hank Janson, *Man of A Thousand Cuts*, pp. 27–33.

From there, he told Parker, it was a short spell in the Merchant Navy. He and another friend, Nathaniel 'Itchky' Simmons, signed on to the Lambert and Holt liner the *Duquesa*, bound for Montevideo, where they landed eight weeks later. According to Spot they went into a bar where they were met by a scowling woman with a revolver. A Polish Jewess herself, she heard them whispering in Yiddish and invited them to stay at her home for as long as they wished. Unfortunately they were due back on ship in two days, and eight weeks later they were back in England. Spot would reminisce about his traditional Jewish mother's traditional Jewish repartee when she said on his return:

'I'm glad you've come back safe, Jack. What've you brought?'
'I bought a tie.'
'Sixteen weeks and he comes back with a tie he could have bought down the road.'

Jokingly, he would maintain that she claimed he needed hospital treatment. For his part he was quite happy to be considered something of what, in those politically incorrect days, was known as a loony. He would hang around the Premiere Boxing arena in Bethchurch Street, the Reform Club in Bow – which was a haunt of the young tearaways – and the Rowton House in Fieldgate Street. A local café was run by Mr Silver, another Polish Jew, and it was here that Spot met some of the other men with whom he would be associated for the next thirty years. The core members of what could be described as a fledgling gang were his cousin Solly Kankus – also known, because of his complexion, as Solly the Turk – Morris Goldstein, Bernard Schack, 'Sonny the Yank' who now carried a sword-stick and looked like Glenn Miller, and Hymie Rosen, 'Little Hymie'. Perhaps Rosen, regarded as a great fighter both in the ring where he fought as Kid Rosen, and outside, tends to be underestimated and is usually only referred to in an oblique way. Mickey Bailey, the East End hardman who died in 2003, when speaking of Bill Ackerman, thought of that Kray henchman, 'He was a man with a fucking big mouth. He couldn't have licked Spotty's boots nor those of Hymie Rosen, the one we called Hymie the Yid.' Over the years others, the cream of London's East End villains, came and went, but until Spot's final fall these men stuck with him.

It was at Silver's that a curious incident occurred, and it was one which would show Spot the bright lights beyond the East End. A pale, thin boy came into the café and begged for money. He had, he said, walked from Leicester. Solly Kankus was the only one with money and he gave the youth a few shillings. He was also given tea and rolls and sent on his way.

A week or so later a Daimler drew up at the café and a liveried chauffeur asked for Mr Solly the Turk. Kankus and Spot left the room to see what this was about and in the back of the car was the youth, now for a brief period a high-paid rent boy, who had come to take the men into the West End as a thank you for their kindness. The boy's protector paid out for suits and camelhair coats, and Spot and Kankus were taken to a series of clubs. The story does not seem to have had a particularly happy end, for the boy fell out with his lover and was soon back on the streets. However, in later years Spot would say how much of an eye-opener the event had been.

For a time Spot worked with an older boy he names as Jumbo who ran a protection racket in Petticoat Lane. Spot claims he did not know exactly what was happening and when he found out he challenged and beat Jumbo in a drawn-out fist fight. 'I was King of Aldgate at 16.' Fighting, thought Spot, 'was better than a good dinner'.[4]

Spot did not acquire his first conviction until at the age of nineteen on 1 February 1933 he was bound over in the sum of 40 shillings for loitering with intent to steal from motor cars. It was the first of a bare handful of court appearances; if he was ever an active thief, he led a charmed life. His infrequent appearances in court also led to the taunt that he was not a proper thief. 'He had never tasted porridge,' was the derisory comment.

[4] *Sunday Chronicle*, 16 January 1955.

It was in Silver's café that he met a burglar, Frank Henry 'Taffy' Osmond, who employed him as part minder and part lookout. Between them they carried out a number of successful burglaries until two years after Spot's first conviction. Their partnership ended when, at the beginning of March 1935, Osmond was arrested following a break in at the house of Sol Birnhak in Coverdale Road, Brondesbury; they had broken a ground-floor lavatory window. The value of the silverware and other property taken was £200. Two days later Spot followed Osmond into custody. A fingerprint belonging to Osmond was found, and it seems clear that he gave up Spot who somewhat stupidly had himself left a wet suit and overcoat behind. Their statements to the police were shown to each other and Spot said, 'I cannot help what he says. I am only going to admit one.' Osmond replied, 'All bunk. He helped me to get in.'[5]

It was now that according to Wensley Clarkson Spot met a young woman from the East End. She became pregnant and they married, moving into a flat in Aldgate. There was a son, John. Neither marriage nor fatherhood seem to have converted him to domesticity at this stage of his life. Nor is the marriage recorded at the Family Records Centre under any of his usual names.

On 4 April 1935 (under the name Comor) he was placed on probation for two years, this time at Middlesex Sessions, and bound over in the sum of £10 for the same period. He had been in custody since his arrest over the Willesden burglary. Osmond, who had previously had a three-year spell in Borstal, received two years with hard labour. That was Spot's last conviction for dishonesty until he was well past his prime. From now on it was protection more or less all the way.

For the moment, he turned to bookmaking and the racecourses. In his memoirs Billy Hill, who calls Spot 'Benny the Kid', wrote:

As a boy he began to work for various bookmakers. He organised street pitches for them. He worked hard and got on well in

[5] *Willesden Chronicle*, 22 March 1935.

the business. Then he was given the job of running a club in the East End on behalf of a wealthy bookmaker named Moshe Cohen. Moshe was a powerful man. His name is not known to the public. He is not a tearaway or a thief or anything like that there. He's just a shrewd business-man who's made a stack, and has kept it. And now he's got a stack he can do with money what money always does. Buy services. Cohen can buy the services of most things, and men. He bought Benny the Kid. He paid him a couple of centuries a week to look after his bookmaking interests and run speilers (sic).[6]

Maurice or Mo(i)she Cohen was one of a number of brothers – Harry, Frank and Jackie were the others – who lived in Brighton and worked as bookmakers on the South Coast. Moishe traded as Major Collins. 'People thought he was a real Major until he let out a few fucks,' recalls Gerry Parker, who was Collins' nephew by marriage. Cohen later also had a betting office in Percy Street in Soho.

For a time Spot also ran a typical fairground scam called 'Take a Pick' at the major race meetings. The mug punters paid 6d to pull a straw with a winning number from a cup. If they were extremely fortunate they won a cheap prize, while Spot cleared between £30 and £40 a day. Later the enterprise was extended to Petticoat Lane where 'Take a Pick' earned him another £50 a morning. He was also an active bookmaker on the free courses. On a bad day he welshed, leaving before paying out on the last race; he was lucky not to have been caught. Welshing was a considerable problem in the 1930s and Tom Divall, the police officer turned racecourse inspector, presented a case to Chartres Biron, the magistrate, arguing that a bookmaker with insufficient money to pay out could be charged under the Vagrancy Act with being a suspected person loitering with

[6] Billy Hill, *Boss of Britain's Underworld*, p. 7. Hill may have been constrained by the libel laws in his assessment of Cohen's honesty. Frank Fraser says that Cohen worked with Charlie Barwick, whose real name was Hyman Romatsky. Together they took an amount of good stolen jewellery to a receiver. He threw some on the fire saying it was rubbish, paid a pittance for the remainder and took the pieces from the grate as soon as they had gone. Frank Fraser, *Mad Frank and Friends*, p. 36. Barwick is also mentioned as a good office thief recruited by the old-time villain Arthur Harding to fight the Sabinis at Brighton racecourse in around 1925. Raphael Samuel, *East End Underworld*, p. 184.

intent to commit a felony. Biron had accepted the argument and sentenced the men to terms of imprisonment with hard labour.[7]

At the time, in both social and criminal terms, the East End was divided into small areas possibly consisting only of a few streets controlled by one team or one family. One of the most powerful of the teams was the long-standing, mainly Irish, Watney Streeters, originally a fighting gang which had been in existence since the docks were built in the nineteenth century.

Mickey Bailey, whose family had long been members of the Watney Streeters, remembered:

> In those pre-war days the Streeters did a lot of work with the Jews in Aldgate and they did for many years probably until Jack Spot started to look after his own. There were lots of clubs in that area run by the Jews, gambling clubs, drinkers, brothels. There were places for paedophiles. The police weren't really interested. It was all so wide open that the police didn't take any notice. The Irish protected them. Then they'd get in disputes with the Sabinis who were the Italian mob from Clerkenwell.[8]

Now Spot was moving upwards.

[7] Tom Divall, *Scoundrels and Scallywags*, pp. 186–7. At Brighton races in 1931 James Button ran away after the 3.15 race and as a result received two months hard labour. Thomas Foster and Joseph Fisher, both from Hoxton, received three months hard labour after being convicted of obstructing the police and frequenting a racecourse with intent to commit a felony. They had torn up winning tickets proffered to Button by punters. *The Times*, 12 August 1931. Systematic welshing continued to be a problem until well after the Second World War. In 1948 there were between fifty and sixty cases at Epsom alone. By 1955 it had been stamped out almost completely, something for which the now seemingly respectable Spot took a deal of credit. *Sunday Chronicle*, 17 July 1955.
[8] Conversation with the author.

2

Young Billy Hill

Billy Hill – in turn Spot's friend, partner, rival and nemesis – was born in 1911 in Seven Dials, near Leicester Square, then one of the rougher parts of the West End. John Capstick, who later became a Detective Chief Superintendent and was said rather romantically to have placed a red rose on the grave of the early gangleader Darby Sabini, joined the police in 1925. After his training he was posted to Bow Street and on his second night allowed to go out on the beat alone. He was patrolling Monmouth Street when he was lured to the now very fashionable Neal's Yard where he was given a good beating and kicking by the locals. When he limped back to the station he did not receive much sympathy. The station sergeant, on being told where the incident had happened, nodded, saying, 'I thought so. That's where they break all you young coppers in.'[1]

Hill's childhood could not have been more different from that of Spot, who was brought up dirt poor in a respectable Jewish family. Hill wanted for little. One of some 21 children, his family had a fine criminal pedigree. His mother was a receiver and, of his sisters

---

[1] Edward T. Hart, *Britain's Godfather*, p. 214. John Capstick, *Given in Evidence*, p. 37; he does not deign to mention Sabini in his memoirs.

and brothers who were thieves, the star turn was Maggie – one of the best shoplifters of her generation and known as 'Baby Face, the Queen of the Forty Elephants'. She took the name partly from the shape she assumed by the time she had packed her bloomers and coats with stolen merchandise, and partly from the Forty Thieves team of shoplifters of which she was at one time the leader. She married the celebrated Birmingham thief and general villain Reuben 'Brummy' Sparkes.[2] Capstick described her as:

> . . . the life and soul of their parties . . . She was one of the slickest thieves I ever tried to follow. Utterly fearless, she knew every trick in the book and she could put away three fur coats and a bolt of cloth in the time it took any of her team-mates to snitch a pair of cami-knickers. A stout, handsome woman, she liked to work with a slim young woman not much more than half her age, and a highly efficient pair they were. I hate to think how much money they made on their regular trips to the Midlands.[3]

The Forty Thieves was a long-standing gang of mainly women shoplifters who had been in operation since at least the turn of the century. The great thief James Lockett, who was born in the same area as Hill, was said to have been one of the few male members. On his release from a four-year sentence imposed in 1898 in America he had returned to England and was an original member of the Forty Thieves, owing allegiance to a woman known as 'The Swan-Necked Beauty' or 'The Queen of the Forties' – of which over the years there were a number.[4] In general,

---

[2] In later years Sparkes took to behaving badly towards Maggie Hill. As a result he was badly beaten in Shaftesbury Avenue and disappeared into comparative obscurity.
[3] John Capstick, *Given in Evidence*, Ch. 9.
[4] Given the arrest rate it is not surprising that there were a number of Queens. One, Helen Sheen, was arrested at Kensal Green Cemetery for a theft of jewellery worth around £100. On the arrival of the officers she sank to the ground and when challenged replied, 'How dare you come and arrest me when I am praying over my dear father's grave.' It was pointed out that the grave was that of a woman. The court adjourned sentence to give her the opportunity to disclose where the jewels had gone, but she declined. Sentenced to 18 months she said to the judge, 'That won't break my heart, old tallow face. Good-bye, dearie.' *Morning Leader*, 19 May 1906. For an account of the hierarchy of the gang and its workings see John Capstick, *Given in Evidence*, Ch. 9.

however, men played a subservient role, being used as decoys and chauffeurs.

Membership of the Forty Thieves was highly prized and carefully controlled. If not a case of waiting for dead women's shoes, it was very much a case of 'once in, never out' until retirement. Defection was punishable.

At the time when Hill was growing up the undoubted leader was Alice Diamond, a regular visitor to the Hill household. Another visitor was the celebrated Eddie Guerin who, at the turn of the century, had organised a number of highly successful bank robberies on the Continent, but was now very much on the slide and working as an hotel thief. There was no question of Hill lacking sailor suits; they were simply stolen for him. As he says, it is easy to understand how he did not aspire to Holy Orders. He claims to have cut a man at the age of 14, stabbing him in the back with a pair of scissors. If the story is true, there seem to have been no reprisals. Shortly afterwards he was arrested for the first time. He claims he was sent to an approved school for five years after having been caught burgling a tobacconist's kiosk in Regent's Park. On appeal the sentence was reduced to one of two years' probation. There was also a condition of residence and he went to live with one of his sisters. His record shows that in fact he had received one day's imprisonment on 15 May 1928, in the name John Cow.

By the time he was 16 he was a fully-fledged burglar working with his sister, Dolly. Hill worked for a greengrocer and, in their innocence, customers would tell him not to deliver their orders until such and such a time because they would be out. Dolly had a telephone, and he would be on the blower to her so that she and her husband could burgle the place safely. He was also carrying out burglaries on his own.

The early part of his career came to an end in 1927 when he and a man he names as Albert Smart were robbing a flat in Golders Green. Smart used the lavatory and then foolishly pulled the chain. The noise was heard; a neighbour telephoned the police and the pair were arrested a few streets away. On 5 January 1929, as Herbert Williams, it was off from Inner London Sessions to Borstal for three years.[5] In his memoirs compiled with the considerable help of his Boswell, the journalist Duncan Webb, Hill wrote of life in the Portland Borstal, which was set on a headland on Chiswell Beach, near Weymouth:

> We had to carry loads of stones in baskets on our backs up a quarry face nearly ninety degrees steep. Every night our backs were washed down with iodine to prevent infection from the cuts, abrasions, sores and scabs. We were harnessed to trucks like horses and we had to pull these trucks along like beasts of burden.

Then there was the crushing of the stones and bones. The youth had to fill a bucket full of powder in his morning shift and a second in the afternoon:

> At first when they gave me bone to pound I would have been sick had there been anything in my stomach to be sick on. The stench of the decaying bones was vile. Then I got used to that because once or twice when I was sick and when I did spew I hurt my stomach. I was sick all over myself.[6]

The stone pounding came after his attempted escape with a boy named Lawrence Edward Harding on 18 September 1929. It was hopeless from the start; because of the geographical location at the end of a spit, successful escapes from Portland were rare. They were dressed in the regulation grey shorts and shirts, a certain giveaway if they were seen. They had to find some clothes and about three in the afternoon broke into the house of a Commander Basil Bowen

---

[5] The ex-Detective Superintendent Fred Narborough claims that it was he who secured Hill his first prison sentence as such. Narborough and two companions were working in St Pancras Way near King's Cross when they saw three men approach a Sunbeam motor car and arrested them. Apparently none of the arresting officers knew where the nearest police station was and Hill directed them. He received three months as a suspected person. Fred Narborough, *Murder On My Mind*, p. 38.
[6] Billy Hill, *Boss of Britain's Underworld*, pp. 21–3.

which they were ransacking when they were heard by his maid Valetta Mary Matthews. She poked her head into the kitchen where Hill was hiding behind the door and he hit her with a pastry-covered rolling pin, cutting her head and stunning her. In his memoirs Hill says that the pair, alarmed at what he had done, then tried to revive her and waited for the police. The prosecution's version was not so heroic. They stole a mackintosh and were trying to find other clothes when she managed to escape from them to an upper room and called Bowen who was doing some gardening. Bowen caught hold of Hill with no difficulty and called to Valetta Matthews to get some help. She ran into the street and a passer-by caught Harding.

Harding, who was now over 21, and who had already received twelve strokes of the birch for stealing money from his father, received twelve months hard labour on top of his sentence and twelve strokes of the cat to go with it. Hill had a more modest nine months along with twelve strokes of the birch. In general prisoners favoured the cat, which was applied to the shoulders rather than the buttocks and was thought to be less humiliating than the birch. 'I am going to stop this sort of thing and stop it with an iron hand,' said Mr Justice Charles. 'I trust this will be a lesson to rascals of your sort that they cannot commit crimes without being dealt hardly with.'[7]

According to Hill:

> They sent a special birch down from the Home Office as they always do and soaked it in brine to make it more pliable. The birch is a bunch of twigs about three and a half feet long. Into them is inserted a handle also about three and a half feet long, making the whole contraption about seven feet in length overall. I was taken into the prison yard and handcuffed by my wrists, which were crossed, at the top of the triangle. My ankles were outstretched at the base and handcuffed at each corner separately.

[7] *Dorset County Chronicle and Somerset Gazette*, 24 October 1929.

I was not allowed to see the screw who birched me, though we always knew who it was. They gave me the strokes on my bare backside and afterwards dressed the bleeding wounds with a medicated pad, and sent me back to hard labour.[8]

Other former inmates tell similar stories of the Portland Borstal. Things had not changed much by the time Hill's protégé, Frank Fraser, was sent there in 1942:

In punishment we did stone pounding, out in the open and too bad if it was raining. The screws sat under a canopy and watched us. Two-and-a-half hours in the morning and another three in the afternoon. When you finished the screws would give you a little shovel and they'd watch while you put all the stuff you'd pounded into a sieve and shook it into a box. If you hadn't filled it up, then you was reckoned to be slacking and you did a bit more time on punishment to teach you.[9]

On Hill's release it was his sister Maggie who helped him. She herself was serving another sentence in Holloway, but she had left some money for him and with it he bought some first-class burglar's tools. However, Hill did not last long on the outside; having completed two successful burglaries, on the seventh day he was found in Maida Vale and charged with being a suspected person. On 19 September 1931 he received 21 days imprisonment at Marylebone Police Court, just long enough for the authorities to revoke his Borstal licence on 23 September, and he was back to Portland. He had only a short time to serve and, by his account, he already had the nucleus of a team around him which loosely formed the Camden Town Gang. He names some of them as Odd Legs, Button and Square Georgie. Now it is almost impossible to give all of them their correct names, but Odd Legs was Teddy Hughes, sometimes known as Teddy Odd Legs because of his limp, the result of a motorcar accident. Square Georgie was George Ball. As was often the case, Borstal had in no

[8] Billy Hill, *Boss of Britain's Underworld*, pp. 21–2.
[9] Frank Fraser, *Mad Frank's Britain*, p. 65.

way improved the inmate's conduct and on 14 February 1932 at Clerkenwell Police Court Hill received three months for loitering with intent.

Just as Spot would write that he was the first person to realise the necessity of every man in a team fitting in and doing his own job, so Hill claimed he had been the first to do so some dozen years earlier: 'I was fond of timing jobs to the second, dwelling upon and figuring out all the details beforehand, and planning it to a schedule.'

In contrast to Spot, Hill was a good paymaster. Importantly, he did not then take more than his share of a job: 'If we were five-handed on a job I split the wages five ways. I did not take two shares for myself and divide the remainder between the other four.'[10]

By 1933 Hill was taking £70 a week, something he thought was good money – which indeed it was. That was when he came a cropper while burgling a doctor's house in Bromley. He was disturbed, and in his escape as he ran down the railway track he stumbled and fell, badly burning himself. This time, on 11 January 1934, it was three years penal servitude from West Kent Quarter Sessions.

It was on his release that Hill took lessons in smash-and-grab from the great thief Charlie 'Ruby' Sparks, so known because after stealing rubies in a burglary in Mayfair he disposed of them, thinking they were worthless. Sparks, who had been involved in smash-and-grab raids as far back as the middle 1920s, had been fortunate not to be charged with murder when a woman died after being knocked down following the first ever smash-and-grab raid in New Street, Birmingham; he stayed away for so long that there was no hope of a successful identification. Now in 1934 Hill set about improving the technique, and was so successful that by the early months of 1935 the newspapers were reporting major thefts on an almost daily basis. Questions were being asked in the House of Commons and,

[10] Billy Hill, *Boss of Britain's Underworld*, p. 27.

as a counter-measure, the Flying Squad was expanded.[11] Hill began to look for alternative employment.

And that alternative was safebreaking. He may never have been the top man, but he certainly ranked in the first half-dozen. Generally, because of their experience with explosives, safebreakers came from the North East, Scotland and Wales, but Hill was soon in demand. He claimed to have lost count of the number of safes he blew and he was also in demand on the Continent. On one occasion a safe was removed from a big store, but the men could not open it. Would Hill go over? Of course he would: 'The same day a private plane arrived for me and we took off after lunch. By eight o'clock that night I was back (by air, of course), the safe was open and I had collected £800 for my services.'

Whether he was quite as good a safebreaker as he made out is questioned by the former Northern safecracker, Albert Hattersley, who thought that London breakers in general were crude in their methods, packing in too much gelignite and so jamming the lock when the handle was blown off. Nevertheless there is no doubt that Hill undertook some highly profitable jobs. These came to an end when on 23 October 1936 at the County of London Sessions he received 21 months for shopbreaking, followed smartly by a concurrent four years at Middlesex Quarter Sessions on 9 December that year for a similar offence.

And that ended Hill's pre-war criminal career.

---

[11] See e.g. *Daily Mirror*, 8 February 1935; *Daily Herald*, 11, 12 February 1935; *Sunday Express*, 10 February 1935. The Flying Squad had its first cars in May 1927, six Lea Francis 14 h.p. convertibles each with a maximum speed of around 75 m.p.h. For an account of the development of the squad see Neil Darbyshire and Brian Hilliard, *The Flying Squad*.

3

The Sabinis

To understand the position Spot and Hill attained in the criminal hierarchy of London, it is necessary to look at their spiritual and practical forefathers. Racecourse gangs of touts, bookmakers' bullies and protectors, dopers, welshers, pickpockets, three-card tricksters and general fraudsters existed from the 1700s. In 1839 the Constabulary Commissioners noted that travelling criminals worked the Midland Beat, which consisted of racecourses.[1] In the 1880s, at a time when many small meetings were being closed because of hooliganism, Jerome Caminada, the celebrated Manchester detective, thought that violence had changed in the composition of racecourse undesirables.[2] Racecourse violence reached its apotheosis in the years immediately after the First World War and through to the mid-1930s. The principal and longest lasting of the gangs was variously known as 'The Italians', 'The Raddies' and most often as 'The Sabinis'.

The criminal father, or at least Godfather, of both Spot and Hill was the half-Italian Darby Sabini from the Saffron Hill area of

[1] First Report of the Constabulary Commissioners, 1839.
[2] Jerome Caminada, *Twenty-Five Years a Detective* (1983) Warrington, Prism Books. For an excellent and entertaining account of racecourse hooliganism and trickery in the nineteenth century, see Carl Chinn, *Better Betting with a Decent Fellow*, Ch. 6.

Holborn. Over two decades, he and his brothers along with their Hoxton and Hackney allies and opponents dominated street and racecourse crime until the beginning of the Second World War. Then Darby together with his formidable friend, Papa Pasquale, known as Bert Marsh, were interned as enemy aliens, appropriately enough at Ascot racecourse internment camp. It is fair to say that, in modern terms at least, Darby Sabini is rightly regarded as the first of the gangland bosses.

While the brothers are mentioned regularly enough in books on London crime[3], it has not always been clear how many there actually were. For example, Charles and Darby Sabini are often referred to as the same man when in fact Charles was an older brother. Darby, when it suited him, was quite prepared to be known as Fred Sabini who was actually the eldest of them.

Their parents were the Italian Charles Sabini and the English-woman Eliza Handley. In all there were six of them beginning with Frederick born in 1881, who, according to police files, traded as Bob Wilson at the Harringay greyhound stadium and apparently took no part in the other brothers' affairs. There is no note on the files as to what he did before greyhound racing became popular at the end of the 1920s. Next came Charles, who was two years younger and was a list supplier working for the bookmaker Joe Levy in what the police saw as a protection racket. He owned shares in West Ham Stadium and was thought to be 'slightly mentally deranged'; certainly by 1940 he had spent some time in mental hospitals. Then came Joseph, who on paper at least was the villain of the family. He served in the First World War in the Royal Welch Fusiliers and then the Cheshire Regiment and was wounded in France; he was then invalided out and awarded a pension of 12 shillings a week. On 12 October 1922 he received three years penal servitude for his part in the shooting of a rival Fred Gilbert in Mornington Crescent. However, the police thought that after that he had split from his

[3] See e.g. Raphael Samuel, *East End Underworld*; Edward T. Hart, *Britain's Godfather*.

brothers, and there was no evidence that he was operating behind the scenes. He traded as a bookmaker Harry Lake at Harringay. George Sabini was the youngest of the brothers – there was a sister who was a cripple – who had no convictions and worked at both Harringay and White City. He was not regarded as being any part of the gang, but it was noted that his name alone would provide him with protection. Of all the brothers it was principally Darby and Harry (known as Harryboy) who provided what euphemistically was called protection and what, in reality, was demanding money with menaces from the bookmakers.[4]

Ullano, better known as Darby Sabini, was born in 1889 in Saffron Hill, Little Italy. His Italian father died when he was two and the family was raised by their English mother. Sabini left school at the age of thirteen and joined Dan Sullivan, a small-time boxing promoter and bookmaker who later worked for Bella Burge at The Ring at Blackfriars. At one time it was thought that Sabini could, in the words of Marlon Brando, 'have been a contender'. While still in his teens he had knocked out the fancied middleweight, Fred Sutton, in the first round. Unfortunately, he did not like the training required and instead became a strong-arm man for Sullivan's promotions at the Hoxton Baths.[5] Later, he was employed by George Harris, a leading bookmaker of the time, again as a strong-arm man.

Harry, born in 1903 (the year before his father died) and always known as Harryboy, was educated at St Peter's Roman Catholic School in Clerkenwell and then went to work for an optician. During the First World War he worked in a munitions factory. He then

[4] Nat. Arch. HO 45/25720.
[5] There is no trace of this bout in boxing records. However, it is possible that the contest took place at a fairground booth. Until the 1960s, when it was officially banned by the British Boxing Board of Control, it was common for licensed boxers to take on all comers at booths. Indeed the ban was never seriously enforced and until the 1970s boxers were using the booths to provide them with summer work. Dan Sullivan was himself part Italian and on one occasion broke up a fight at The Ring between the Sabinis and the Hoxton element. He almost ruined Bella Burge, the promoter at the arena, by failing to keep proper records, leaving her liable for a substantial amount of tax. Since he was almost illiterate this was not surprising. Despite this and other deficiencies, for a time he was a steward of the British Boxing Board of Control and also managed the Irish boxer Jack Doyle.

became a bookmaker's clerk, working first for Gus Hall and later for Walter Beresford; when the latter died he became a commission agent. By 1940 he was a wealthy man with money in bonds for his children's education, bank accounts and a number of properties. Regarded by his solicitors as a 'conveyancing client', he was also a life Governor of the Northern Hospital.

Just what were Darby Sabini and his brothers like physically? A photograph taken of them with their friends and later rivals the Cortesis sometime before the Fratellanza shooting shows Enrico Cortesi – who was often said to be the smartest of them all – in a straw hat sitting in the middle of the group like the captain of a cricket team. To his left is Darby, less than middle height, with the flat cap he always wore and a shirt with no collar. He wore a dark brown suit with a high-buttoned waistcoat, a black silk stock and the light checked cap. He had selected this outfit when he was twenty and wore it for the rest of his life – indoors, outdoors and, so it is said, sometimes in bed. To Cortesi's right and in the background is handsome Harryboy Sabini, who wore highly polished springsided boots. Brother Joe liked cherry checks, while George wore a grey fedora.

After the First World War attendance at racecourses boomed, particularly at the Southern tracks at which trotting was also a popular spectacle. Before the war the Birmingham gangs had established a hold on racecourse protection and now they sought to advance their empire. Under the leadership of Billy Kimber from Bordesley in Birmingham, who described himself as a bookmaker and punter, and the heavy gambler Andrew Townie, they metamorphosed as the Brummagen Boys despite the fact that most of the members came from the Elephant and Castle area of London. The Boys had a fearsome reputation, said to be willing and able to kill rats by biting them. Their organised racecourse protection began in around 1910, and for a time Kimber's mob took control of Southern racecourses such as Newbury, Epsom, Earl's Park and Kempton. There were also other gangs operating from Leeds, known as the Lunies because of their addiction to drink,[6] Uttoxeter and Cardiff, with links throughout the country. Later Kimber's men also had a loose alliance with one of the metamorphoses of the Hoxton Mob. In fact Kimber was not a layer but instead controlled the best pitches on the courses, leasing them out on a half profit but no loss-sharing basis. It was a course of action which would later be enthusiastically pursued by both Spot and, to a lesser extent, Hill. Kimber, according to some accounts, was well regarded, and it was looser elements out of his control who terrorised the mainly Jewish bookmakers in the cheaper rings at the Southern courses. The Southern bookmakers accepted the imposition fairly philosophically.

Racecourse protection worked in a number of ways. First, there was the question of the pitches themselves. The Sabinis and their rivals simply bullied the hapless bookmakers away from their spots and then sold or let them to their cronies. One way of preventing a bookmaker from attracting any business was to surround his stand with thugs so that the punters could not get to it to place their bets. Then there was the bucket drop. If a bookmaker wished to avoid this trouble, he would drop 2/6d in a bucket containing water and a sponge which was carried up and down the line between races. The sponge was also used to wipe out the odds next to the printed sheet of runners on the board. If the tribute was not paid, then the odds would be wiped off at inappropriate and totally inconvenient times. The sheets of runners had themselves to be purchased; costing about a farthing to produce, they were retailed by the Sabinis to the bookmakers for another half a crown (2/6d). Chalk had to be bought, and a stool cost ten shillings to hire for the day. Other manoeuvres included starting fights near a bookmaker's pitch, claiming a non-existent winning bet, and having other pitches put so close to the

---

[6] On 29 November 1926 one of their members, Joseph Burns, was sentenced for two counts of demanding money with menaces. He had already served a five-year sentence for manslaughter. He appealed to Justice McCardie for leniency, claiming his wife and children would be destitute. The judge had little sympathy: 'I always think this world would be a better place if men who intend to commit these crimes would think of their wives and little ones before they acted.' *The Times*, 30 November 1926.

non-paying bookmaker that he physically could not operate. Quite apart from that, there was the straightforward demand for a non-repayable loan of £5 or £10. Today these sums may seem small but in the 1920s, added up, it came to big money. The racecourse business was a profitable one; when a gang went to a course like Brighton they could clear £4,000 or £5,000. At Epsom on Derby Day, it could be as much as £15,000–£20,000.[7]

Now the Sabini brothers, later known as 'The Italian Mob', who were said to import gangsters from Sicily, began to put together their organisation. It was fashionable for Italians to box under English names and many of the gang were ex-boxers. A long-serving Sabini man was Angelo Ginicoli, who boxed as George Thomas, and who had failed to return to France after leave during the First World War. He had a number of *noms-du-ring* including Bill Shelton's Unknown and George Langham. Others included the completely bald James Ford and Thomas Mack, as well as Pasquale Papa (who boxed as Bert Marsh) and Silvio Massardo, known as Shonk because of the shape of his nose.

The statement that 'there wasn't an Englishman among them'[8] was something of an exaggeration. There was. However, it certainly did not mean they could speak anything but English. Once when Mr Justice Darling, who fancied himself as a linguist, addressed one of them in Italian the man stared in amazement.[9]

The Sabinis may have had no great command of Italian but they had command of the police:

> Darby Sabini got in with the Flying Squad which had been formed about 1908 or 1909; they got in with the racecourse police, the special police, and so they had the police on their side protecting them. Directly there was any fighting it was always the Birmingham

---

[7] Raphael Samuel, *East End Underworld*, p. 184.
[8] *Ibid.*, p. 182.
[9] Apparently until this moment in the case Darling had been taking a close interest. Now he confined his remarks to the jury to the effect that the witness must be descended from the Sabinis, and went on to tell the story of the Sabine women. *The Times*, 12 September 1923.

mob who got pinched. They was always getting time, five-year
sentences and that.[10]

In some versions of the legend, the meteoric rise of Darby Sabini
can be traced back to a fight he had in 1920 with Thomas 'Monkey'
Benneyworth, known as The Trimmer, a leader of the Elephant Gang.
After he deliberately tore the dress of an Italian girl, Carmen Cardoza,
who was serving behind the bar of the Griffin public house in Saffron
Hill, Benneyworth was knocked out and humiliated by Sabini. When
his broken jaw had mended he returned with members of the
Elephant Gang to seek retribution, but they were driven out of Little
Italy by Sabini with the help of young Italians who looked on him
as their leader.[11] Now, with them behind him, he saw the opportunity to muscle in on some of the smaller gangs who were providing
protection around the racetracks. Although the big gangs such as
the Broad Mob from Camden Town, the mainly Jewish Aldgate Mob
and the Hoxton Mob could boast a membership of up to sixty, they
could be spread thinly because they were obliged to operate on
several tracks a day. The Sabinis moved in, in force.

   With the arrival of the Sabinis and their superior relationship with
the police, Billy Kimber and his gang temporarily retreated to the
Midlands. For some time the factions lived in an uneasy relationship. Kimber and Co. worked the Midlands and Northern tracks;
the Sabinis, along with a gang called the East End Jews, the London
and Southern ones.[12]

---

[10] Raphael Samuel, *East End Underworld*, p. 183.
[11] Thomas Benneyworth is something of a shadowy and unsung figure who reappears
over the years from 1917, convicted mainly of small theft and racecourse violence.
Monkey Benneyworth and Dodger Mullins, together with two others, were accused of
attacking and cutting Moey Levy in Aldgate on 15 February 1925. It was another matter
which was soon straightened out. The case was dismissed eight days later. *The Times*,
18, 24 February 1925. On 8 August 1935 he was involved in the beating of a pickpocket by the name of Flatman in the Waterloo Road. For an account of this and countless other racecourse battles, see Nat. Arch. HO 144 10430; London Metropolitan
Archives, Calendar of Prisoners, County of London Sessions 1927.
[12] There were numerous tracks in the South, many of which, such as Gatwick, Lewes,
Alexandra Park and Hurst Park, have now closed down. In addition trotting was popular,
with courses at such places as Greenford and Hendon.

The next five years saw a long-running battle over control of on-course bookmakers. On the one side were the Sabinis allied to the Jewish bookmakers from Aldgate. On the other were Billy Kimber, George 'Brummy' Sage and – a one-time Sabini man – the welterweight Fred Gilbert from Camden Town who boxed as Fred Clancey.

Kimber's Brummagen Boys did not give in easily and the fighting continued throughout the year. The file on Harry Sabini's appeal against internment at the beginning of the Second World War provides a good, although probably incomplete, list of the major outbursts of violence.[13]

A bookmaker under the Sabinis' protection was threatened at Sandown Park and was beaten up when he refused to pay a £25 pitch fee. Darby Sabini sent a retaliatory force to Hoxton. He himself was caught at Greenford trotting track on 23 March 1921 and escaped a bad beating from the Brummagen Mob by shooting his way out of trouble.[14] It was one of the few occasions when he was arrested. Charged with unlawfully and maliciously endangering life, he was acquitted after arguing self-defence, fined £10 and bound over to keep the peace on a charge of possessing a five-chamber revolver without a certificate. Inspector Heaps told the court that about twenty Brummagen people tried to get at Sabini, shouting, 'Come on, we've got them on the run. The police are frightened of us too.' Sandy Rice and Fred Gilbert were charged with being suspicious persons, but since they could not be linked to the Sabini incident they were discharged the following week.[15]

On 26 March, Robert Harvey was beaten up at London Bridge station. He had been suspected of welshing at Greenford. The next day there was a serious piece of violence when Billy Kimber, 'accompanied by a number of other roughs' who may (or more likely may not) have been trying to pour oil on the troubled waters, was found shot on the pavement outside Darby Sabini's house in King's Cross.

[13] Nat. Arch. MEPO 3 158.
[14] *Glasgow Herald*, 25 March 1921.
[15] Nat. Arch. MEPO 3 366. HO 144 10430.

He had apparently gone to 70 Colliers Street to remonstrate with Alfie Solomon and produced a revolver. Solomon took it away from him and Kimber was shot with his own weapon. On 27 April 1921 Solomon was acquitted of attempted murder when the jury accepted his claim that it was an accident. Kimber had declined to give evidence.

Reprisals for the Greenford incident came quickly. On 4 April the police were informed of a likely showdown at 'The Ascot of North London', Alexandra Park, a small frying-pan-shaped track which closed in the 1960s and which was known as Ally-Pally. By one o'clock, all they had found were two Birmingham bookmakers' touts who had been beaten up. Tom Divall says that it was he and the boxing referee Moss de Yong who cleared out first the Sabinis and then the Birmingham men.[16]

As a reprisal, however, two Jewish taxi-drivers, chauffeurs to the Sabinis, were caught in the Silver Ring at Alexandra Palace by the Birmingham men. One was shot twice as he lay on the ground; he too could not identify his shooter. A further reprisal came later that spring at Bath when Billy Kimber and his men attacked the East End Jews found in the Two Shillings Ring.[17]

The newspapers followed the entertainment with some enthusiasm. *The Times* reported that it was being whispered at Doncaster that there was likely to be trouble at Yarmouth: 'The Birmingham gang have obtained the better of their enemy which may make for a temporary peace.'[18]

The quarrel between Sabini, plus the Jewish element in his contingent, and outsiders continued throughout the summer. Fallers included David Levy of Bethnal Green who was sent to prison for three months at one of the magistrates' courts which were specially

---

[16] Tom Divall, *Scoundrels and Scallywags*, p. 200.
[17] Divall, whose attitude to both Sabini and Kimber was ambivalent to say the least, credits Kimber with clearing out the Birmingham Gang. This is curious since he headed it. Most likely is that he saw no point in continuing the operation when under observation from Divall. *Scoundrels and Scallywags*, p. 200.
[18] *The Times*, 14 September 1921.

convened behind the stands at the Derby meeting. He had been found carrying a pistol with soft-nosed bullets. His explanation was that he had been told that if he and his brother Moses went to Epsom they would be shot by 'The Sunderland Kid'. Nothing daunted, they had gone to the course. Levy had eighteen previous convictions for assault and two for larceny.[19]

This was clearly a small part of the celebrated battle on Derby Day. It appears to have been engineered by Reuben Bigland, the Birmingham tycoon known as 'Telephone Jack', following a complaint by the publisher (and later convicted swindler) Horatio Bottomley. He maintained that it was wrong that Italians such as the Sabinis should be depriving 'our boys' of a living, particularly after the latter's gallant fight in the First World War. The outcome was a punitive expedition by the Brummagen Boys, who were fuelled by the knowledge that some time previously two of their men had been attacked by the Solomon brothers, James Wood (later a Spot and Hill man) and Alf White in Covent Garden. One had needed seventy stitches in his legs alone.[20]

After the Derby itself, won by Steve Donoghue on the ill-fated Humorist, the Birmingham boys left the course and blocked the road with their charabanc to lie in wait for Sabini and his friends. Unfortunately for them, the Sabinis had already left the scene and the first cab in sight which was duly attacked contained their allies from Leeds. In the ensuing fracas one man lost three fingers. Twenty-eight men were arrested by a Sergeant Dawson, who at first thought the affray was a Sinn Fein riot and so removed the sparking plugs from the charabanc. He then held the men at gunpoint until help arrived.[21]

It is curious how throughout the history of organised crime the

[19] *Star*, 1 June 1921.
[20] One version of the story is that it occurred on the eve of the Derby, but the Home Office file gives it as 23 February 1922. Nat. Arch. HO 144 10430.
[21] Nat. Arch. MEPO 346. It is often suggested that Jack 'Dodger' Mullins was one of those involved in the attack. If so, he escaped arrest. Humorist began to haemorrhage after the race and died within a few weeks; a post-mortem showed he had won with only one sound lung.

victims will align themselves with their oppressors who, in turn, through that alliance somehow gain a quasi-respectability. After bookmakers at Salisbury races had been forced at gunpoint to pay a levy for the privilege of having a pitch, in 1921 they formed themselves into the Racecourse Bookmakers and Backers Protection Association, today a highly respected organisation. Eight stewards were appointed at a wage of £6 per week including Darby Sabini, his henchman Alf White and Philip Emmanuel – son of Edward, a noted Jewish gangster from the first decade of the century – who became the association's vice-president. Another curious steward was Fred Gilbert, while the Sabini hardman James Ford would claim at one of his regular trials to be an honorary steward (whatever that might mean).[22]

A partial explanation was offered when Ford and George Langham were committed for trial on a charge of causing grievous bodily harm to one of their regular opponents, John Thomas Phillips, at the Chatfield Hotel in Brighton.[23] A witness, Harry Cohen, explained that Harry Sabini was a member of the association, 'whose stewards are people who could use their fists to prevent bad characters from blackmailing bookmakers. In consequence a racecourse is now a garden party compared with what it was years ago.'[24] Any improvement did not last long, for it was soon apparent that the stewards had reverted to their old ways and were demanding a shilling for every list sold.

By now, it was said that at the time Darby was earning the fantastic sum of £20,000 a year. This may be an exaggeration but, taken at the lowest level, 60 sheets sold at 2/6d made a working man's wage for the week, and there is no doubt the brothers did far better than that.

---

[22] The Racecourse Bookmakers and Backers Protection Association, *What It Has Done and What It Can Do with YOUR Help* (NAB File, 'History' 1921); The Racecourse Bookmakers and Backers Protection Association General Committee, Minutes, 12 September 1921.

[23] Over the years Phillips was himself in the courts on a number of occasions, including one appearance following an affray at the Admiral Duncan public house in Old Compton Street.

[24] *The Times*, 12 September 1922.

Emmanuel senior also set up a company providing the book-makers with tickets to hand to the punters. There is also a suggestion that in 1922 he was now controlling the Sabinis, but this is probably incorrect. In September of that year their services were dispensed with by the RBBPA.[25]

Violence may have spread away from the racecourse, but that year was a vintage one in the battle for supremacy on them. On 23 February 1922 Michael Sullivan and Archie Douglas, both of them Brummagen Boys, were slashed in Coventry Street by a Sabini team consisting of Alfred Solomon and his brother Harry, Alfred White, James Wood and a man named Mansfield.

On Good Friday Fred Gilbert was slashed about the legs in the New Raleigh Club in Jermyn Street by the Italians, led again on this occasion by Alfie Solomon who often worked with his brother. Gilbert declined to bring charges. The Derby meeting that year, when Captain Cuttle won after spreading a plate on the way to the start, passed off quietly enough, but two months later the Sabinis were back in the dock charged after a fight in Mornington Crescent, Camden Town, during which shots were fired at Fred Gilbert who had been out walking with his wife and some friends when he was ambushed. For once the Birmingham men were able to give the names of their attackers to the police, but by the time the case was heard they had forgotten them.

Things did not stop there, and the Jockey Club gave serious consideration to shutting down the courses on which there was trouble. There have been persistent stories that a son of the boxer George Moore, a Gilbert man from West London, was stabbed to death in a club off the Strand, or perhaps in Tottenham, but the police report specifically denies this. What is clear is that the Sabinis and their rivals fought for supremacy on street corners, on trains, on the roads and at the racecourses.

---

[25] South PA Folio 47, 15 May 1933, 'Printing of Lists'; The Racecourse Bookmakers and Backers Protection Association General Committee, Minutes, 15 May, 12 June, 4 September 1922.

On 29 July 1922 there was an affray just outside the Red Bull in Grays Inn Road. William John Beland said that on that date he had heard shots fired from the public house; he went to the scene but was stopped by Fred Gilbert who said, 'Go the other way or I shall blow your fucking brains out.'

Beland had also been down at the canal bank off Caledonian Road at the beginning of 1920 when he saw Gilbert and George Droy fighting. When Gilbert was getting the worst he took out a razor and slashed Droy across the shoulder. Trixie Droy, a manufacturing optician, came to his brother's assistance and for his pains Gilbert shot him also in the shoulder.

On 22 August 1922 Jewish bookmakers actually went to the police complaining that George 'Brummy' Sage and Gilbert had demanded £10 from them as they waited for a train to the races. One of them, Samuel Samuels, said that he was at Waterloo station on 19 August when George Sage came up to him and said, 'You Jew bastard. You're one of the cunts we're going to do. You're a fucking bastard Jew and we are going to do you and the Italians and stop you going racing. I want to be the governor here.'

Jack Delew from Yorkton Street, Hackney, said he had been in the Rising Sun at Waterloo on the same day when Sage, Jim Brett and Gilbert approached. Sage caught hold of another bookmaker Harry Margolis and said, 'This is one of the bastards, do him, Fred, through the guts.' Gilbert then pressed a large service revolver into Margolis's body and said, 'Give us a tenner and you can go.' Jim Brett, aka Stevens, pulled a butcher's knife on Delew and asked, 'Shall I do him?' when a man named Sullivan entered and said, 'Let them alone. They'll do later.' Sullivan then said that there were fifty of them and the Sabinis and Alf White would be done in for certain.

Earlier that same day the Sabinis, including the increasingly powerful Alf White – now Chief Steward of the Racecourse Bookmakers and Backers Protection Association – Joseph Sabini, George West aka Dai Thomas, Paul Boffa and the long-serving

Tommy Mack, arrived at Mornington Crescent in a fleet of taxis and shot at Fred Gilbert.

There was a good deal of ducking and diving by friends of the Sage and Brett contingent in respect of their bit of bother, as a result of which on 24 November John Gilbert, Joseph Smith, Thomas Ackroyd and George Moore were found not guilty of perverting the course of justice by getting Margolis to give false evidence. It had been alleged that on 12 October, when Margolis went to the Old Bailey to testify, he was met by George Moore whom he knew from the races. Moore said he was ashamed of him giving evidence. Margolis went with him across to the Wellington Coffee Shop and there saw Joe Smith and John Gilbert. Later he went with Gilbert to meet Fred Kimberley and was offered money to change his story. Overall neither of the cases could be seen as noted successes by the prosecution. On 1 November, Gilbert, Jim Brett and Sage had all been found not guilty of demanding with menaces. No one seems to have bothered about the shooting of George Droy.[26]

Meanwhile most of the Sabini gang involved had been acquitted of the Gilbert shooting in Camden Town. Alf White was convicted but acquitted on appeal. 'The sooner the Bookmakers Protection Agency is disbanded the better,' said Mr Justice Roche. Joseph Sabini was not so fortunate. He received three years which he was serving in Maidstone when Alf White, together with a George Drake and another unidentified man, decided his conditions should be improved. To this end they approached a warder Matthew Frygh and offered him £2 to deliver letters for Sabini. Frygh reported the matter and the recently-released White found himself back in the dock along with Drake. The police wanted to charge George Sabini, but there was no evidence against him. He had been thought to have masterminded the whole thing but, on closer inspection, it turned out that the 'George Sabini' who had visited his brother in prison had been another of White's men. This time White received

[26] Nat. Arch. MEPO 3 366.

eighteen months and Drake six months more. They appealed, and because White had an arguable point of law he lost no remission when his appeal was dismissed. Drake apparently had a good service record as the batman to a Regimental Sergeant-Major in the British Expeditionary Force in France. Now Lord Justice Swift had a little judicial fun at his expense: 'It is clear that society is not safe unless Drake is in the army or in prison and as the court cannot send him into the army what are we to do? One thing is certain. If the sentence stands he will not be able to bribe another warder from outside.'

The unfortunate Drake lost his appeal and with it his remission.[27]

At the Doncaster St Leger meeting the Brummagen team sent word that no bookmakers or their employees would be allowed to attend Town Moor. As a result, in open defiance, Sabini and his men 'protected' the London bookie Walter Beresford, putting him safely on the train to Doncaster where it was met by Kimber's men who then allowed only him and his staff to go to the racecourse. It is often suggested that this was an act of generosity by the Sabinis, but Beresford had employed Harryboy Sabini – or was it the other way around? – for years.

The next trouble spot was at the Yarmouth autumn meeting, a course claimed by the Sabinis as theirs. They arrived the day before the meeting to search the public houses in the town to see if the Brummagen men had arrived. They had not. Instead they were met by Tom Divall, formerly a Chief Inspector of the CID but now working for Wetherbys. Divall, something of a supporter of the Midland team, calmed things down.

Later Divall wrote of Kimber that he 'was one of the best' and of another incident: 'Just to show what generous and brave fellows the aforesaid Sage and Kimber were, they would not give any evidence or information against their antagonists, and stated that they would sooner die than send those men to prison.'[28]

[27] Nat. Arch. MEPO 3366.
[28] Tom Divall, *Scoundrels and Scallywags*, p. 200.

One explanation of the Sabinis' success and longevity comes from Billy Hill:

There were more crooked policemen about than there are today. The Sabinis received protection from certain elements of the law. If a thief or pickpocket was seen on a course, a Sabini man would whiten the palm of his hand with chalk and greet the thief with a supposed-to-be 'Hello'. In doing so he would slap the thief on the shoulder, just like a long-lost friend. The whitened hand-mark would identify him to the law. Then they knew without doubt that this man was safe to be nicked for being a suspected person.[29]

According to Divall it was Beresford who in 1923: '. . . brought the two sides together, he is still continuing in the good work, and I am very pleased to see the two crews are associating together, and, in addition, to have their principals assuring me that no such troubles will ever occur again.'[30]

The Sabinis and Kimber did agree to divide the racecourses between them and the racecourse wars died down. With the Sabinis now controlling the South, where there were more meetings, and Kimber and his friends the rest, the bookmakers were firmly in their hands.

But if by then Darby Sabini had made his peace with that fine fellow Billy Kimber, for some time he had been under threat from other sources inside his own organisation. Some of the troops decided to seek a higher percentage of the takings. The four Cortesi brothers (Augustus, George, Paul and Enrico, also known as the Frenchies because they were born in France) were deputed to act as shop stewards to put the case. Almost immediately afterwards part of the Jewish element in the gang, to become known as the Yiddishers, also formed a breakaway group. In true business fashion the Sabinis negotiated. The Cortesis would be given a greater percentage. The

---

[29] Billy Hill, *Boss of the Underworld*, p. 4.
[30] Tom Divall, *Scoundrels and Scallywags*, p. 205.

Yiddishers were given permission to lean on one – but only one – of the bookmakers under protection.[31]

However, peace did not last long. The Yiddishers began to side with the Cortesis and, with defections to the Frenchies amongst the troops, the Sabini position was substantially weakened. In the autumn of 1922 the new team had effectively hi-jacked the Sabini protection money from the bookmakers at Kempton Park. Retribution was swift. As a result of the reprisals, Harry Sabini was convicted at Marylebone Magistrates' Court of an assault on George Cortesi. More seriously, one of the other leaders of the breakaway group was attacked, for which five of the Sabini troops were sentenced to terms of imprisonment for attempted murder.

Then, just before midnight on 19 November 1922, Darby and Harry Sabini were trapped by the Cortesi faction in the Fratellanza Club in Great Bath Street, Clerkenwell. Darby was punched and hit with bottles, while Harry was shot in the stomach by Enrico Cortesi. They were saved from more serious injuries by the bravery of Louisa Doralli, the manager's daughter, who was said to be in love with the handsome Harry. First she pushed away the hand of Augustus as he tried to shoot Darby, and then tried to shield Harry before being pushed aside. Darby, however, suffered a greater indignity. As he told the magistrates' court, his false teeth were broken as a result of the blows from the bottles. He was also able to confirm his respectability:

> I am a quiet peaceable man. I never begin a fight. I've only once been attacked. I've never attacked anyone . . . I do a little bit of work as a commission agent sometimes for myself and sometimes for someone else. I'm always honest. The last day's work I did was two years' ago. I live by my brains.

He had only once carried a revolver, and that was the time when he was attacked at Greenford Park where according to the police all

---

[31] Arthur Tietjen, *Soho*, p. 48.

the trouble had started. Indeed, he turned out his pockets in court in confirmation that he was not carrying a gun. It must have been one of the few occasions when he was not doing so, for he was certainly being economical with the truth. The general view of Sabini was that he carried a loaded gun all the time and slept with it under his pillow. If that is right and he did carry a gun around London, it says something for his relationship with the police; he does not seem to have been continually worried by them with a series of arrests and charges of possessing an offensive weapon.

The Cortesi brothers, who lived only five doors from the Fratellanza Club, were arrested on the night of the attack and, at the Old Bailey on 18 January 1923, Augustus and Enrico each received a sentence of three years penal servitude. George was found not guilty, as were Paul and Alexander Tomasso, the latter known as Sandy Rice. Mr Justice Darling now wanted to know about race-course protection. 'We are told that people blackmailed bookmakers and that the latter established an association to protect themselves but that they were blackmailed by their own stewards?'

> *Inspector A. Gosse:* I have never heard of such an allegation being made by bookmakers. Since the stewards have been employed the police have received no complaints of bookmakers being black-mailed. There is no doubt that the Bookmakers' Protection Association has done a considerable amount of good. For eighteen months I did practically nothing else but look after gangs at race meetings.

A recommendation by the Grand Jury that the Cortesi brothers should be deported was ignored by the somewhat eccentric Mr Justice Darling:

> I look upon this as part of a faction fight which has raged between you and other Italians in consequence of some differ-ence which the police do not entirely understand. There is nothing new about that. Anybody who has read Italian history – and I happen to have read a good deal of it – knows perfectly

well that to determine the cause of the differences between the factions which existed in Italy in the Middle Ages passes the skill of most people who later tried to investigate the matter.

You appear to be two lawless bands – the Sabinis and the Cortesis. Sometimes you are employed against the Birmingham people, and sometimes you are employed against each other. On this occasion you were carrying out a feud between you and the Sabinis. I have the power to recommend an order for your deportation. I am not going to do it. I can see no reason to suppose that you two men are worse than others who have been convicted in these feuds and have not been recommended for deportation.

There was, however, a warning that the Italian colony should know in future that if this kind of lawless conduct went on, those who were convicted would be turned out of the country with their wives and children.[32] A rather sour note on the Home Office file reads, 'It is a pity that the Cortesis were not charged with the murder of the Sabinis.' Nevertheless, after that they faded from sight.

Meanwhile anonymous letters to the police detailed a series of incidents for which the Sabinis were said to be responsible. The principal correspondent was 'Tommy Atkins', who said he had been victimised, and if the police cared to contact him by putting an advertisement in the *Daily Express* he would reveal all. Meanwhile he alleged that Edward Emmanuel and a Girchan Harris were financing the Sabinis, and that they had a number of members of the Flying Squad in their pay as well. The police inserted the advertisement suggesting a meeting, which was declined by 'Atkins' who, nevertheless, did supply details of some twelve incidents including an account of an attack by James Ford and George Langham on a bookmaker named John Thomas Phillips in Brighton. This was, of course, common knowledge, and charges had been brought even though the case fizzled out with disappearing

---

[32] *The Times*, 19 January 1923.

witnesses.[33] He also reported the story that the brother of George Moore had been killed and that the *Evening News* racing correspondent 'JMD', who wrote as Beaumont, had been attacked at Newmarket. There was a suggestion that Billy Westbury had been injured so badly that he was now 'mentally insane'.

The police could find no trace of the death of Moore's brother and reported that poor Billy Westbury had suffered 'minor injuries'. It was correct, however, that 'JMD' had indeed been attacked. What had happened was that this journalist who campaigned against the racecourse gangs had been waylaid on the way back from the course to the railway station and had been plastered with flour, red ochre and soot. To his credit, he was not deterred and carried on his campaign.[34]

In June 1923 Darby and Harry Sabini, along with George Dido, were arrested at Epsom races and charged with wounding Jack Levine, known also as Maurice Fireman. The allegation was that they had used knuckledusters on the unhappy bookmaker. They were fortunate that the incident had been witnessed by Sgt.-Major Michael O'Rorke VC, a resident of a local veterans' hospital, who saw no knuckledusters and believed Fireman was the aggressor. Dido gave evidence that he had been wearing a ring which might have seemed at a glance to be a knuckleduster. Asked where it was, he said rather piteously that he had pawned it to pay for the defence. 'Not Guilty.' Those who cannot remember history are condemned to repeat it. It all seems to be echoed in the Dimes-Spot fight over thirty years later.[35]

One of the most serious incidents came in 1924 when the Sabini man Alfie Solomon stood trial for the murder of Barney Blitz, known as Buck Emden, who had nine convictions for wounding and assaults on the police including one at Old Street Magistrates' Court when, on 20 July 1916, he had been ordered to pay £20

[33] *The Times,* 19 January 1923.
[34] W. Bebbington, *Rogues Go Racing,* p. 98.
[35] *News of the World,* 24 June 1923.

compensation for striking an officer with a bayonet. Emden had died in a fight at the Eden Social Club, a spieler in the Hampstead Road, which was really over the sometime Sabini friend, sometime Sabini enemy Edward Emmanuel. Emden thought, probably correctly, that Emmanuel, a noted mixer, had grassed him over an affray at Epsom races the year before, and now he sought at least an explanation and preferably a grovelling apology. He threatened Emmanuel with a broken glass and Solomon, carving-knife in hand, leaped to his friend's defence. The one-time boxer died in hospital some days later.[36]

The police only managed to persuade a bare half-dozen out of the forty-odd present in the club to come to give evidence. One defaulter was the fishmonger – soon to be boxing promoter – Jack Solomons. He wished he could help, but since he had been drinking all evening he could not give an accurate recollection (even though he had been sober enough to play faro when he arrived at the premises).

The story is that Darby Sabini arrived unannounced at the flat of Sir Edward Marshall Hall KC in Marylebone, brandishing a bundle of white £5 notes in an endeavour to persuade the great man to appear for Solomon. He was sent to see Hall's clerk and Sir Edward accepted the brief. Solomon's defence was that he had seen Edward Emmanuel being assaulted and had struck a blow with a knife to save his dear old friend. As for his part, Emmanuel, who had now left behind his East End upbringing and was living in Golders Green, said he wished he could cut off his own hand if the act would bring Emden back to life.

Some felt that the real villain of the piece and the person who had set it all up was indeed Emmanuel, who was alleged to have controlled things from the Tichbourne Club in Paddington, and Scotland Yard received another anonymous letter.

[36] The old-time villain Arthur Harding regarded Emmanuel as the Jewish Al Capone of his era. Raphael Samuel, *East End Underworld*, pp. 135, 204–5.

I feel (rec 25 Sept) I must write and tell you something about the poor man that was stabbed in the Eden Street Club. The man who started the row was Edward Emmanuel who I know went there with Solomons. He is making his brags all over the East End that his money will keep him out of this affair. I know him and know he paid this man Solomons to do this poor man some injury. The police must know this Emmanuel, he has had gambling houses all over London and it was because he had a previous row with this poor man that took him there with Solomons who is also a villain and this is not the first one he has stabbed. Make Solomons say who he went to the club with and who broke the glass and hit the poor man on the head. Please take notice of this letter and make this Emmanuel come forward. I only wish I had curage [sic] to come and see you and tell you more you will find out this is true. He professes to be a very good man by helping poor jews and that is why they will never say anything about him you have got his photo at Scotland Yard if you look it up I am a poor woman who has suffered through these gambling dens.[37]

Without their leaders the Cortesi opposition to Darby Sabini had folded, but 1925 was a vintage year for gang fighting and the list of incidents is formidable. According to the newspapers, on 15 February there was a razor slashing in Aldgate High Street, and another slashing took place at Euston Station on 24 April. On 21 May ten armed men raided a club in Maiden Lane looking for the Sabinis or their men. Later that night shots were fired in the Harrow Road. On 30 July, three men were wounded in a club in Brighton. There was an incident when men fought on Hampstead Heath on 3 August. Five days later a man was attacked in the Marshalsea Road in the Borough, and on 16 August twenty-four men fought in Shaftesbury Avenue.

The police were called on to comment and replied that the fight in Shaftesbury Avenue was total invention. They accepted the Maiden Lane incident, and that Monkey Benneyworth had been involved.

[37] The Solomon referred to is obviously Alfred rather than Jack Solomons. The whole saga appears in the file Nat. Arch. MEPO 3 373.

As for the Hampstead Heath fight, there was no evidence that race gangs were involved. With respect to allegations that Flying Squad officers were standing by watching some of the incidents, this was totally incorrect. Indeed, the newspapers should be ashamed of themselves for such irresponsible reporting.

In the House of Commons, in a statement which anticipated a subsequent denunciation of Jack Spot by some thirty years, Home Secretary William Joynson Hicks vowed to stamp out the race gangs. And just as swiftly as they had arisen so, for a time, did the street fights die away.

In 1926 a new sport of greyhound racing arrived. The crowds at the early meetings were enormous; 17,000 were reported at Belle Vue, Manchester, in the autumn of that year. Career criminals have shown time and time again that they are entrepreneurs who are able to identify new opportunities. Now dog racing provided yet another avenue for the Sabinis, and it was one they were quick to seize. Both London and provincial tracks came under their control as rivals were dealt with in the same way as racecourse bookmakers. There were, of course, casualties along the way and in February 1929 the faithful James Ford received two months hard labour for an attack the previous November on William Farmer, who was said to be taking control of Belle Vue Greyhounds.[38]

It was not until the 1930s, by which time the Sabinis had fully extended their territory into greyhound racing, that they again came under serious threat from another team.[39] This time it was from their former ally Alf White whose family and friends had been getting stronger over the years and were now set to expand their King's Cross-based territory. Trouble had been brewing for some time and Sabini had not been able to control the disparate interests of the Jewish members and the Whites, the more right-wing arm of the enterprise.

---

[38] Two months seems to have been a fairly standard sentence for racecourse fighting. Ford received the same at Salisbury on 18 July 1921. *The Times*, 20 July 1921.
[39] *The Times*, 25 February 1929.

There was also the small matter of the pitches on the open courses at Epsom and Brighton which were outside the control of the race-course stewards, as well as bookmaking at point-to-points – let alone the dog tracks where, according to the son of a man who ran a pitch, 'they terrorised the bookmakers'. Just as bookmakers' pitches on the racetracks had been controlled, so it was with the new sport of greyhound racing.

Meanwhile, from the 1920s onwards the Sabinis had been branching out, taking interests in the West End drinking and gambling clubs, and installing and running slot machines. They were also extending their protection to criminals. If a burglary took place, the Sabinis would send round for their share. They had become thieves' ponces. Billy Hill, who was now beginning to make a name for himself in criminal circles, thought:

> Burglars and thieves had no chance. If they wandered Up West they had to go mob-handed. And they had to be prepared to pay out if they were met by any of the Sabinis. If they went into a club it was drinks all round. The prices were usually especially doubled for their benefit. If they did go into a spieler they never won. They knew better than to try to leave while they were showing even a margin of profit. If one word was spoken out of place, it was all off. The Sabinis, who could rustle up 20 or 30 tearaways at a moment's notice anywhere Up West, stood for no liberties, although they were always taking them.[40]

Members of the family were also undoubtedly behind one of the best of the bullion robberies of the 1930s, the very carefully planned snatch at Croydon Airport. Gold used to be shipped from the airport and, on 6 March 1936, three boxes of gold bars, sovereigns and dollars – intended to be sent by Imperial Airways to Brussels and Paris – disappeared.

There is no doubt that security at the recently opened Croydon Airport was lax, as was the discipline with the pilots. In theory the

---

[40] Billy Hill, *Boss of the Underworld*, p. 5.

buffet-cum-restaurant was open only to passengers and other customers, but the pilots kept overcoats in their lockers to wear over their overalls so as to gain access. Nancy Johnstone, who worked in the canteen-cum-restaurant, recalls that one pilot, Paddy Flynn, used a code 'a little more sugar this morning' to mean a measure of whisky in his coffee before he flew. He lost a leg in an air crash while flying for Imperial Airways in the early 1930s.

Opposite the restaurant was the bullion room in which gold bars, the universal currency, were stored. If a transfer of currency was made between countries, then the gold bars were literally moved. The security was in the hands of guards of the Civil Aviation Transport Organisation, but from time to time the door to the bullion room was left open with the key in the lock. The staff had previously noticed a man hanging around the airfield, and it is thought that he was there to take a wax impression of the key. Nancy Johnstone remembers locking up the canteen one afternoon after the last flight – there were no such things as late-night departures – and when she returned to the premises the next morning she found it in an upheaval. The gold due to be flown to France was gone.

The boxes had been placed in the safe room but amazingly only one man, Francis Johnson, remained at the aerodrome overnight. He had to leave the actual building at 4.15 in the morning to receive a German airliner which was landing and, while he was on the tarmac, the gold was stolen.

So far as the police could reconstruct events, a cab had been hired from King's Cross and driven to the airport where the boxes were loaded and brought back to Harringay. Cecil Swanland, John O'Brien and Silvio 'Shonk' Mazzardo were arrested. The police found wrappers and seals from the gold in Swanland's room, but there was not a trace of the gold itself. The evidence included identification and, since this was clearly not strong, the then mandatory confession to a cellmate. Mazzardo and O'Brien were acquitted. Swanland's defence was that by the time the boxes arrived at his home they were empty.

He had a number of old convictions, mainly for forgery, and had already served sentences of seven, five and six years penal servitude. This time he received another seven. None of the gold was recovered. The astute Bert Marsh was suspected of being the actual mastermind.[41] Shortly afterwards a Sabini bookmaker, in tribute to or financed by the robbery, began betting using the name Nick Gold.

But the Sabinis and the Whites were not without other rivals. In 1937 the crime writer and novelist Peter Cheyney wrote in the *Sunday Dispatch* that there were five major London gang districts; Hackney, Hoxton, North East London, North London and the West End, this last being 'worked over' by a loose alliance of the Hoxton, Elephant and Castle Boys and the Hackney Gang as well as the West End Boys.

Until 1927, wrote Cheyney: '. . . the Hackney Gang was supreme in the West End. Then came the battle of Ham Yard when the gang suffered a severe reversal in terms both of blood spilled and prestige lost.'[42]

Cheyney was writing a decade later, and in fact the battle took place at the end of 1923. The following January George West and the omnipresent James Ford had wrecked the New Avenue Club in Ham Yard, for which they went to prison. West had a long record beginning in 1898 when he served two months for larceny, interrupted by a career when he boxed as Dai Thomas. In October 1922 he had been acquitted of the attempted murder of Fred Gilbert in the Mornington Crescent shooting. This time West received nine months and Ford six.[43]

Apart from the gangs which ran their areas, there would be splinter

---

[41] James Morton, *Gangland*, pp. 20–21.

[42] Reprinted in *Crime Does Pay*. In February 1927 Freddy Ford, no relation of James, who ran the Musicians and Artists Club, an *alter ego* for the New Avenue, went to prison for receiving along with a man named Chandler. The club was described by Inspector Wesley as patronised almost exclusively by thieves – male and female. If, by mistake, a genuine patron stumbled into the club it was rare that he left with his money. *Empire News*, 13 February 1927.

[43] Tom Divall suggests that James Ford eventually reformed, retired from the racecourses and from his earnings was able to buy himself a freehold house. *Scoundrels and Scallywags*, pp. 214–15.

teams such as the squad of pickpockets from Aldgate who worked the nearby City. There was talk, emphatically denied by the authorities, that there had been an increase in the use of knives and weapons in Soho by aliens in the two years prior to 1929. Nothing could be further from the case, said the Home Secretary. In fact no such incident had occurred (or been reported) during those two years. A look through the Home Office file, however, shows a number of well-known names in cases which for one reason or another never came to court or, if they did, were withdrawn or the charges were dismissed.[44]

After his unfortunate incident at Maidstone prison, Alf White had maintained a low profile as far as the courts were concerned until in July 1935 he and his sons William and Alfred jnr each received twelve months hard labour for assaulting John McCarthy Defferary, the licensee of the Yorkshire Stingo in the Marylebone Road, at the Wharncliffe Rooms on 17 April that year. The fight had been at a dance in aid of St Mary's Hospital and Defferary lost the sight of his left eye. There was a suggestion that Carrie White, Alf's daughter, had been given £12 taken from the victim, and that the Whites had robbed a number of people that night.[45]

On 28 April that year, a Frederick Ambrose had written to the police alleging that Alf White was 'one of the Worse Race Course Pests and blackmailers that ever put foot on a racecourse'. The file contains another series of letters suggesting White had the police in his pay.

Now when the Whites appeared at the Old Bailey they were supported by some forty members of the gang and fighting broke out, but there were no arrests. The guilty verdict was thought to be very much against the weight of the evidence. An internal Scotland Yard memo said 'success in such an appeal would, in the matter of Law and Order, be a catastrophe'. There had been a threat against

[44] Nat. Arch. HO 144 10430.
[45] The White appeal against his conviction in the Gilbert incident appears in the Law Reports under (1922) Cr. App R. 60 and also in Nat. Arch. MEPO 3 910.

prosecuting counsel Horace Fenton and, for a time, he was given police protection.[46]

As for the racecourses, the last major pre-war fight took place when, at Lewes racecourse on 8 June 1936, the Bethnal Green Gang in alliance with the Hoxton Mob, and almost certainly sponsored by Alf White, ran riot.

According to the racecourse inspector William Bebbington, there had been bad feeling between a man known as Conky and another 'D.' who had been badly slashed in the Bedford Hotel off Tottenham Court Road some two years earlier.[47] Nothing happened until a row blew up between them, this time at Yarmouth races on 4 June 1946. This was followed by an incident at the Shades Hotel near Liverpool Street station when a member of the Whites had his throat cut. Now thirty members of that firm went to Lewes races with the specific intention of injuring two of the Sabinis. They did not find them and instead set upon the bookmaker Arthur Solomon and his clerk, Mark Frater, known to be friendly towards the family. This was also, at least in part, a reprisal for the death of Bernard Blitz at the hands of Solomon. Solomon knew that this would happen sooner or later, and perhaps the interesting thing is how long it had been in coming. After his release from prison he had written to the police saying he was now a respectable bookmaker and asking for protection from his former friends and in particular Arthur 'Dodger' Mullins who had threatened him at Clapton greyhounds. The police thought otherwise; a note in the case file reads that Solomon is a 'dangerous rascal and his enemies are far more in need of protection than he is'.[48]

After a running battle sixteen men were arrested. As always serious money was available and they were defended privately at Lewes Assizes by the very fashionable J.D. Cassels KC and G.L. Hardy, but on pleas of guilty the ringleaders – who included the long-standing

---

[46] See also HO 144 10430.
[47] W. Bebbington, *Rogues Go Racing* pp. 102–4.
[48] Nat. Arch. MEPO 3 373. Dodger Mullins ran a series of protection rackets for many years. For an account of his career see James Morton, *East End Gangland*.

criminal offender Jimmy Spinks, friend of Mullins – drew five years
penal servitude from Mr Justice Hilbery who imposed a total of 53½
years on the defendants. Spinks had compounded his crime because,
the day after he was released on bail, he had approached Frater
saying, 'You don't recognise me, do you?' There is possibly some
truth in the suggestion that the Sabinis tipped off the police and
were not therefore the first targets for arrests. Their long-time Sabini
man Thomas Mack seems to have been one of the few Sabinis who
was caught. He received three years.[49]

The year 1936 was busy and almost wholly successful for Bert
Marsh, the organiser of the Croydon Airport bullion robbery. On 1
September Massimino Monte Columbo was stabbed to death at
Wandsworth greyhound racing track which had opened some four
years earlier. A fight broke out in the 2/6d ring witnessed by Jim
Wicks, who thirty years later was to be the manager of boxers such
as Henry Cooper. 'His boss J. Wicks should be ashamed to employ
him [Marsh],' wrote one fan at the time. But in all probability Marsh
employed Wicks or at least protected him. In turn Massimino,
described as the idol of the girls in Little Italy, worked for Marsh.
A popular bantamweight, Marsh had fought at Lime Grove Baths
and Shepherd's Bush. He was described by the officer in the case
as, 'Quick-tempered, excitable and easily provoked'.

Once Marsh was appointed to work at the stadium he had
obtained jobs for the Columbo brothers there, and Wicks employed
Camillo at Marsh's behest – an indication of who exactly was the
master. The quarrel was allegedly over the employment by a bookmaker Samuels of another Monte Columbo brother, Nestor. Instead
of Nestor the job had gone to Bert Wilkins, described as having

---

[49] For an account of the battle, see Edward Greeno, *War on the Underworld*, Ch. 4.
Greeno, on whose recollections it is not always safe to rely, gives credence to the story
that a Sabini man was killed in the Benneyworth raid on Maiden Lane. In *Britain's
Godfather*, Edward T. Hart has it that Arthur Solomon deserted Sabini and effectively
led the Yiddishers as an opposing group. In a rather romantic story he has George
Sewell, known as the Cobblestone Kid, after Sabini's death, going to Solomon's favourite
public house and giving him a beating in front of his supporters. As with Greeno,
Sewell's recollections cannot be wholly relied upon.

'Ivor Novello looks', and the Columbo family objected. They were also looking for more money from Marsh. Fighting broke out and Massimino was stabbed in the neck.

Marsh had undoubtedly suffered kicks and punches in the fight and when he and Wilkins were surrendered to the police by their solicitor J. A. Davies, he sensibly asked that the fingerprints on a life preserver or cosh were checked as, 'It'll show they weren't mine. I was nearly killed,' he told Divisional Detective Inspector John Henry.

Marsh had a number of previous convictions, dating back to 1917 when he was bound over at Clerkenwell Magistrates' Court for stealing a quantity of brilliantine and a tricycle. More seriously, on 12 November 1922 he received six months with hard labour at the Central Criminal Court for unlawful wounding; he had stabbed a man in the hip and then hit him. This was followed in 1924 with an appearance at Ashford Magistrates' Court on a charge of common assault, which followed an incident at Wye races. Harry Sabini was acquitted but Marsh, along with Antonio 'Babe' Mancini and Thomas Mack, each earned a month with hard labour. On 27 November 1928 Marsh was fined the substantial sum of seventy guineas with twenty guineas costs for selling intoxicating liquor at an unlicensed premises. His last outing in the courts before the murder charge had been another bind-over for common assault at Clerkenwell in 1934. In the murder file there is a letter saying that Marsh had said how sorry he was that he had not shot Inspector Burbridge who closed his drinking club.

At the Old Bailey Marsh and Wilkins were defended by a team of eight barristers including three silks led by Norman Birkett KC who was said to have received £3,000 as his brief fee. The funds for their defence were thought to have been subscribed by racing men, and the 'pretty young Mrs Marsh, mother of eight' had pawned her jewellery and drawn out her savings to retain Birkett. 'A loyal citizen' wrote to the police that the money had been raised by terror and extortion. Most probably a good deal of it came from the

Croydon Airport bullion robbery. Whoever provided it, the money was well spent from the donor's point of view.

While on remand in Brixton prison, on 28 October Marsh and Wilkins had assisted Prison Officer Payne during exercise when, according to reports, he had been seized by a powerfully built man and been bitten and kicked. This was something which stood them in good stead throughout the trial.

When it came to it the only real witness was Camillo Monte Columbo who made a poor showing, arguing with and berating counsel during his questioning. He had already told the police he had been offered £300 and £3 per week for life if he altered his evidence. None of the other supposed eyewitnesses was able to help. The murder charge was dismissed and Marsh, as the older man with his criminal record of assaults and unlawful wounding, received a modest twelve months for manslaughter; Wilkins got three months less. The judge specifically took into account the part they had played in assisting the warder who 'might have been killed'. Not everyone was convinced about that either. Later it was alleged that friends had organised the 'attack' so that the two Berts could step in and obtain credit for their efforts. This sort of 'put-up attack' was by no means new, nor was it the last time it was used. The police do not seem to have questioned that the assault was genuine. Newspapers noted that many bookmakers and even film stars were in court for the verdict.[50]

There are a number of letters complaining about the Whites and Marsh in the file. For example: 'Who is the head of this gang who run night clubs in the West and East of London and employ all these crooks. Ask Mr W Chandler of Wandsworth and other Dogs (sic) tracks and the leading light of the Jews.'[51] Another writer thought that Edward Emmanuel was still exercising control, and it was also suggested that he had some of the Croydon bullion. But, by and large, the police seem to have ignored these helpful suggestions.

It was after this and an attack on Harry White and Danny Gray

---

[50] Nat. Arch. MEPO 3 912.
[51] Letter, 10 November 1936, in Nat. Arch. MEPO 3 912.

at White City greyhounds that an accommodation was reached. The Sabinis would have the West End, the Whites the King's Cross area. They became known as the King's Cross Gang and Alf White would hold court in the Bell Public House or Hennekeys in the Pentonville Road, exercising strict discipline amongst his followers. 'No bad language was allowed,' says John Vaughan, a former police officer from King's Cross. 'First time you were warned. The next time – out.' It had been the same with Darby Sabini: women were to be treated properly; Italian youths could not drink before they were twenty. His had been a reasonably benevolent dictatorship.

Very occasionally the Sabinis could be seen acting for the forces of good, but even then their actions were not wholly altruistic. Darby saved Tom Divall, then working as a racecourse inspector, from a beating by some members of a Northern gang at the pony racing track at Hawthorn Hill, after he had refused to allow two of their number to take bets. 'I have often wondered what would have been my fate if such a good ally as Darby had not popped up at that critical moment.'[52] He arranged for some purloined binoculars belonging to an Epsom trainer to be returned to him, and Harryboy Sabini came to the rescue of the jockey Jack Leach when he was riding at Ostend and withdrew the English-trained Americus Boy. The horse had left the paddock for the Prix Eclipse and had therefore technically come under starter's orders, so bets were lost. The Belgian crowd believed that Leach had deliberately defaulted but Sabini, who admitted losing money, said, 'We know the owner and trainer did too, so we were on your side.' He then produced two razors and a hammer and said he had a gun as well.[53] There are similar stories of the Sabinis intervening when three-card tricksters lit on jockeys travelling to races by train, whom they thought were easy pluckings.

Darby Sabini made a great mistake repeated by countless criminals when, following a series of unfavourable articles, he sued D.C. Thomson, the proprietors of the offending *Topical Times*, for libel.

[52] Tom Divall, *Scoundrels and Scallywags*, pp. 209–10.
[53] Jack Leach, *Sods I Have Cut on the Turf*, pp. 183–4.

The article commented: 'No story of the turf wars could be complete without reference to one or two men whose activities have made themselves notorious. The Sabini brothers, Harry and Charles Darby Sabini have earned themselves enough publicity.'[54]

On 15 December 1925, the day of the action to be heard before the Lord Chief Justice, Darby failed to appear and costs of £775 were awarded against him. He did not pay and bankruptcy proceedings were commenced.[55] By this time it was heard he had moved to Brighton where, he said, he was living in furnished accommodation.

On 28 October 1929, he appeared in court there charged with assaulting bookmaker David Isaacs. It was something of a curious case. After an incident at Hove greyhound stadium, when Sabini thought Isaacs was welshing on a bet, at about 11.40 p.m. they had met in Porky's restaurant where each said the other attacked him. Isaacs went to the police, who patched him up; then instead of going straight home to bed he felt faint and went for a cup of tea at a billiard hall. Outside by mischance he met Sabini again, who called him a copper's nark and challenged him to a straight fight. Isaacs said Sabini then launched himself at him and knocked him down and unconscious. When Isaacs was asked why he had not brought witnesses, he replied, 'How can I get witnesses against a man like this, when everyone goes in fear of their life of him?' Sabini called four witnesses who said Isaacs was the attacker, along with the ring inspector from the dog track, William Shepherd, who thought just as highly of him as did Tom Divall: 'So far as I know he seems ready to do anybody a good turn. He has assisted many when they have been in financial difficulties.' His evidence did not assist Sabini because the Chairman of the Bench, in a curious little judgement, said there was no doubt 'a serious assault was committed although there might be some mitigating circumstances'. Sabini was fined £5 with the alternative of 28 days hard labour.[56]

---

[54] *Topical Times*, 12 April 1924.
[55] *The Times*, 16 December 1925.
[56] *Evening Argus*, 29 October 1929.

Even if they declined to speak against him, Sabini was not all that popular with the local residents. Former bookmaker Morrie Peters recalls, 'If he went into a pub he'd sit in a corner with his back to the wall so no one could attack him from behind.'

According to Saffron Hill legend his daughters were educated at Roedean; but there are no records of the girls there, at least under the name Sabini. He is also said to have had a penthouse flat in the Grand Hotel on the front financed by two sacks of gold which he is believed, again according to Saffron Hill residents, to have taken with him to the South Coast.

4

The Battle That Never Was

Jack Spot's reputation as the 'Champion of the Jews' is based on a single incident which has attained legendary status over the years. It is a totally spurious story, but one on which Spot successfully traded for the whole of his career as King of the Underworld.

His rise to fame in the East End in the mid-1930s coincided with that of the British Union of Fascists led by Sir Oswald Mosley. More particularly, according to Spot's memoirs, it can be traced to the so-called battle of Cable Street on 4 October 1936 when, so the story goes, the whole of Stepney rose as one to prevent a march by the Fascists.

Spot claimed he played a great part in stemming this tide of evil which threatened to engulf the East End and there is no doubt what-soever that he traded on the story of how he felled Roughneck, a professional wrestler bodyguard of Mosley, so becoming the Champion of the Jews, a self-proclaimed position he maintained for the rest of his life.[1]

---

[1] The wrestler said to be involved was in fact 'Rough House' King Curtis. Curtis was a top-class all-in wrestler in the days when the sport bore some resemblance to reality. On 11 November 1933 at Lanes London Club he lost to Atholl Oakley for the British

As the years have passed, however, it has become clear that he did no such thing and his story, as indeed was much of the event, is simply folk legend. Perhaps more importantly, it is becoming increasingly accepted that the so-called battle between the East Enders and the Fascists which resulted in the expulsion of the latter never took place. There was certainly a confrontation, but it involved the police on one side and left-wing sympathisers on the other. Mosley and most of his men simply stood by and watched.

Mosley was born in 1896 and educated at Winchester before going to Sandhurst. In the First World War he was commissioned in the 16th Lancers and sent to Ireland from where, on his application, he was transferred to the Royal Flying Corps. In 1918 he was elected to Parliament as Conservative member for Harrow, and for a time was regarded as a young high-flyer. By 1922 he had quarrelled with the hierarchy and stood as an Independent, defeating the official candidate. In 1920 he married Lady Cynthia Curzon, daughter of the statesman Lord Curzon, a lady of Jewish extraction who was an ardent socialist. Under her aegis he converted to socialism and won the Smethwick seat for the Labour party in 1926. In 1928 he succeeded to the baronetcy, and from then on moved right and was duly expelled from the party. In 1932 he founded the British Union of Fascists, known as the Blackshirts – the uniform was said to have been copied from that worn by fencers at which sport Mosley, despite a limp following a flying accident, was of almost international standard. At its height, the movement had some 20,000 members, mostly young, white and light-blue-collar workers, in 400 branches throughout the country.

A meeting at Olympia in June 1934 provoked considerable opposition from Communists, and with police presence at a minimum there were angry complaints at the way demonstrators and hecklers were handled by the Blackshirt security forces. In September of that

All-In Heavyweight title. Towards the end of 1936 he appeared in the well-received film *All-In*, starring Ralph Lynn. There is no evidence that he took part in the Cable Street march.

year Mosley endeavoured to hold a meeting in Hyde Park, but with an estimated 150,000 anti-Fascist demonstrators present the meeting broke up before he spoke.

A series of well-supported marches through the East End attracted little opposition until in the late summer of 1936 the local community – supported by the Communists – began to strike at the increasingly hostile presence in the area by the British Union of Fascists. On 30 August there had been fighting at a march by Jewish ex-Servicemen to Victoria Park in Hackney. Rotten eggs, soot, flour and apples had been thrown at the marchers, and in turn the residents had fought with the Fascists.[2]

Buoyed by his progress in the East End, Mosley decided to hold a major rally on 4 October 1936 to mark the fourth anniversary of the founding of the party. The intention was that the Blackshirts should assemble at Royal Mint Street at 2.30 p.m. for an inspection by Mosley. This would be followed by a march through the East End and he would speak at Salmon Lane in Limehouse at 5 p.m., Stafford Road in Bow half an hour later, Victoria Park Square at 6 p.m. and Aske Street in Shoreditch at 6.30 p.m. Even his greatest detractors regarded him as a mesmeric speaker and the meetings were bound to be well attended. Now opposition began to mount against him and his march.

The popular view is that it was the local community which rose spontaneously against this right-wing leader, but this is not so. It required a great deal of organisation by the Communists to achieve their undoubted success. Speaking a decade later H. W. Carver, Chairman of the Stepney Borough Communists, took the credit on behalf of his party: 'It was the Communist Party which organised that struggle and it was in the face of the opposition of their own leaders that many Labour people joined the fight.'[3] Commenting on the situation and a counter-march the following week, *The Times* thought that 'many small shopkeepers seemed

[2] *The Times*, 1 September 1936.
[3] *East End Advertiser*, 26 December 1947.

to resent this disturbance of the East End by political processions of whatever sort'.[4]

Appeals by the Mayors of the East London boroughs for the march to be banned were ignored by Sir John Simon, the Home Secretary, who relied on the police to keep the potential combatants apart. The Commissioner, Sir Philip Gale, set up field headquarters off Tower Hill, and 6,000 constables and the whole of the mounted division were drafted in to the area.

The Blackshirts began to assemble at 1.25 p.m. but they had been pre-empted by a group of some 500 anti-Fascists who were already there, with the *Daily Worker* being sold in Leman and Cable Streets. By 2.15 it was estimated there were around 15,000 anti-Fascists in the Aldgate area, about half of whom had blocked the Commercial Road at Gardiner's Corner, making clenched-fist salutes and shouting – in echo of the French at Verdun – 'They Shall not Pass'. At 3 p.m. it was thought that the Blackshirts, still in Royal Mint Street, now totalled around 1,900 including women and cadets and four bands. About 300 of them were in ordinary dress.

Mosley arrived to review the troops at 3.30 p.m. and shouting by his supporters was countered by the singing of the 'Internationale'. Now the Police Commissioner Sir Philip Gale decided things had gone far enough and banned the march; instead, Mosley would be allowed to march West through the deserted City. The Blackshirts moved off at 4 p.m., ending at Somerset House in the Strand at 4.30 p.m. Later Mosley spoke from the BUF Headquarters in Great Smith Street, Westminster:

> Brother Blackshirts. Today the Government of Britain has surrendered to Red Terror. Today the Government of Britain has surrendered to Jewish corruption. The British Union will never surrender . . .

And more in the same vein.

[4] *The Times*, 12 October 1936.

The actual battle did not concern Mosley and his men. A barrier
had been erected in Cable Street and a lorry was overturned; timber
was expropriated from a builder's yard, along with bricks with which
to pelt the police. Broken glass was strewn across the road to hamper
and injure the police horses.

One old member of the BUF recalls:

> The so-called Battle of Cable Street never took place. The
> only people involved were Tommy Moran and a few who had
> arrived with him to set up the assembly point. Hundreds fell
> on them.
>
> I had just arrived in London from Lancashire and went to the
> place of assembly. None of the thousands of supporters there
> were involved. The battle was between the police and the
> Communists who had been organising all over the country for a
> fortnight.
>
> Mosley's attitude was to obey the law until we could change
> it, so when Sir Philip Gale ordered him not to march he obeyed
> that order.[5]

For Mosley it was a case of *reculing* to *sauter mieux*. Ten days later
he did march effectively through the East End. A Special Branch
report of November 1936 concluded:

> The general cry . . . that the entire population of East London
> had risen against Mosley and had declared that he and his followers
> should not pass and that they did not pass owing to the solid
> front presented by the workers of East London. This statement is
> however, far from reflecting accurately the state of affairs . . .
> There is abundant evidence that the Fascist movement has been
> steadily gaining ground in many parts of East London and has
> strong support in such districts as Stepney, Shoreditch, Bethnal
> Green, Hackney and Bow.
>
> There can be no doubt that the unruly element in the crowd
> . . . was very largely Communist-inspired. A number of well-
> known active communists were seen at, or near, points where
> actual disorder occurred.

[5] John Warburton, conversation with author, July 1999.

While attempts by the Communist Party to raise enthusiasm over the 'Fascist defeat' were comparative failures the BUF, during the week following the banning of their march conducted the most successful series of meetings since the beginning of the movement. In Stepney, Shoreditch, Bethnal Green, Stoke Newington and Limehouse, crowds estimated at several thousands of people (the highest being 12,000 assembled) and accorded the speakers an enthusiastic reception; opposition was either non-existent or negligible and no disorder took place.[6]

And so for the next few months Mosley and men marched through the East End, creating an atmosphere of terror amongst the Jewish community until they were banned. Parker recalls: 'I was about six at the time. I was terrified; there was drums banging; they broke our windows. They knew who to look for because Jewish houses had the Mezzuzah – a strip with the scroll – outside the front door.'

Wensley Clarkson recounts the October 1936 story in vivid detail and bases it on Spot's own account in the *Sunday Chronicle*, but it is simply wrong. According to Spot, he played an heroic part in the fight against Fascism. In Clarkson's version Spot led a charge which included his stalwart friends Moishe Blueball and Sonny the Yank. He had armed them with weapons and himself carried a chairleg lined with lead. Scattering Fascists left and right, he was finally overpowered and clubbed to the ground by police officers. When he recovered consciousness he was in hospital and was told, 'You're nicked.' He was charged with grievous bodily harm, taken from his hospital bed to court and there was remanded in custody for a week. He was unable to finance his defence and so local Communists provided a 'legal adviser'. His wife tried to see him, but the police told her she had missed

---

[6] Nat. Arch. MEPO 2 3043. The report went on to say that membership of the BUF had increased by 2,000 since the march. Other meetings during the month held by anti-Fascist bodies such as the Young Communists League had been closed by the police, either to prevent breaches of the peace or because of lack of support.

visiting time and would not be able to see him for another five
days. At his next court appearance the Communist legal adviser
did not mitigate for him but ranted on about provocation and
urged the police commissioner to ban marches. Spot was convicted
and received six months imprisonment. It was then, he maintains,
that he learned his trade, being taught by some of the greatest
practitioners of the time in varied occupations such as
safebreakers, counterfeiters and confidence tricksters. Here he had
a road to Damascus experience:

> I met crooks from every branch of the criminal profession, and
> while I learned from them, anxious to know as much as any
> one of them, one fact became increasingly obvious to me. It
> was so obvious I wondered why no one else had ever realised
> it.
>   No one man is capable of possessing all the various skills that
> the 'perfect' criminal needs. But to achieve perfect robberies, beau-
> tifully executed and with no fear of failure, the separate skills of
> *all* these men should be welded together into one concentrated
> effort.[7]

In fact four months seems to have been the maximum handed out
– to a man who attacked a police officer shielding a fallen Blackshirt
from the crowd – by any of the magistrates, who seem to take a
dim view of the behaviour of some of the Jewish members in the
crowd. Sentencing one man who had urged the crowd to free a man
and woman who had been arrested, the stipendiary commented: 'I
do not understand the attitude of you people. You expect the police
to protect you from the people you regard as your enemies – the
Fascists – and yet when the police are endeavouring to keep order
you do your best to create a disturbance and riot urging people to
attack the police.'[8]

   According to Clarkson, Spot had married a young woman named
Mollie Simpson in 1936, and they had a son. By the time he was

[7] Hank Janson, *Jack Spot*, p. 43.
[8] *The Times*, 11 October 1936.

released his wife was involved with another man.[9] If Spot did marry her at that time, it was not under any of his usual names. Nor is there any record at the Family Records Centre of a child being credited to Comer or his normal aliases during that period. Clarkson says that later, when Spot was in financial difficulties, Mollie Simpson gave an interview to the *Sunday Dispatch* saying that he had only occasionally contributed to the upkeep of their son: 'Those years leave a mark in any life. They ruined my health. I was a pretty and healthy girl when I married Jackie. I could tell of the years we spent together, where we went and whom we knew – I knew them all. I can fill in the gaps in the public story of Jack's life. But, though I don't think he would harm me, there are always his friends . . . and I've got to be careful.'[10] Spot's marriage cannot, of course, have broken up because of his imprisonment over fighting Fascists in 1936.

Unfortunately Spot's memoirs, and the subsequent accounts which have relied on them, are very often completely untrue. He paints the picture of himself as a young, enthusiastic freedom fighter who was, he says, nineteen. But he was not; he was twenty-six when he was released from his sentence. On 23 January 1955 the *Sunday Chronicle* published a retraction of his story, admitting it to be a complete fabrication. Nevertheless, as James Stewart says in *The Man Who Shot Liberty Valance*, 'Print the legend.' It is the legend which has lived on, and it is on this that most of Spot's reputation is based.[11]

In fact, it was not until 31 March 1939 that Spot was actually convicted of malicious wounding at Mansion House Justice Room and received his six months imprisonment. When – years later at his trial for slashing Tommy Falco – he was questioned about the

[9] Wensley Clarkson, *Hit 'em Hard*, pp. 36–42.
[10] Wensley Clarkson, *Hit 'em Hard*, pp. 244–5. Clarkson gives the article as having appeared shortly after the Rossi, Blyth and Dennis trial. I have been unable to trace it for that period.
[11] Robert Murphy in *Smash and Grab*, p. 158, says that Spot was fined for his part in the battle of Cable Street, but a conviction does not appear in his criminal record.

conviction, once more he claimed that it was for fighting with Fascists. Again no one bothered to look at his criminal record and he managed to avoid being unmasked.

The truth was that he, Morris Goldstein and Bernard Shackter had been running a protection racket in the East End for some time. They were arrested on 22 March 1939 on charges of causing grievous bodily harm and were held in custody. The next day they appeared at the Mansion House Justice Room and were remanded to appear the following week. On 31 March their case was heard by the Lord Mayor, Sir Frank Bowater. They pleaded not guilty. The fight had been at the Somerset Social Club in Little Somerset Street, E1. One man had been slashed and the other hit over the head with a milk bottle. Passing police officers had heard cries of 'Murder' and had gone to investigate. Hall Halkin, representing the three men, said that it was a question of one gang defending itself against another. The Lord Mayor thought there was a doubt in Goldstein's case and discharged him. Detective Inspector Jordan then told the court that Comer and Shackter were members of a gang who terrorised shopkeepers and café proprietors in the East End; they levied blackmail and their victims were afraid to appear against them. Spot and Shackter were sentenced to six months apiece. This time their victims were Hyman Jacob and Spot's former friend Nathaniel 'Itchky' Simmons. The case had nothing whatsoever to do with the fight of good over evil; it was a simple and straightforward matter of club protection. When it came to it, business was business.

After the pair were sentenced Comer tried to get out over the dock rails, and fighting broke out between the rival gangs in the well of the court. The police eventually broke up the fight while others struggled to get Comer and Shackter down to the cells. After that there was another bout of fighting outside the court.[12]

---

[12] Mansion House Justice Room register 1939. Prior to 1967 the Lord Mayor and Aldermen of the City of London were allowed to sit as single justices. 'Gangsters fight in court' in *East London Observer*, 8 April 1939. In the report Spot appears as Comar and Shackter as Shackster.

About two years earlier, however, Spot had been involved in an incident which was held against him for the next twenty years; he is said to have given evidence against Jimmy Wooder. Once more it is difficult to disentangle myth from reality. Wooder ran an Islington-based protection team and again Itchky Simmons was the victim. As the doorman of the New Moulin Club, owned by the former world champion boxer Ted 'Kid' Lewis, he was attacked by Wooder and given a kicking. Then in December 1936 he took another beating from him and three others – this time in Fox's, a billiard hall in Dean Street. It is now that Spot is said to have given evidence on his behalf. The case was a curious one, involving the once great boxer from the East End, Lewis – who at one time misguidedly was a Mosley man – as well as the boxing promoter Jack Solomons. Simmons was said to be Lewis's minder, which was a bit odd because of all people Lewis should have been able to deal with any trouble himself. In his memoirs Lewis suggests he was simply the doorman.

At the end of the case, the Recorder Sir Holam Gregory had some strong words to say:

> We have had to listen to an unpleasant case which arises out of an affray in one of those horrible and vile places that exist in the West End under the title of a club.
>
> Those places exist and do untold harm to the community. Young men are still being corrupted there; fights are taking place nightly.[13]

Wooder then gave evidence in the case against the former boxer Ted Lewis[14], who was charged with conspiracy to pervert the course of justice. It was said that he had taken £50 to help Wooder with an identification parade and, in the fashion of the day, to persuade Simmons to change his evidence. Three men had been charged in

---

[13] *The Times*, 18 February 1937.
[14] Morton Lewis, in his account of the affair in his biography of his father, suggests the name was the Moulin Rouge. *Ted Kid Lewis*, pp. 223–8.

the December with an assault on Simmons, but it was not until 5 January that Wooder was put on an identification parade. Three days before he was arrested Lewis had told him, 'I have the handling of the case and if you can get the money I can prevent them picking you out. They can be straightened out for half a hundred.' A meeting was arranged at The Ring, Blackfriars, but Wooder did not turn up. On 5 January Wooder was indeed picked out on a parade and Lewis attended the remand hearing. Afterwards he was alleged to have said to Wooder's mother, 'Jimmy is a little fool. If he had come and seen me as promised he would not have been picked out.' He told her he would do all he could and when asked whether it was not too late was apparently full of assurances: 'No, I can do anything I like with Simmons.'

On 19 January there was a meeting at the New Moulin Club when Wooder's father told Lewis, 'My old woman has got £40 and I will part up £10.' Lewis replied that he would get the boy out of it. 'I won't let you down. You trust me.' There was another meeting the next day when Wooder senior handed over the money and, with the police watching the transaction, Lewis was arrested.

At the Old Bailey Lewis was represented by a phalanx of top barristers led by G.D. 'Khaki' Roberts who would later represent Dimes in the 'no-fight' trial. At the end the Recorder pointed out that there was no evidence that Lewis had approached any of the witnesses, and the jury retired for a bare fifteen minutes before returning a not guilty verdict. 'If it is any satisfaction to you,' said Sir Holam Gregory, 'you are quite right.' Curiously, on the first hearing at the magistrates' court the stipendiary had suggested that there could be an alternative charge of obtaining money by false pretences, but the prosecution had ignored it.[15] Lewis went on to open the El Morocco club in Dean Street.

Parker has the story that Wooder and others then gave Spot a bad beating with the butts of cues in a Soho billiard saloon when

---

[15] *The Times*, 13, 14, 15 April 1937.

he was again trying to help Simmons. Later Spot learned that Wooder drank in Whitechapel at a club, Pancho's. Spot caught up with him in the lavatory and cut him from ear to ear.[16]

It was while Spot was serving his six-month sentence in 1939 for the assault on Simmons that he came to the notice of the one-eared – it had been bitten off in a fight – Arthur Skurry, and earned this very hard man's approval. Spot told Parker that the incident which gained him recognition stemmed from Antonio 'Babe' Mancini and his dislike of Jews which manifested in his habit of spitting in their prison food. Mancini was a long-term Sabini man who served a number of short sentences, mainly resulting from thefts and fights at racecourses.[17] Spot at first refused to eat the food which Mancini had fouled. Mancini had also been appointed the prison barber and Spot was sent to him: 'Time you had a haircut, Abe', the officer is alleged to have said. When he found that Mancini was the one to cut his hair, fighting broke out and Mancini came off badly. He also suffered a second time at the hands of Shackter. 'Skurry was a diddicoy. He saw Jack do up "Babe" Mancini and that's when he said he didn't realise Jews could fight. Skurry was like the King of Upton Park,' says Parker. Unlike a number of Spot stories this cannot be disproved. Mancini was certainly in prison at the time, serving a sentence of one year's hard labour imposed at Folkestone Quarter Sessions for stealing a wallet.

In any event Spot must have impressed Skurry, for he forged an alliance with the Upton Park gypsies who generally 'protected' small market stallholders. Fighters they may have been, but they were not

[16] Robert Murphy dates this as 1938 and places it in 'Foxy's', with Spot's revenge taking place in 1946. Frank Fraser places it in 1943. The correct name of the club was Fox's. Wooder, along with his brother Charles, was a member of the Islington Mob. Charles, who described himself as a boxing promoter, was an expert pickpocket. One occasion when he was less than successful was when he earned six months at Dover Magistrates' Court. He had been caught in an attempt to relieve an American tourist Henry Schmidt of his wallet and £155 on the gangway of a cross-Channel steamer. The Times, 1 July 1935.

[17] These included a sentence of one month passed at Ashford Magistrates' Court on 13 October 1924 for assault on a bookmaker at Wye races. Harry Sabini was acquitted but Bert Marsh and another long-time Sabini supporter, Thomas Mack, were also convicted. The Times, 15 October 1924.

smart and effectively the Upton Park Mob with luminaries such as Skurry, Teddy Machin, Porky Bennett and Jackie Reynolds became his boys.

Spot was always recruiting hard men when he could find them. Wassl Newman was one candidate, Parker remembers:

> Jack wanted Wassl Newman on his team but Newman wouldn't wear a suit. He was an old Toby with a toggle scarf round his neck and a cap. He was cut up by four brothers from Bethnal Green. He'd been nipping and they did him. He had a sister in the Bethnal Green Road and she sewed him with a needle and cotton. He didn't care that she'd used white cotton.
>
> Newman's greatest enemy was an ex-boxer Albie Day, and once a week they'd have a fight in the Roman Road market. Wassl pulled a chain off a cart and gave Albie a God awful hiding and after that Albie didn't bother him.

The stories of Newman are legendary. About 5'7" tall, he had a set of fine white teeth which he attributed to eating hard crusts of bread, something he did daily to keep them polished and sharp. When he was a young man the locals would offer him a slice of bread and jam if he would put his hand through a window pane. He would always take up the challenge, but if the bread and jam was not forthcoming there would be serious trouble. It was said he would walk miles to seek out a fight. On the debit side he was also reputed to have thrown a cat into a fish-fryer when the owner of the shop refused to pay him protection.[18] It is easy to see how he would have fitted in with Arthur Skurry and the others from Upton Park.

Another man Spot wanted on his firm but failed to attract was Billy Howard, said by some including Frank Fraser to be one of the best street fighters in London. Parker recalls:

> He was one of the few people Jack respected. They had respect

---

[18] The same story is told about Jimmy Spinks. See Bryan Magee, *Clouds of Glory*, p. 138. And no doubt about many others as well.

for each other. If Billy was on the door at Winston's no one would have a row with him. He hated Billy Hill. He was quite a good-looking boy, not a liberty taker although he once cut a fellow to pieces. All over a girl it was. Jack wanted him on the firm but Howard liked his own little kingdom.

It was probably after Spot's period of imprisonment that his relationship with Mollie Simpson broke up. She told him she had become involved with one of the West Ham boys. Spot is said to have returned to live at his parents' flat.

5

The Fortunes of War

The Second World War provided the greatest single opportunity for organised crime in Britain and, led in London by Billy Hill, criminals now took advantage of it. One significant factor was the expansion of their markets. Just as middle-class America would not have thought of consorting with criminals until Prohibition, so the war narrowed the class boundaries. With dozens of prohibitive Emergency Orders being made in Parliament, there were opportunities beyond their wildest dreams. In his book *Boss of Britain's Underworld* Hill wrote, 'So that big, wide, handsome and oh, so highly profitable black market walked into our ever-open arms.'[1] Now middle-class women were prepared to deal with black marketeers to obtain extra food, clothes, cigarettes and petrol coupons. Government offices were raided for ration books. The bombing provided a great opportunity for looting and, dressed as ARP wardens, thieves were often inadvertently assisted to clear stock from damaged shops by members of the public. The blackout and consequent ban on car lights helped the getaway drivers enormously.

[1] Billy Hill, *Boss of Britain's Underworld*, p. 73.

Seeing the opportunities available, people who would not normally commit crime helped themselves. In 1943 thefts from railway stations exceeded £1 million (£40 million in today's terms) and the next year the figure almost doubled. A new generation of criminals was born.

There was also more co-operation between criminals throughout the country. The Scots, known as talented safebreakers but not gifted when it came to disposing of the proceeds, now took advice. Any city with docks was a particular target of thieves and black-marketeers. The pillaging of military stores continued throughout the war, and whole consignments of commodities such as razor blades and cigarettes simply disappeared.

A by-product of the arrival of troops from overseas was that it required more work from prostitutes and those in the vice rackets. Marthe Watts, a senior employee of the Messinas – the brothers who controlled most of the organised prostitution in Soho and Mayfair – recalled that once the United States forces landed, the girls were required to work fourteen hours a day. In turn the ranks of profes-sional criminals swelled with deserters, of which there were esti-mated to be over 20,000 from British services and later from overseas forces, all of whom had to exist without a proper job. They needed false papers, identity cards and army passes to survive and so, in addition to forged ration books etc., a market now developed in counterfeit papers. Organised crime came into its own.

But first the war saw the effective end of the Italian Mob. The night when war was declared against Italy there was rioting in Soho with Italian-owned property being destroyed. The Sabinis were dealt some rough treatment, not only by rival gangs but also by the British government. Some of the brothers were interned as enemy aliens. Darby was detained on 6 June 1940 and Harryboy eight days later, which left the Whites very much in control of things. Aligned with them were the Yiddishers. One of the Sabini men who remained outside the sweep was Babe Mancini, the man whom Spot claimed to have attacked in Brixton prison. It was he who would lead what was left of the group to maintain Italian interests.

By the November Darby Sabini had still not appeared before a tribunal to determine whether the reasons for his detention were justifiable. He was described as being in semi-retirement and was believed to be a man of considerable means.[2] Harryboy (alias Harry Handley, Henry Handley and a few other names), partial to highly polished springsided boots, was detained a few days later. Off they both went to the Ascot internment camp.

It is apparent that the authorities were using the war to smash the Sabinis by portraying them as enemy aliens. Such evidence as there was showed they spoke little Italian and had few convictions between them. It seems improbable that they would lead an insurgence. Like all the best gang leaders, Darby had no convictions. Harry's were modest in the extreme, and actual evidence of his bad character was minimal. The worst that could be said about the family conviction-wise was that Joseph, another of the brothers, had been sentenced to three years penal servitude in 1922. There had also been a small matter of the attempted bribery of prison officers while he had been in Maidstone.

The police report leading to Harryboy's arrest described him as:

> . . . one of the leading lights of a gang of bullies known as the Sabini gang who under the cover of various rackets have by their blackmailing methods levied toll on bookmakers . . . He is a dangerous man of the most violent temperament and has a heavy following and strong command of a gang of bullies of Italian origin in London.

It concluded:

> We have no knowledge that he has previously engaged in any political activities but . . . he can at best be described as a dangerous gangster and racketeer of the worst type and appears to be a most

[2] *Daily Express*, 8 July 1940.

likely person who would be chosen by enemy agents to create and be a leader of violent internal action.

Harryboy appealed against his detention under Regulation 18B. The reasons for his internment were given as 'hostile associations' but more likely he, together with Bert Marsh, had been detained as a reprisal by the authorities for the successful bullion raid at Croydon Airport.

The appeal was delayed and so Harryboy, ill-advisedly as it transpired, applied for a writ of *habeas corpus*. He had already offered his home, worth some £15,000, as surety if he could be granted bail. In his affidavit in support of the application for leave to be granted, the writ said he had never been known as Harry Handley. However, the evidence of his arrest was that the police had gone to his house at 44 Highbury Park, Highbury New Barn in North London on 20 June 1940, and asked Sabini's wife where Harry Handley was. The reply had been 'upstairs'. It was also successfully argued that he could be described as being of 'hostile origin' even though he had an English mother and his father had died when he was a child. His brother George Sabini had a daughter in the ATS and a son in the RASC who had joined up immediately after war had been declared with Italy. So far as he was concerned, he would be prepared to enlist at once. The authorities were none too pleased when Harry was released from detention on 18 March 1941. He was promptly rearrested for perjury and on 8 July that year he received a sentence of nine months imprisonment.[3] So for a time the West End interests were shared by the Whites, Jack Spot and the Elephant Gang – with the Whites increasingly the dominant force.

Before the Second World War protection had been something of an art form. A fight was started in a club and a certain amount of damage was done. Perhaps a foot went through the skin on the drum, tables were overturned, a few glasses were broken. The next

---

[3] There is a full and highly critical account of the Regulation 18B process, under which the Sabinis and many others were detained, in A.W. Brian Simpson's *In the Highest Degree Odious*, Chs 13 and 14. Nat. Arch. Home Office papers TS27/496A.

day came a visit from a sympathetic representative of the Sabinis or others who would point out how disruptive such incidents were in frightening off punters and how they could be avoided by payment of a small weekly sum. By 1941, however, the rules of the game had changed. Now it was thought best to inflict the maximum amount of damage possible on a rival's premises. If the club closed for good, so much the better. There was one less competitor.

On 20 April 1941, the Russian-born 'Fair Hair' Eddie Fleischer (known as Eddie Fletcher) and Joseph Franks were involved in a fight with Bert Connelly, the doorman of Palm Beach Bottle Parties, a club in the basement of 37 Wardour Street which also housed the Cosmo on the ground floor and the West End Bridge and Billiards Club on the first. Now Fletcher was given a beating and banned from the club by the manager Joe Leon, whose real name was Niccolo Cariello. Fletcher had been involved in protection and violence for years. In January 1931, along with Harry White, he had been charged with assaulting Fred Roche as he left the Phoenix Club in Little Denmark Street.[4]

Ten days later Fletcher returned and Sammy Lederman, a Soho denizen of thirty years – he was a friend of Jack Spot and gave evidence against the Kray Twins – came to the Palm Beach to tell Mancini, now the dinner-jacketed catering manager and doorman for the night, that 'They're smashing up the [Bridge and Billiards] Club.' What had happened was that Fletcher and other members of the Yiddisher Gang including Moishe Cohen had been playing pool and cards in the club when in walked Joseph Collette, Harry Capocci and Albert Dimes, then currently AWOL from the Royal Air Force. Fighting broke out, started – said the witnesses, who may not have been wholly impartial – by Albert Dimes. The police thought that the intention was to destroy a rival club. The unfortunate Fletcher received another beating and was taken to Charing Cross Hospital, then a matter of minutes away.

[4] *The Times*, 23 January 1931.

Quite what this was to do with Mancini is not clear and, according to a statement he later made to the police, this is what he told Lederman. Joe Leon however asked Mancini to go to the door of the Palm Beach and let no one in. He stood inside the door and then changed out of his evening clothes and went upstairs to see the damage.

As he was on the stairs he heard someone say, 'There's Babe, let's knife him.' Mancini thought the speaker was Fletcher, who had returned to the club to retrieve his coat; he sensed someone was behind him and went into the club followed by Fletcher, Harry 'Little Hubby' or 'Scarface' – although no prosecution witness would accept that latter soubriquet for him – Distleman and another man. Little Hubby had managed the Nest Club in Kingly Street for four years from 1934 but had apparently not worked since, supporting himself – according to his brother 'Big Hubby' Distleman – by successful betting on the horses and greyhounds.[5]

It was then that fighting broke out yet again, with Albert Dimes being restrained by his elder brother, Victor. Distleman was stabbed. Few of the forty people in the club saw exactly what happened, but the consensus of such witnesses as were prepared to speak up was that it was Mancini who stabbed Distleman. In fact Distleman had said to two companions, 'I am terribly hurt. Babe's done it.' This did not have the same evidential strength as a formal dying declaration, but it certainly did not help Mancini. There must have been more than a grain of truth in the belief by the police that trouble had been deliberately caused, because just at the end of the fight who should arrive but the one-time Sabini man, Thomas Mack?

Mancini had then chased after the unfortunate Fletcher and had almost severed his arm. When he was interviewed he told Detective Inspector Arthur Thorp, 'I admit I stabbed Fletcher with a long dagger which I found on the floor of the club, but I don't admit

[5] 'Big Hubby' Distleman ran a string of brothels in the West End, as did his prematurely deceased brother. He died in the 1980s, reputedly leaving £4 million in safety deposit boxes.

doing Distleman. Why should I do him? They threatened me as I came up the stairs and I got panicky.' The next day, however, he said he had the dagger wrapped in a rag with him when he went up the stairs. In fact, Mancini had known 'Little Hubby' Distleman for about fifteen years.[6]

Mancini was unlucky at his trial. The brief to the prosecution suggested that if he offered a plea to manslaughter, 'Counsel will no doubt consider it, as the witnesses of the assault on Distleman are vague and shaky.' It is not possible to say now whether any such plea was offered, or whether the prosecutor did not accept it. It was argued that if self-defence was rejected, a death in a gang fight in such circumstances should only be manslaughter – and indeed the judge Mr Justice McNaughten summed up to that effect. In fact, in a not dissimilar case three months earlier this is exactly what had happened. However, after a retirement of a bare fifty-five minutes the jury convicted Mancini of murder – a decision with which the judge concurred – and an appeal met with no success at all. The judge had, if anything, been too favourable in his summing-up, said the Lord Chief Justice. A further appeal to the House of Lords also failed, and Mancini became the first London gangster to be hanged for nearly twenty-five years.[7]

Following the Mancini trial Dimes, Collette and Capocci were again arraigned, this time before the Recorder of London, Sir Gerald Dodson. One by one the witnesses for the prosecution failed to identify them, and the trial effectively collapsed. Capocci was acquitted, but Dimes and Collette were bound over in the sum of £5 to come up for judgement in the next three years. 'You were probably

---

[6] See Arthur Thorp, *Calling Scotland Yard*, pp. 111–13.
[7] The last to be hanged prior to Mancini was Joseph Jones, a man with a long record for violence who along with two Australian deserters preyed on soldiers on leave in London towards the end of the First World War. Under the pretext of taking a man to a gambling club or brothel, he would be lured into an alley and beaten and robbed. On 8 November 1917 Gilbert Imlay was attacked on leaving a drinking club in the Waterloo area and died from his injuries. One of the Australians, Ernest Sharp, turned King's Evidence and received seven years. The other, Thomas Maguire, was sentenced to ten years. Jones was hanged at Wandsworth by John and William Ellis on 21 February 1918.

expecting prison,' said the Recorder, 'and no doubt you deserve it.' Dimes was returned to the RAF, where he did not remain for very long.

On the other hand Spot and Hill had very different wars; neither of them much to their credit, but each in its way very profitable. At the beginning of the war Hill was inside, finishing off a sentence which was cut short by the discharge of prisoners who had only a few months left to serve.

By the time he came out things had changed. Frank Fraser recalls: 'The war organised criminals. Before the war thieving was safes, jewellery, furs. Now a whole new world was opened up. There was so much money and stuff about – cigarettes, sugar, clothes, petrol coupons, clothing coupons, anything. It was a thieves' paradise.'[8]

Ever the organiser, Hill set to with unmatched enthusiasm. Writing of the black market he would recall, 'It was the most fantastic side of civil life in wartime. Make no mistake. It cost Britain millions of pounds. I did not merely make use of the black market. I fed it.'

And one way in which he fed it was by the theft of bed-sheets from a services depot in the south-west of England. Lorryload after lorryload was taken; he estimates that thousands of pairs were stolen each week and sold at £1 a pair. He also raided a warehouse full of fur coats which were sold at £6 each. Whisky went for £500 a barrel, the same price as a barrel of sausage skins. Hill was, he said, clearing around £300 to £400 a week, a fantastic sum for the time.

It is a wonder he had any time for his other career. He had also become the master of the smash-and-grab raid, something he learned from the burglar Charles 'Ruby' Sparks who had developed the technique in the 1920s. Now in 1940, with the blackout in force and a complete boon and blessing to criminals, a series of daring raids took place. Frank Fraser, yet to meet his hero Hill, recalls:

[8] Frank Fraser, *Mad Frank*, pp. 18–19.

You could nick a car, take the back seats out, take it to the West End, do a job, and the chances of getting caught were just about nil. I'll never forget one in Hanover Square. It was a high-class gentleman's tailor, a very high-class one at that. We had on wardens' helmets with the letters 'A.R.P.' on them and armbands. We smashed the windows in with the car and when people came looking asked them to stand back, saying, 'Control, please stand back.' People were helping to load the car up.[9]

The police were convinced that Hill was behind – if not an active participant in – most of those early raids. On 1 February 1940 Ciro's Pearls in Bond Street lost almost its entire stock. The windows had been covered with screens and so provided protection from view as the burglars, who had forced the metal grille and front door, ransacked everything. The next month Hill was arrested after a mid-morning raid on Carrington's, the jewellers in Regent Street. At about 10 a.m. on 20 March a small maroon car was driven over the pavement into the shop doorway, blocking access. A second bigger, black car pulled up and the driver smashed the window with a car-jack. Rings worth some £6,000, which in today's terms would be estimated at about £250,000, were stolen. Hill was placed on an identification parade but not picked out.

Hill was arrested again after a car mounted the pavement in Wardour Street on 21 May. At first passers-by thought the vehicle was out of control, but a man in the passenger seat stood up and, leaning out of the sunshine roof, robbed the shop through the broken display window. It was a technique devised by Hill. Another robbery was one at Phillips in New Bond Street when jewellery worth £11,000 went. This time the second car which had been stolen had the engaging new number plate MUG 999. Hill survived yet another identification parade.

His luck ran out on 26 June 1940 when he and two long-standing friends – Harry Bryan, nominally an Islington bookmaker, and 'Square Georgie' Ball – were arrested in a failed robbery on Hemmings

[9] Frank Fraser, *Mad Frank*, pp. 18–19.

& Co. in Conduit Street.[10] A PC Higgs threw his truncheon through the windscreen and, with the crowd joining in, Bryan and Ball were arrested. Hill fled down Bond Street into Bruton Street, but by now the crowd and two more policemen were after him. He managed to get on to a roof and despite the old trick of saying to a policeman who climbed after him, 'He's in there', in almost pantomime tradition the crowd shouted, 'That's him.' Bryan and Ball drew three years apiece, but Hill managed to negotiate a charge of conspiracy which carried a maximum of two years. For him it was off to Chelmsford, where he worked as the prison barber and where he met the man who would become his enforcer, Frank Fraser: 'I was in trouble the whole time, on bread and water, and Bill was very kind to me. He took me in the cell they used for haircutting and told me to try and keep my head down. I got in with him marvellous. We had the same birthday, December 13th, although of course he was twelve years older.'[11]

The food in the prison was poor and Hill managed to organise a series of thefts from the kitchen with Fraser as the distributor. When he was discharged from the prison he gave him his watch, and from then on Fraser was his man.

A one-month sentence at Marylebone for being a suspected person followed Hill's release and then, in the terms of the trade, it all came on top when he was given information about a potential armed robbery. On 15 July 1942 a postmaster in Islington was to be the target during the lunch hour. Jock Wyatt and Teddy Hughes went with him; Wyatt as lookout. The robbery went well until a lorry driver rammed their getaway car. Hughes and Hill were caught in the car and Wyatt, instead of sauntering away, tried to run and was also arrested.

---

[10] Bryan had previously been convicted in the celebrated 1936 Clerkenwell bullion robbery when £2,000 of gold ingots were stolen in a snatch from a lorry. John Murray, also known as Hoppy McCarty, who had convictions going back to 1902, received two years as the planner. Charlie Barwick was another involved but was not charged. *The Times*, 16 July, 25 September 1936.
[11] Frank Fraser, *Mad Frank*, pp. 30–31.

In those days it was possible to exchange part of a sentence for strokes of the cat, and Hill and the others asked Sir Gerald Dodson, the Recorder of London, if this could be done.[12] Unfortunately Hughes had a weak heart and it was not thought he could stand the punishment. It was a question of twelve strokes or none for all, and so Wyatt and Hill received four years and Hughes a year less. For Hill now it was off to Dartmoor.

Meanwhile, what had Spot been doing? In fact, to his intense dislike he had actually been called up: not the sort of thing that should happen to a self-respecting gangster. In fairness to Hill he had signed up for the Royal Air Force on the basis that he thought it was less daunting than the 'Kate Carney', but he was never called up. According to Spot's memoirs, he himself was an active soldier for three years in an anti-aircraft regiment waiting for a chance to get at the Germans: 'I'd have known how to deal with one of those German storm-troopers if ever I could have got my hands on him. But the nearest they ever let me get to the Germans again was the British coast, this side of the Channel.'[13]

Disappointed that he never received a commission, Spot raged on about how demeaning and wasteful it was for a man of his ability being obliged, for three years, to shine his boots and buttons, having to suffer from a sergeant's temper and taking orders from 'pasty-faced little runts with officer's pips'. He implies the hostilities would have been over a great deal sooner had he been in charge of the war effort.

In fact for Comer, all in all his war was much lower-key than that of Hill, but he was nevertheless making money in his own way. He served for a short time in the Royal Artillery stationed at Norton

---

[12] One robber, sentenced along with Alfie Hinds senior for a £23,000 robbery of Lloyds Bank in Portsmouth on 23 April 1932, asked Mr Justice Avory, 'If you can give me corporal punishment and so lighten my sentence so I can come out to my children, I hope you will.' He received fifteen strokes and five years from the judge, not known for his leniency. *Portsmouth Evening News*, 16 August 1932. Although generally a flogging did no lasting damage, Hinds is said to have been broken by his own lashing and never recovered his health.
[13] Hank Janson, *Jack Spot*, p. 55.

Manor Barracks, Taunton. Later he told Gerry Parker that in the camp he met the same anti-Semitism as was prevalent in the outside world. Another East Ender had told him, 'Jew-boy – you've come here to fight and you want luxury? You won't get no luxury here. You sleep up there where I put you.'

Spot did nothing until the man went into the lavatory, when he followed him with his army boots slung over his shoulder. He started belting him with them and in turn the East Ender began calling out for help. Spot was transferred, but fight followed fight and he gained a reputation as a troublemaker. Eventually, following a short time with the Marines, he was sent to see a psychiatrist who recommended him for a medical discharge in 1943. He returned to the East End to find his parents dead and his brothers and sisters scattered. One brother was, in fact, serving in the RAF.

Now it is impossible to trace the accuracy of most of Spot's stories but, according to him, after his discharge he returned to London and gravitated to the West End where in November that year he became involved in a fight with a man known as 'Edgware Sam' – in all Spot's stories the men are Manchester Mike, Bristol Bert and so forth – in the grandly named Piccadilly Club, in reality a spieler in the Edgware Road. Parker was told that the quarrel appears to have been over the serious matter of who should be served their tea and butty first. Other accounts suggest there was anti-Semitic bullying of the barman over not putting enough sugar in his tea, which certainly makes for a more heroic account. Spot intervened and, after knocking Edgware Sam, hit him with the metal teapot. Sam ran out of the club, some said to get a gun.

Whether Spot believed this or thought that Sam had gone to the police, he feared a prison sentence and, advised by his friend and mentor, the London club owner and receiver Abe Kosky, fled North to a land where the black market and organised crime were rampant. Goods were being stolen from the ships at Hull docks and the cash had to be spent somewhere.

Where illegal gaming and drinking clubs are established, protection is sure to follow. According to Spot he helped a club owner, Jack Marks (known as Milky), of the Regal Gaming Club in Brunswick Street, Chapeltown, Leeds, to clear out a Polish protection racketeer from his club, became the owner's bodyguard and, as a reward, was given a pitch at the local greyhound track. He dealt severely with an ex-coalman who looked like the Swedish singer and film star Carl Brisson and wore a bowler hat and pinstripe suit. The man seemed to believe he had a no-loss betting account, expecting a payment when he won and his losses to be erased, and Spot swiftly disabused him. He also dealt with Liverpool Jack, said to be the leader of the toughest gang in Leeds, and apparently another formidable man called London Alf who was also in the North at the time.[14] Whether these men existed or were merely good stories for the Sunday readers is a moot point. He certainly went to Leeds where local recollection of what happened differs from his own. One habitué of Milky's recalls an elderly kibbitzer being smacked for criticising the card skills of one of Spot's men. A local, 'Fatty' Fineberg, remonstrated and was rewarded by being threatened with a knife.

Whichever version is correct, from then on Spot's future in Leeds was assured. He undertook to protect members of the local Jewish business community against anti-Semitism, and he certainly brokered a partnership between a leading Northern bookie Jack Ashe and Abe Kosky. Meanwhile Milky continued to prosper. He had a close relationship with the wife of a senior police officer while, in turn, the man had his pick of the club girls. Spot found the North an exciting place.

He also worked as what he described as a 'troubleshooter' for various other Northern clubs until he heard that Edgware Sam, with whom he had fought, had been jailed for fraud. Perhaps fraud is too grand a word. It seems to have been for working the tweedle, a short-time con trick of taking a ring into a jeweller's for valuation and then declining to sell it. At the last moment the grifter changes

14 *Sunday Chronicle*, 23 January 1955.

his or her mind and offers the ring once more. This time, however, the ring appraised by the jeweller has been switched and he is now offered a fake in the hope that he will not bother to examine it a second time. In any event Spot returned to London, pleaded self-defence to the assault charge and was acquitted.[15]

Now he was in great demand and was repeatedly called to help club owners in the major Northern cities. Spot was seriously big in Leeds, but he also had interests in Manchester and Birmingham. Gerry Parker recalls:

Jack got his start back in Manchester. Gus Demmy, the old man, that is, wanted a pitch and he couldn't get one. The man who was running them wouldn't talk to him. Jack called a meeting with him in the Midland Hotel and asked why his 'cousin' couldn't have a pitch. Everyone was Jack's 'cousin'. Jack gave him a dig – and remember a lot of big men can't punch their weight but Jack was well over six foot and 17 stone and he could. He had a very hard body. After that Gus got his pitch and Jack was made.

He had trouble in getting a pitch for himself at Doncaster races, standing up to another racecourse bully, and later assisted racecourse officials in the North to allocate pitches in a fairer way. It was something which he claimed stood him in good stead when there were troubles at Ascot shortly after the war.

Spot was also well regarded in Birmingham and he moved, as required, between the cities. He was certainly back in London by the end of 1943. When there were signs of trouble from the authorities it paid him to adopt a low profile. Gaming was frowned on in the courts as being against the war effort, and as such the promoters were dealt with severely. On 5 January the next year, now described as a doorman at the Apex Social Club, Beaumont Grove, Spot was fined £2 along with his cousin Solly Kankus and another dozen or so punters who, when asked, chorused, 'We all

---

[15] The story appears in all Spot's accounts of his career but I have been unable to trace the actual case under any of his usual names in the court records at the London Metropolitan Archives.

plead guilty.' Two weeks later Mrs Ettie da Costa, the proprietress, was fined £250.

With the bombing over, things in London gradually returned to normal, and with normality came the opportunities beloved by any criminal. In his book *Jack Spot, The Man of a Thousand Cuts*, Comer – echoing Billy Hill's earlier memoirs – claims modestly that:

> I was the first man to realise that criminals could be organised, each crook becoming a small part of a master plan in which every cog and spindle operated perfectly.
> I became the planner and master mind.
> I became the Boss of the Underworld!

It was this sort of attitude which would lead to his downfall; but for the moment things went accordingly and, by the end of the war, Spot was doing very well for himself. He claimed he had met with the American gangster Sam Clynes, said to be a former member of Murder Incorporated, and received a good deal of advice from the great man.[16] The advice included how to treat members of his team if they went to prison. Clynes suggested a weekly pension of £20 for wives, and showed him how to run a dice game. The advice on payment to the wives was sound when, in fact, a policeman's wage was between £9 and £11. Unfortunately, too often Spot failed to pay and in turn paid the penalty for it. After Clynes' death he paid for a funeral service and a headstone.

One problem with this story is that it is another almost total fabrication. The name Clynes is probably an amalgamation of James Hynes and Harry Kleintz. Hynes was certainly an American and, it was claimed, he was shot when the gangster 'Little Augie' Orgen was killed. Later, together with Kleintz, he came to England where following a robbery on a jeweller's they both received five years on 28 June 1928 at Newcastle Assizes. At the end of their sentences both were deported, but they re-entered Britain from France. In

---

[16] *Sunday Chronicle*, 20 February 1955; Robert Fabian, *Fabian of the Yard*, pp. 154–61; Arthur Sharp, *Calling Scotland Yard*, pp. 81–90; Nat. Arch. MEPO 3 901.

1934 Hynes was sentenced to five years penal servitude at the Central Criminal Court for school-breaking and possessing housebreaking implements by night. In November 1937 he then stole some £20,000 worth of jewellery from a Mildred Hesketh-Wright at her home in Park Lane. According to various police officers' memoirs, the implication is that he was arrested in a Turkish bath where he could not conceal a weapon. Clearly the police themselves were not averse to printing the legend when it suited them. In fact he was arrested on 16 November 1937 in the Mile End Road outside Stepney Green tube station. He was another who is said to have asked for the cat in order to reduce his sentence, but Mr Justice Goddard told him the injuries he had received in the shooting would not allow this. At the time of his arrest he was wanted by police in a number of countries in Europe. He died in Parkhurst on 12 April 1943. Spot can never have met him, but it is conceivable that he knew Harry Kleintz and it was possibly from him that he obtained the advice. However, there is no record of Kleintz being a member of Murder Incorporated. According to Scotland Yard records James Hynes was indeed shot in the assassination of Orgen in Brooklyn in 1927, when it was suggested he was a bodyguard. Neither Hynes nor Kleintz rates a mention in J. Robert Nash's *Encyclopaedia of Organised Crime*, or indeed in any of the other standard books on the era. But why should that get in the way of a good story?[17]

What was much more accurate was that Spot was running Botolph's, a gaming club masquerading as the Aldgate Fruit Exchange in the daytime, on behalf of Abe Kosky (now a black market millionaire), and running it extremely profitably.

During the daytime clerks in white collars and bowler hats arrived at their desks. Some empty fruit crates decorated the premises and the

[17] Orgen was shot in the back of the head while talking to his bodyguard, the legendary Jack 'Legs' Diamond. His cherry-red coffin bore a silver plaque: 'Jacob Orgen Age 25 years.' He was in fact 33, but when he had formed his gang eight years earlier his father regarded him as already dead. For a full account of his career see James Morton, *Gangland International*. The reports of the killing in the New York papers make no mention of Hynes.

clerks began to answer letters sent, said Spot, by his friends. At 5 p.m.
they put on their hats and coats and left and the transformation began.
The desks were shifted into an ante-room, the blinds were pulled down
and soft lights were switched on. By 7 o'clock the place had been
turned into 'the biggest gambling club London had ever known'. Play
continued until 7 a.m. the next morning. 'We never had an argument
much less a fight.' This was not surprising because apart from Spot,
on the door was the fearsome Arthur Skurry who, despite fearing 'he
would look like a poof', had been persuaded to exchange his cap and
choker for a suit. The fact that half an ear had been bitten off only
enhanced his status. 'My old pal Julius was in charge of the eats.'

Chemin-de-fer, faro and rummy were the games played and, with
the house taking a cut of two shillings in the £1 on the bets and
the kitties running into the thousands, there was so much money
about that, Spot said, there was no need to fiddle. Spot claimed that
black marketeers would call the bank at chemin-de-fer at £5,000
without a blink:

> When a man got cleaned out he just got up and walked out of
> the joint as if he were going for a breath of air. If it had been a
> bad smash you didn't see him again.
>   I remember one regular customer tossing his last handful of
> notes on the lay-out at faro. He lost his lot and strolled out with
> a nod to me. Three days later he shot himself. Of course, he may
> have had other troubles.

If there was a big winner Spot would arrange for him to be seen
home by little Hymie Rosen, Goldstein or George Wood.[18]

To give the story verisimilitude the *Sketch* published a short confir-
matory rider from ex-Chief Superintendent John Sands: 'Jack Spot's
spieler was typical of the bigger clubs though those in the West End
used to be moveable and would open in different and lavish premises
every week or even every night to avoid the attention of the police.'[19]

[18] Jack Spot, 'My Life as a Gangster' in *Daily Sketch*, 1 October 1955.
[19] For an account of these card games see Robert Fabian, *London after Dark*, pp. 31–2.

Hill himself ran a number of these parties and the police spent a great deal of time and trouble tracking them down in order to prosecute the organisers. In his memoirs Gilbert Kelland, former head of the CID, recalled one potential raid on a house in Grosvenor Crescent. A minimum of twelve people were required to be on the premises in order to defeat a defence that it was a private party, and prior to the Gaming Act in 1960 a Commissioner's Order in Writing (which was valid for a month) was necessary before a raid could be carried out. Hill frequented the Star Tavern in Belgrave Mews, and a check on the cars in the area showed his Ford Consul had been parked nearby on the last night when the order would be valid. With a matter of minutes to go before midnight, when the order would expire, three men went into the house thus making up the required minimum, but almost immediately three others came out. Then three more and a further two left. Kelland thought the first three had been acting as lookouts and had spotted the police. The raid was aborted.[20]

Quite apart from the pretence of masquerading as the Aldgate Fruit Exchange, the real reason Spot's club stayed open and untouched was the huge sums being paid weekly in bribes to the police. Parker recalls:

> Jack was the bagman going to pay off the police. He would take the money to Victoria station. Presumably they didn't want to be paid on their own patch. It must have been the only place you could ask a policeman directions how to get to the club. 'Left, second right and left again'.

And Hill? He claimed that, more or less at the end of the war and now out of prison, he was within a hair's breadth of a £7 million robbery of savings, insurance and postage stamps. A van left Harrow and drove to High Wycombe where the stamps were collected. Then it was driven to a side street while the men went into a café for

[20] Gilbert Kelland, *Crime in London*, pp. 54–5.

lunch, with only one remaining to guard the van before it was taken to the railway station for the stamps to be loaded onto a train for countrywide distribution. Hill regarded the robbery as no more difficult than shelling peas for his team of four, and thought that the whole swoop on the van would take no more than ninety seconds. Then, however, it was a question of careless mouths cost jobs; somehow the police came to hear of the plans and the route was switched. Hill was still prepared to go ahead but then he learned that Superintendent Robert Lee, 'one of the smartest bogies in the business', was 'sniffing around'. The job was abandoned. And, lied Hill, 'I packed up active crime soon after that, and carved my way to the top of the Underworld in London to settle down to a quiet career running my clubs and spielers.'[21]

[21] Billy Hill, 'Whispers lost me millions' in *People*, 24 October 1954.

6

Whitewash

During the war, with petrol rationed, there was only limited horseracing at five tracks. The Derby was run at Newmarket after Epsom had been appropriated by the authorities. Ascot became an internment camp. It could not be said that petrol was needed for attendance at greyhound tracks, but there was still the blackout and a track had only one meeting a week, usually on a Saturday afternoon. With peace things returned to normal. The war had also brought with it substantial changes in the Underworld hierarchy. Gone were the Sabinis – interned, ageing, even disinterested. Their place had been taken first by Jewish gangsters and then the Whites. Up and coming on the rails were Spot and Hill.

The Whites had an uneasy tenure in office. Despite their fearsome reputation in the early and middle 1930s, they were not really hard enough men. As early as 1939 their leader, old Alf White, had taken a bad beating at Harringay dog track from some young tearaways from Stoke Newington, and the expected swift reprisal had not materialised. Their serious and rapid decline began at the end of the war with their ousting from control of Yarmouth racecourse in October 1946.

Moey (or Moses) Levy, a Jewish bookmaker who had once been

part of a powerful family in the Aldgate area, had been warned off his pitch at the course by the Whites.[1] The Levys, of Spanish-Portuguese extraction, had been strong in the 1920s and 1930s. They were a family of seven, and Moey had started life working for Jewish gaming clubs. He married an English girl and worked as a bookmaker in Brick Lane in the days when the Jewish people kept to one side of the street and the English to the other. Later he had a club over a confectioner's shop on the corner of Middlesex Street. In 1926 he had been slashed by the East End villains Arthur Harding and Charlie Horricky. Five years earlier his brother David had been sent to prison for carrying a pistol to the Epsom Derby meeting along with Moey. David Levy said they had been told that if they attended the meeting they would be shot.

Over the years Moses Levy was in and out of the wars. He also served a sentence at the time of the 1921 Epsom Derby, and was back in court in the August in breach of a bind-over imposed that March. This time his counsel argued that if the magistrates at Epsom 'had known of the desperate gangs that were visiting Epsom they would have arrived at a different result'. His case was heard on the day that the Brummagen Mob beat up a number of Jewish book-makers including Alfie Solomon at Bath. Some years later Thomas Newman received three years penal servitude for demanding money from Levy with menaces.[2]

Now Levy was getting old and he appealed to Spot for help to deal with the Whites. Spot travelled to the course with his team. In charge of the White operation there was Eddie Raimo from King's Cross, a man who modelled himself on George Raft and who wore a black shirt with a white tie. A hard man, Raimo had previously glassed Billy Hill in a public house in Clerkenwell and during the war had been with Fraser in the glasshouse in Bradford.[3]

[1] See Raphael Samuel, *East End Underworld; Star*, 1 June 1921.
[2] *The Times*, 18 August 1921; 20 September 1927.
[3] He made a number of appearances in the courts including one at the Old Bailey in May 1938 when along with Jock Wyatt, also from King's Cross, he received 18 months for causing grievous bodily harm. He was acquitted on a second matter after a retrial when the prosecution offered no evidence following the failure of the complainant to attend. See also Frank Fraser, *Mad Frank*, p. 26.

Now, faced with Spot, he simply backed down. It was a bad sign for the Whites.

Frank Fraser recalls the family:

Then [pre-war] they had a good team with men like Jock Wyatt and Billy Goller on the strength but now Alf White was old and Harry, his son, was a lovely man but with no stomach for a fight. Harry was in Wandsworth in 1944. He'd hit a geezer with a walking stick and got a few months. That was all the time he'd done and he didn't like it. He was very big, impressive, full of bonhomie, hail-fellow-well-met. And Alf was as well. If you had a crooked copper they were the ideal men to handle it. If anyone was in trouble and could get a bit of help they were the ones to go to, but as for leaders they didn't really have the style. All in all they were a weak mob and they were ripe for taking.

The one who would have been terrific and who would have defended the territory was Alf White's son, also called Alf, but he had died in 1943. The other brothers, Johnny and Billy White, were really racing people and not involved in clubs.[4]

One former Flying Squad officer recalls Spot, Harry White and Dimes from the days when they were providing a united front:

Harry, Albert D, Jack Comer *et al* were in a pub in the Euston Road. It was well 'after time' but nevertheless the obviously homosexual pub pianist had been induced to stay on. This man was something of a flamboyant dresser and at some stage Albert D. produced a cut-throat razor and, as the man was playing, cut off his tie. This, seen as quite hilarious, started a trend: razors were produced and the poor man's lapels, sleeves, waistcoat – in fact everything down to his vest and pants – was cut off, such exercise leaving him with a series of small cuts and nicks, all bleeding, all over his body. The man, well aware of whose company he was in, was petrified and said nothing: he just kept playing. Anyway, at the end, they all had a 'whip-round' and gave the pianist enough for several suits and sent him home in a taxi.

[4] Frank Fraser, *Mad Frank*, pp. 46–7. In July 1935 Alf White snr and jnr and another son, William, each received 12 months hard labour for assaulting John Defferary, the licensee of the Yorkshire Stingo. See Nat. Arch. MEPO 3 910.

Harry was prompted to tell me this one evening in the Premier Club where there was a gay pianist, but whether he was the same man or not I cannot say.

He describes Harry White as: 'Really he was a most gregarious fellow. He was very "hail-fellow-well-met" and cockney in the manner in which Americans expect. He was always smartly dressed, a very heavy smoker and drinker and a nuisance when he had over imbibed.'

Fraser may not have thought too much of Harry White's ability on the street, but there is no doubt that he undertook his fair share of pre-war protection. In January 1931 he could be found with Eddie Fleischer (aka Fletcher) in a fight outside the Phoenix Club in Little Denmark Street. The manager Casimir Raczynski and a man named Fred Roche had been attacked as they left the club, and White and Fleischer were accused of malicious wounding. As did so many of these affairs, the matter blew over. When the case came up for committal, Roche said he had made a mistake while still suffering from the effects of the attack. Now he was sure that, whoever hit him, it was neither White nor Fleischer. The one independent witness, Thomas Jeacock – who had identified White and Fleischer – was pleased to tell the court that Roche assured him he had made a mistake. In such ways were things sorted out.[5]

Now, following his Yarmouth success what Spot really wanted was complete control of the pitches. The financial benefits were almost boundless. The Whites controlled the allocation of the pitches at point-to-points and on the free course at tracks such as Epsom and Brighton. It is portrayed as a benevolent operation, but that is probably far from the case. Alf White had begun the collection of £2 from each bookmaker on the course and Harry White continued the practice. The Whites had already negotiated permission to control the allocation of point-to-point pitches with the local Hunt Secretary after making an alleged donation to the Hunt of £300, but the likelihood

[5] *The Times*, 24 January, 4 February 1931.

is that £50 was nearer the mark. On the face of it bookmakers then paid their modest £2 for the pitch, but there were also the protection fees involved. It was something Spot wanted for himself and with the help of Arthur Skurry and his Upton Park gypsies, including the generally out-of-control Teddy Machin, he took command of the free course at Ascot from his long-time enemy Jimmy Wooder to whom Machin is said to have taken an axe. That still left the other pitches run by the Whites.

The real trouble for the family interests began when in January 1947 Johnny Warren, part of what could be described as their extended family, followed Spot into the lavatory of a public house in Soho and made the mistake of mocking him over the fact that he was only drinking lemonade. He compounded this by making what Spot considered to be an anti-Jewish remark, suggesting that, 'Here was another Sheeney trying to take over.' Later Spot would say he knew the consequences of what would happen if he dealt with Warren, and at first he simply asked him what he wanted. Aggravatingly, Warren replied, 'Anytime,' and 'Bump! Down into the piss he went. I thought I shouldn't have done it and I went out. I don't know what happened but in a minute a mob comes looking for me.' Spot was fortunate. He was joined by Teddy Machin, Georgie Wood and Hymie Rosen; they all went to Al Burnett's Stork Club in Sackville Street.

It was then that Harry White and four or five others including Billy Goller arrived. Accounts vary as to what happened next. Spot's version was:

> Harry had seven of the toughest of his boys with him when I led my pals into the room. There wasn't any politeness this time. They knew what I'd come for. And I sailed right in. At the first smack I took at them Harry scarpered. You couldn't see the seat of his trousers for dust.

Over the years Spot's account of the fight varied and the incidents were telescoped or expanded to suit the teller. Whether this particular incident occurred immediately after the Warren episode or whether it was the culmination of several minor run-ins, one thing is certain, and that is that Billy Goller had his throat cut and nearly died.

Harry White's version as reported after Spot's downfall went as follows. He had been drinking in a club with the racehorse trainer Tim O'Sullivan and a third man when:

> Spot walked in with ten thugs, went straight up to Harry and said, 'You're Yiddified' – meaning he was anti-Jewish.
> White denied it. He said, 'I have Jewish people among my best friends.' Spot wouldn't listen and hit him with a bottle.
> As White collapsed in a pool of blood, the rest of Spot's men attacked O'Sullivan and the third man who was employed by White.
> O'Sullivan was beaten unconscious and pushed into a fire in the corner of the club. The other man was slashed with razors and cut in the stomach.[6]

That night Spot's patron, Abe Kosky – 'he had a name like the Russian for a horse's laugh' – was dining with a senior officer from Savile Row police station when the news came through that Goller had been badly injured. Spot had almost ignored his own maxim – 'You must never cut below the line here, cause, if you do, you cut the jugular – and the hangman is waiting for you . . .' – and Goller received the last rites. Spot was packed off to Southend to a club at the end of the airport runway run by Jackie Reynolds on behalf of one of the Upton Park gypsies, Benny Swan, who was a Spot man through and through. When he recovered, Goller was given £300 and matters quietened down temporarily; but so far as Soho was concerned, the Whites had lost considerable face and Spot had become a man with whom to be seriously reckoned in the Soho hierarchy.

It was then that Harry White's wife came to see Spot at Hyde Park Mansions to ask him to stop the quarrel, saying her husband

[6] Sidney Williams in *Daily Herald*, 3 October 1955.

only got Yiddified when he was drunk. 'Tell him not to drink then,' was the curt reply.[7]

There were other rumbles, including one in February 1947. According to the article by Harry White, the fight in the club had been merely an intimidatory rehearsal. Now, before racing began at Lord Roseberry's point-to-point at Bletchley, Spot backed by thirty men turned up and said he wanted twenty-five per cent of White's takings 'from today, Harry'. Spot's men gave other bookmakers the chance to pay, and if they refused their pitches were overturned and umbrellas sent flying. 'Why are you letting them do this to us, Harry?' asked one small-time bookmaker. But White had no proper answer. Spot had done '. . . what no other man had done. He frightened me to death.' After that, whenever possible, Spot went everywhere with him. On many Saturdays there were a number of point-to-points across the South of England where White kept a book, and one or more of Spot's men would go with him to jot down the winnings. For Spot it was a no-loss account; White had to bear those himself and suffer the admonition to be more careful next time.[8]

Spot however was never a bookmaker. He was into protection. He administered the layout of the pitches, and he took a cut of everything from the bookmakers' profits to the ice-cream concession.

Accounts mark the end of the Whites as coming in the week of 9 July that year. There had been talk of a gang fight at Harringay arena on the night of the Joe Baksi–Bruce Woodcock contest, but Detective Chief Superintendent Peter Beveridge had put a stop to it. Now according to both Hill and Spot – although their versions differ as to who plays the more heroic part – the Whites were ousted in a single night of violence. In Spot's version Harry White simply vanished, while Hill's account written by his amanuensis, the reporter Duncan Webb, who could always tell a good story, has one White

[7] Gerry Parker in conversation with the author.
[8] Sidney Williams, 'The Case of the Frightened Bookie' in *Daily Herald*, 8 October 1955.

roasted over a fire. Whichever (if either) is the correct version, the Whites were ousted.

> 'It's all right,' I said to Benny the Kid (Spot). 'We won't need shooters in this town anymore. Get 'em off the boys and get rid of them.' They collected the shooters and the bombs and the machine gun and destroyed them. They were actually thrown down a manhole.[9]

In Spot's version Beveridge called at his flat in Aldgate and asked him to come to the police station. Spot was quite pleased to comply because upstairs there were the Wood brothers who had a quantity of arms in pillowcases in their room, and the last thing Spot needed was a search. At the station Beveridge explained the facts of life to him.

> When I got back to Aldgate I collected the heavy mob together at once. 'We've got to pack it up,' I said. 'Get rid of the iron-mongery.' So we collected all the Stens, the grenades, revolvers, pistols and ammunition, loaded them into a lorry and dumped the whole lot in the Thames.[10]

The stories that Hill and Spot had a thousand men behind them when they saw off the Whites are of course a complete exaggeration, and some doubt that the clear-out was even approximately on the scale Spot and Hill portray in their respective memoirs. Beveridge's own memoirs are silent on the point. Indeed Spot's version which has him chasing down two White men – one of whom he beats and the other he lets go – is probably indicative of the actual scale of the enterprise.

It does seem, however, that in the 1940s and 1950s there was a mutual tolerance and even respect between the top criminals and the stars of Scotland Yard of the time. Men such as Detective Superintendent Robert Higgins could, and did, walk into public

[9] Billy Hill, *Boss of Britain's Underworld*, p. 7.
[10] Jack Spot in *Daily Sketch*, 3 October 1955.

houses or clubs unmolested and without the back-up required today
to fish out men wanted for questioning or to be put on an identification parade. Hill recounted the story of when Higgins walked
into a club where he and some thirty of his men were drinking.
They offered him a drink, which he declined, and he told Hill that
he and two others were to go to the station with him to be questioned about a robbery. Could they have another drink first? Higgins
waited and then they all called a cab to take them to Tottenham
Court Road police station. They were not picked out on a subsequent parade and returned to their headquarters.

Hill commented:

> But the point I want to make is that we all had real respect for
> Supt. Higgins and there wasn't the slightest risk in his coming
> into a pub alone where thirty villains were assembled.
>
> We could have cut his head off and no one the wiser, but that
> wasn't our idea of playing the game and it wasn't Mr Higgins' idea
> either.[11]

---

[11] Billy Hill, 'Whispers lost me millions' in *People*, 24 October 1954.

7

Hill and Spot Triumphant

Hill's triumph in his part in clearing out the Whites did not last long. Very shortly afterwards he was arrested along with a friend 'Stuttering Robo' over a warehouse breaking, and taken to Tottenham Court Road police station where he was charged. Hill maintains he was innocent and, given his full and frank admissions relating to his other escapades, he is possibly telling the truth:

> I felt choked. I never did mind being nicked for something I had done, but to get picked out for something I hadn't done was as much as flesh and blood could bear. They gave me bail and I decided to go on the run. I decided to leave Britain for ever, even while yet my crown was barely resting on my nut.[1]

He discussed this with his wife, Aggie, who wanted him to take her with him on the basis that she might stop further foolishness on Hill's part. Meanwhile, however, for criminals the purpose of bail is to furnish an opportunity to provide for the future and Hill needed one last quick and profitable job. On the East Coast an RAF officer

---

[1] Billy Hill, *Boss of Britain's Underworld*, p. 120.

was selling gash parachutes as surplus parachute silk to a South
London villain. Hill, dressed as a police officer, and friends including
John Tilly, known as John the Tilter, tailed the villain's lorry and
stopped it. The South Londoners ran away and Hill took the lorry.
He netted over £9,000 from the night's work, and although he was
providing for the wives of some of his friends who were in prison,
he still had more than something left over for himself.[2]

A diplomat friend obtained him a passage and Hill went to South
Africa via Lisbon. Within a week he was in Johannesburg where he
saw that a familiar East End face, Bobby Ramsay – a tricky little
fighter who looked like a pocket edition of Freddie Mills but who
had no real punch – was due to box there.[3] Hill soon made himself
busy. At the time the king of the city's Underworld was Arnold
Neville, a 17-stone ex-wrestler who controlled the gambling with
his partner Sammy Abnit.[4] They fell out and Abnit approached Hill
with a view to opening another club.

So now Hill opened the Club Millionaire as a gambling school
above a restaurant in Commissioner Street. Neville caught wind of
the venture, threatened to break up the club and, according to Hill,
he invited him to do so. He had apparently not realised that Hill
was now in partnership with Abnit. When Hill declined and his
involvement became apparent, Neville said that if the club opened
on the Sunday he would break it up himself.

Hill regarded this meeting as a showdown effectively for control
of Johannesburg. According to his memoirs, he had been given a
revolver by a reporter who disliked Neville and now he carried it
with him. Hill also had a large hunting knife which he gave to
Ramsay, who was told to be on the door.

Neville owned another club, the Stork Room, and Hill had a spy
placed there to warn him when Neville and his team were on their
way. On the opening night of the Club Millionaire on 12 May 1947,

[2] Billy Hill, *Boss of Britain's Underworld*, p. 123.
[3] In the 1960s Ramsay would go on to align himself with the Krays and was later cut
by Frank Fraser.
[4] In *Boss of Britain's Underworld*, Hill refers to him as Abinger, p. 125.

Neville and his team of eight appeared there about 1.30 in the morning.

Two days later there was an account of the ensuing entertainment in the Rand *Daily Mail*:

> Mr Arnold Neville, the former wrestler of Highand Road, Kensington was given nearly one hundred stitches in the Johannesburg General Hospital early yesterday morning after being attacked outside a city night-club. His assailants slashed his head and buttocks with razors and his condition is serious. It is alleged that shots were also fired during the attack. At about 1.30 a.m. when Neville and two friends were standing outside the night-club there was an argument. Blows were struck. Two men drew razors and one a revolver. Neville's friends retreated. When Neville attempted to break away, he was knocked to the ground and slashed. Later, Neville stated, he heard the firing of bullets.

Hill's account more or less follows the general line of the story but is rather more graphic in detail. He had been stopped from shooting Neville by Bobby Ramsay, who knocked his arm in the air. The supporters fled and Hill, firing his revolver, caught up with Neville and scalped him with the hunting knife he had taken back from Ramsay. Knife fights were, apparently, more or less unknown in South Africa at the time. According to Hill, 'His scalp was lifted clean off, just like a strong wind had blown off his wig. He went down like a stuck pig. Bobby grabbed my knife and slashed his buttocks as he was falling.'[5]

Hill and Ramsay were arrested soon afterwards. At the trial in August Neville admitted three convictions, one for assault, and also having escaped from prison. He was a retired wrestler who had earned about £40 a tournament, which was extremely good money. He denied being the minder for a gambling club or that he earned his living as a gambler. So far as another witness – the wrestler Dirk van Loggerenberg – was concerned, he was not Neville's minder and

[5] Billy Hill, *Boss of Britain's Underworld*, p. 126.

he had not received £50 for the night's work. He wished he had.

Ramsay said he had merely been playing cards and had not known there was any plan to defend the club. Harry Snoyman, the 20-year-old bouncer who wrestled – but not for money, he said – as Abe Wiseman, turned Neville away and said he had only used his hands on him. There was no need for him to use a knife. He had been cut by Neville and when he turned aside to wipe off the blood he heard Neville scream.

'Gangsterdom must be stopped,' said the prosecutor. 'I don't think you are a suitable person for South Africa,' said Magistrate J.H. Nolte, imposing a five-month sentence with hard labour on Ramsay. Snoyman received three months, also with hard labour. The charges relating to the alleged attack on van Loggerenberg were dismissed. By the time of the trial, however, Ramsay was the sole British representative. Hill was long gone and making his own way back to England.[6]

After the fight Hill had driven through the night to Durban in a hired car, with a man he describes as his workman. The driver was sent back with the car to Johannesburg where he was promptly arrested and, when falsely told that Neville had died, promptly gave Hill up. Hill had booked into the Waverley Hotel under an assumed name, but it was only twenty-four hours before the police were at his door.

He was represented by Harry Gross, then one of the top defence lawyers in Johannesburg. Neville's name was well known as a villain in the courts and Hill presented himself as a small, mild-mannered bespectacled man. He was given bail of £75, but now came a problem; he knew that it was only a matter of time before an application for his extradition came through, and he pre-empted it by skipping his bail and taking a flight to Egypt. He stayed in Cairo

---

[6] Rand *Daily Mail*, 14 May, 8, 9, 11 August 1947. While serving a sentence in Dartmoor, Bobby Ramsay was one of those who seemingly underwent a religious conversion. In the days when newspapers and wirelesses were not allowed in prison, he is credited with advising the chaplain to read the football results at the end of the Sunday morning service, so ensuring a full attendance. Later he ran a number of clubs in the West End and became a staunch friend of the Kray family.

and made his way back to England and the East End where Spot arranged for him to be hidden out with the Upton Park Mob: 'Benny the Kid was running things his own way, but then Benny was not a screwsman. He was a mobster, a good leader of tearaways, but he could not control the thieves like I could. They were not sorry to know I was back home.'[7]

For the moment, however, it was going to be back to prison. Hill did yet another last job in Manchester with Sammy Josephs and Teddy Machin, netting some £9,000, and promptly fell in love with a nightclub hostess named Connie. He promised that when everything had been sorted out he would send for her, and then he gave himself up. He served three years in Wandsworth, and it was then that he repeated the earlier stunt of Bert Marsh and Bert Wilkins when he saved a screw from a seemingly out-of-control Jack Rosa, a South London hardman. Rosa was awaiting a flogging and, at the time, the prison rules were that no further punishment could be imposed on a prisoner in these circumstances.

The day after his flogging Rosa attacked an officer with a knife in the pouch workshop. Hill intervened and was roundly condemned by the prisoners in the know who chorused that he was a bastard for saving the man's life. Rosa apologised, claiming that it was the effect of the cat which had sent him berserk. He escaped punishment and was said to have been paid £5,000 for his trouble. For his bravery, Hill received six months off his sentence. On his release he was met at the prison gates in 1949 by a jovial and cigar-smoking Spot, now very much the senior partner.

Once on the outside it was back to the gaming tables, and Hill leased the New Cabinet Club from Eva Holder who in 1950 was convicted of defrauding Peter Haig Thomas, a former Cambridge rowing coach who had married into the aristocracy and who now at the age of 68 had fallen in love with this temptress some thirty years his junior. He met her while she was soliciting in Soho and

[7] Billy Hill, *Boss of Britain's Underworld*, p. 133.

paid her £2. 10 shillings, along with five shillings for the maid. From then on it appears to have been love on his part; and in an effort to keep her off the streets, over a period of a year he parted with a total of over £35,000 on the basis that she was investing it in property in Soho or interests in clubs. He set her up in a flat in Lisle Street and intended to take her with him to Kenya, but because of her convictions for soliciting dating back to December 1929 this was impossible. Curiously, despite numerous convictions for soliciting she had none for dishonesty and none for soliciting after he met her. She claimed the money was a series of gifts, and that his complaint was malicious and really because she could not put up with him any more; but the jury and certainly the judge – finding it unbelievable that anyone would part with this sort of money – were against her. She received two years imprisonment.[8] From that moment on, for Hill it was onwards and upwards in the New Cabinet Club.

In the meantime Jack Spot had both reigned supreme and fallen in love. The object of his affections, Rita Molloy, came from a poor Dublin family. Her father died when she was seven and at thirteen she was wrapping soap in a factory, earning 11s 6d a week. She had then become a cinema usherette. On any showing she was outstandingly beautiful. Then aged nineteen, while driving to a football match her head was badly gashed in a car crash at Bray. She received £200 damages: 'The biggest sum I had ever handled until I met Jack . . . I went to Liverpool where most of my relatives live. I wanted to see the world I had read about in glossy magazines.'

And that world included Haydock Park races where she met Spot on one of his protective visits North:

> I looked around for the nicest looking bookmaker, someone I could trust. Then I saw him. I looked appealingly into his eyes. He met my gaze. 'Could I have ten shillings each way?' I asked him. He never took his eyes off me. I wasn't given a ticket. He said, 'I shall remember your face.' Neither of us can remember

---

[8] Victor Cooney, a younger man, who had a conviction for living off immoral earnings, was convicted with her. *News of the World*, 2, 9 July 1950; *The Times*, 4 July 1950.

what happened to the horse I backed. I only know that I had
fallen in love with Jack Spot.[9]

And it was off to the then notorious Adelphi Hotel in Liverpool
where, it was said, more women fell than horses at Beecher's Brook.
In 1948 they moved into Hyde Park Mansions in Cabbell Street
where they lived for the next nine years. The relationship was something of a trial for her devout Catholic mother: here was her daughter
associating with a Jew. For once it was something with which Spot
had to learn to live. Rita and Comer married on 8 July 1954 at
Marylebone Register Office. The gang was not there. They later had
two daughters, Rachelle and Margaret.

One man who was a reasonably healthy, if relatively short-term,
influence on the finances of both Jack Spot and Billy Hill was the
old-time villain Freddy Ford. Then in his eighties, Ford had been
around since the turn of the century as a major Soho player running
a string of illegal drinking clubs both in the West End and in Holborn
which were regularly raided by the police.

Ford's criminal career had more or less run the gamut of offences.
He claimed to have sold Peter the Painter a blowpipe used in the
Houndsditch robbery which led to the siege of Sidney Street on
3 January 1911. He had been sentenced to five years penal servitude at the Old Bailey in 1912 for wounding. In 1921, along with
his long-time partner Hyman Kurasch,[10] he was acquitted of passing
forged notes to a man named Boxer. It was a form of the old Green
Goods swindle, where the mark would be sold a small number of

---

[9] Rita Comer, 'They call me a Gangster's Moll' in *Sunday Pictorial*, 11 December 1955.
[10] Kurasch was himself a master international criminal. Apart from his convictions with
Ford, he appeared on conspiracy charges at the Old Bailey in 1915. In 1924 he was
wanted in Germany, and the next year was sentenced for possessing stolen jewellery in
Hamilton, Ontario. The jewels had been stolen in England. He was then convicted of
counterfeiting in Michigan in 1927. He returned to England and ran greyhound racing
at Portsmouth between 1933 and 1935. Then he moved to London and was involved
in a series of low-class nightclubs, and was thought to be involved in both drugs and
the white slave trade. In January 1937 he received five years penal servitude at Plymouth
Quarter Sessions for deception in a version of the pigeon drop which had netted him
over £2,000. His appeal, at which he was represented by Norman Birkett KC, was
dismissed. *Empire News*, 10 January 1937.

genuine notes on the basis that they were forged and no one could tell the difference. He would then be sold a substantial quantity of what would turn out to be blanks. Three years later in 1924 Ford was again acquitted, this time of manslaughter. It was alleged he was driving a taxi while drunk when his passenger William Taylor had been thrown out of the vehicle and killed. In 1926 Ford's clubs were in trouble. Weekday patrons of his Soho drinkers were sent at the weekend to Cursitor Street, just off Chancery Lane, where black-tie parties were held. He was given three months imprisonment over that club in March, and in the May he was explaining to a jury that magistrates were biased and would not listen to his defence that he was running a genuine club, the New Avenue in Ham Yard. It did him no good and he received a month's imprisonment, followed by a four-month sentence over the Havinoo club which had opened on the same premises the day after the New Avenue closed.

The next year he was sentenced to five years for receiving. In February 1927 – by which time the Havinoo was known as the Musicians and Artists Club – Ford went to prison for receiving along with a man named Chandler. The club was described by Inspector Wesley as patronised almost exclusively by thieves – male and female. If, by mistake, a genuine patron stumbled into the club, it was rare that he left with his money.[11] Finally, Ford served ten years for safebreaking.

However, by the end of the war Ford was a rich man who owned a number of hotels in King's Cross mainly used by the streetwalkers of the area. He had had the bright idea of making the women take suitcases along with their clients into the hotels, so providing the manager with an instant defence to allowing the premises to be used for the purposes of prostitution.

Now Ford decided that he wished to have the best spieler in London, and to have someone run it for him. Premises were found back in Ham Yard and Spot and Hill took over. Naturally Ford did

---

[11] *Empire News*, 13 February 1927. Freddy Ford, *King of Crooks*.

not see the share of the profits he expected and, after a series of raids, the club was closed. Hill and Spot then opened a club at the end of the airport runway at Southend, managed for them at various times by Benny Swan, Teddy Machin and Jackie Reynolds from the Upton Park Mob, and they also joined with two Greeks to open another club in Dean Street. It is sometimes suggested that Billy Howard partly bankrolled the Ford spieler and that, while there was no need for protection from other criminals, as with the Botolph club in Aldgate large amounts were paid out weekly to bagmen from Scotland Yard, West End Central police station and council officials.[12]

Quite apart from the clubs Hill and Spot were putters-up of robberies, often working with the Jewish thief Sammy Josephs. The Jewish connection particularly suited Spot and, as Parker says, 'Billy Hill was never anti-Semitic.'

However, there was one relatively small incident in 1948 which would have significant repercussions. A small but game Glasgow hardman Victor Russo, known as 'Scarface' from the slashings he had received, came to London. He had met Spot at the end of the war when Comer helped him financially in Manchester. Now Spot took him on a tour of the clubs and he became attached to a girl named Maisie. Soon it was a question of having to put up money for Maisie's brother's bail after he had been arrested for rolling a businessman. There was another incident during the visit when, in another club, Billy Hill's brother Archie and the old villain Dodger Mullins began to bait Russo. It was their early-week entertainment to tour the clubs and terrorise the ponces; that Russo was not a ponce did not matter; he was a 'foreigner' and that was what counted. When Hill and Mullins went to the lavatory, Russo followed them and cut them both before vanishing.

It appears that Russo had been hoping to share a bed with Maisie, but when this was not on offer he slept on a bench and then made his way to the Piccadilly club where the barman telephoned Spot.

---

[12] Michael Connor, *The Soho Don*, pp. 59–61. The book claims that it was Billy Howard who found the club and put together a syndicate.

He was told to give Russo £20 and send him to a barber's for a shave and clean-up. Long-term, Spot can rarely have invested £20 in a better way.[13]

The time when Hill was abroad or in prison was, perhaps, the high point in Spot's career as King of the Underworld. These were pre-Rita days when he could stay out all hours. Parker recalls: 'Jack used to go to the Corner House in Coventry Street in the early hours of the morning. Birmingham Phil who was an ex-copper was on the door and when this was slack about 3 a.m. he'd come and sit with us.'

Not exactly the high life, but it suited him. Now Spot was in control of the bookmaking at the racetracks and he had acquired the reputation as someone who could sort things out. And he did so. One story told about him is of a man who, having run up a big betting account in Australia which he could not pay, returned to Leeds and, still pursued by Australian heavies, was told he had to go to Spot, the overlord of the Leeds gangs, for help. He is said to have paid £5,000 to get them off his back, and the money was well spent. Spot, without paying anything to the Australians, had them apologise to the man.[14]

Even though this was Spot's heyday there were unnecessary hiccoughs. Parker recalls:

> Dick Hutton was a fellow my uncle used to employ at the races. People used to say to Jackie Cohen, 'Don't you employ Jews?' And he'd reply, 'Dick suits me.'
> Then in the late 1940s Jackie was going to put on a charity boxing show in the Withdean Stadium, Brighton. He was always doing this. He put the singer Billy Daniels on at Brighton Hippodrome; Julie Andrews was a little girl on the same bill. When Jackie Cohen did the boxing I had a phone call from him:

[13] As with all good stories, there are a number of versions of the Hill-Mullins cutting. Frank Fraser attributes it to 'Flash' Jimmy Emmett who was then cut by Billy Hill. Emmett later was sentenced to ten years for having a firearm near the Café de Paris in Coventry Street. Part of the severity in the sentence came from the fact that it was a favourite watering-hole of Princess Margaret. See Frank Fraser, *Mad Frank's London*, p.5.
[14] Gerald Byrne, 'The Truth about the Racings Gangs' in *Empire News*, 9 October 1955.

'Don't sit anywhere near Dick Hutton.' What had happened was that Dick had hit a Yiddisher boy with his binoculars outside either Ascot or Sandown Park, I forget which, and Jack was going to put it on him. Jackie Cohen heard through the grapevine what Spot was planning and told him not to come down, saying it was a charity night and it shouldn't be spoiled. Jack didn't come down, but Hutton walked about with a gun for weeks.

Spot had a special pocket made for his razor and he was free with its use:

> Big Benny Fox was a big man from the East End who liked going to Southend, and he liked paddling. Fox was a nuisance. He'd sit behind you at the fights and he'd never stop calling out, 'Hit him with a fucking left' in a very gruff voice. It got on your nerves. There was an argument out in the street and Fox said something out of order and Jack did him. Jack cut him on the chin. But nuisance or not he shouldn't have done; he was a Yiddisher boy.[15]

Nor was it possible for Hill to expand the empire. Spot had built up a formidable network of friends and allies in Northern cities but Hill, like many a Southern comedian who failed north of Watford, was never able to do so. Manchester had never really had a boss as had London, and the locals did not want one. The nearest had been the King of the Barrowboys, Bobby McDermott, along with Bobby Critchley who was said to drive in a bulletproof car, but these men did not operate on anything like the scale that Hill and Spot did in London.

However, Hill does appear to have looked seriously at potential opportunities in and around Manchester. What he seems to have wanted were tip-offs of wealthy patrons in the clubs, particularly the very fashionable Cromford Club run by Owen Ratcliffe. The idea was that while they were watching the cabaret, provided by performers of the calibre of Joseph Locke and Charlie Chester, their houses would be burgled. The spotter was promptly banned from

[15] Conversation with the author.

the Cromford, and Hill had a minion telephone Ratcliffe to express his annoyance. In turn Ratcliffe, operating on his own territory, threatened to have a meat cleaver put in Hill's head if he tried to move into Manchester. According to Ratcliffe's former partner Paddy McGrath, Ratcliffe even went to London to brace Hill in front of Albert Dimes.[16]

In the Underworld, however, accommodations are often reached. Matters must have been patched up between them because a decade and more later, when Ratcliffe was having trouble with the Hayward family over his Catford club, Mr Smith and the Witchdoctor, he sought the advice of Hill and Dimes. He was recommended to use the services of Eddie Richardson and Frank Fraser, something which led to the disastrous fight in the club in March 1966 which destroyed Charlie Richardson's thriving operation.

---

[16] Peter Walsh, *Gang War*, pp. 6–7. See Frank Fraser, *Mad Frank*; James Morton, *Gangland*; Robert Parker, *Rough Justice*. The healthy dislike shown by both Manchester denizens and the police to Southern villains was repeated when the Nash brothers and later the Krays were shown the way to the train. For an account of the Manchester clubs of the period see Frank Fraser, *Mad Frank's Britain*.

8

The Airport Disaster

The job on 28 July 1948 which was to have been the first major
post-war robbery took place at Heathrow Airport – then called Heath
Row, and from the number of thefts which took place there was
known as Thief Row. The robbers included the cream of the Upton
Park Mob, the Wood brothers, Franny Daniels and Teddy Machin,
mainly men then aligned with Jack Spot. So, not necessarily correctly,
he has been given the credit for planning the robbery. It took place
while Hill was still serving his three-year sentence, and although
there have been stories that he advised from his cell, these really
are fanciful given conditions in prison at the time.

Sammy Josephs, the thief with whom both Spot and Hill had
worked previously, had discovered that cargoes were kept overnight
on a fairly regular basis; the target was to be the bonded warehouse
which contained nearly £250,000 worth of goods including
diamonds and was due to receive £1 million in gold the next day.
The job had been meticulously laid out with inside help, and the
gang maintained a twenty-four-hour watch on Heath Row over a
two-month period. Dummy parcels were sent from Ireland and
Franny Daniels checked they had arrived when, as an authorised

driver, he was allowed in the Customs sheds. Then a warehouseman approached Donald Fish, chief security officer of BOAC, to report that he had been offered £500 to dope the warehouse staff. The Flying Squad was called in.

The plan had been to drug the guards at the warehouse, and at first the raid seemed to go according to plan. The messenger with the tea was intercepted, and barbitone was dropped in the jug. But at the last minute the guards had been switched and replaced by members of the Flying Squad; the tea was put on one side and the three 'guards' lay on the floor seemingly unconscious. Members of the gang entered, hit one of the detectives with an iron bar to ensure he was unconscious and then took the keys from his pocket. At the same time other members of the Squad attacked the robbers. Of the detectives, John MacMillan had his nose broken and a robber broke DI Peter Sinclair's arm. Five of the robbers escaped. Teddy Machin fell into a ditch, was knocked unconscious and as a result was overlooked in the search for the escapers; Franny Daniels held on to the underside of a van and instead of being dropped off at the first set of traffic lights as he hoped was carried to Harlesden police station from where he made his way home. Scorched by the exhaust, he carried the burn on his shoulder for the rest of his life. The great burglar Billy Benstead also escaped. The next day a patched-up collection of the remainder went into the dock.

Sir Gerald Dodson, the Recorder of London, had a field day:

> All of you men set your minds and hands to this enterprise. You were, of course, playing for high stakes. You made sure of your position by being ready for any situation with weapons of all kinds. This is the gravity of the offence. A raid on this scale profoundly shocks society. You went prepared for violence and you got it. You got the worst of it and you can hardly complain.

Edward Hughes received twelve years' penal servitude, Sammy Ross one less, and Alfred Roome of Ilford received ten years. The very respected Jimmy Wood of Manor Park collected nine, George Wallis (who was really George Wood, Jimmy's brother) and Sidney Cook of Stratford picked up eight, while William Ainsworth of Dagenham collected a more modest five years.

Some of those captured lived to fight again, but Roome became more and more off-balanced during his imprisonment. After his release, on 20 January 1956 – the day before his eldest daughter's wedding – he attacked his wife and her employer John Wirth at his newspaper stall outside the main gate at Ford's Dagenham with a knife and a hatchet. He then committed suicide on the spot by swallowing a potassium cyanide capsule. Although he had worked on the stall himself for a few days, he believed his wife was having an affair with Wirth and had tried to persuade him to sack her. Roome had already tried to set fire to his daughter's trousseau.[1]

Frank Fraser, who knew many of the men, recalled:

> Those men on the airport were such a good firm; really getting dough. They were organised and sensible and intelligent enough to be doing very well. When they were nicked and so many got such bird it took the heart out of their organisation. Teddy Machin was never really the same after it. He was a Spot man.[2]

When the Wood brothers came out of prison they transferred their allegiance to Billy Hill. Billy Benstead had already moved. As for Spot, the police could never prove that he was the organiser, but his interests were disrupted and under pressure his gambling club in St Botolph's Row was closed.

Sometimes Spot claimed responsibility for the robbery, sometimes not. In his book he wrote that his friend whom he calls Smokey had betrayed them and that as a result he beat him badly. This does not seem to have terminated their friendship, however:

---

[1] For an account of the case see *The Times*, 18 September 1948. Shifty Burke's *Peterman* is an inside account of the robbery.
[2] Frank Fraser, *Mad Frank's Friends*, p. 34.

Three days later when Smokey had got over the worst of this beating I went round to his apartment again. He'd lost a couple of teeth, one eye was closed to a slit and he wouldn't be recognisable for another week. He ought to have hated me. He ought to have been burning with resentment and the desire to be avenged.

But when I offered him my hand to shake and wheedled: 'It was a misunderstanding, Smokey. Let bygones be bygones. Let's forget it', he only hesitated a moment before he took my hand.

And Smokey added that he understood the strain Spot had been under: 'Your nerves must have stretched to breaking point.' Spot claimed he never again trusted him.[3]

In the East End it was said that the betrayer of the scheme was the former wrestler Man Mountain Dean, who had also appeared as an extra in films such as *Ben Hur*. Shortly before their release Dean took to his bed, so it was said, to keep out of the way of those on whom he had informed. 'He just layed there the rest of his life. He died a few years ago – a very wealthy man. By the end he'd got some skin disease and it just used to come off in flakes', recalls one East Ender.

Dean certainly had police connections, for he sorted things out for Arthur Maffia over the death of his brother Tony, known as the Magpie because of his hoarding of stolen property. Through Dean's negotiations, and in return for Arthur's cooperation into the inquiry into the death, an outstanding fraud case against him was dropped.

It is difficult to accept the reason for Dean taking to his bed as gospel. After all, a number of men on the robbery had escaped capture and had not sought him out over the years. That he took to his bed is certainly correct; when he was charged with selling condemned Argentinian beef, a court was convened in his bedroom. 'Everyone was selling it. There must have been a container full in Romford market alone,' commented one East End face.

Was Spot really the organiser? Many – and Parker is one – doubt

[3] Hank Janson, *Jack Spot*, p. 111.

it. Despite his claims of organisational ability, they do not think he had the brains to pull off such a coup. There is no doubt that many of his associates were involved and that Spot knew of the robbery. Parker says that Spot told him his club had been used for the organisation, and in his articles in the *Daily Sketch* Spot says merely, 'Well, I had nothing to do with that, but as I say, two of my pals were silly enough to get talked into the job and they got sent down.' Years later, as an old and possibly confused if still boastful man, Spot told a reporter how his entire mob of pure-blood gypsies had been arrested in one go: 'They went to London airport to do a robbery,' he recalls as if they'd gone out for a picnic, 'and the police was waiting. They got 12–15 years apiece. F——g bastards turned my mob in.'[4]

Shifty Burke in *Peterman* gives the nickname 'King Solly' as the putter-up and goes on to say that he looked after the families of the captured men. If this latter is correct, then it is unlikely to have been Spot, who was a notoriously bad payer. Could King Solly possibly have been the boxing promoter Jack Solomons? He certainly had the money, but it is unlikely. Spot was definitely close to Solomons at the time, but the promoter was very much on the fringes of the Underworld. There was no word about that he was wrong. Parker believes a very credible alternative is Abe Kosky. The plan was certainly hatched at Botolph's club. He had sufficient funds, and it was said of him that he could not even lie straight in bed.

Almost all gang leaders – whether in London, New York, Chicago, Melbourne or Macau – have come a cropper when they raised their heads into public view, and for a time Spot observed the rule that his should stay firmly below the parapet. True he was on good terms with the *People's* columnist Arthur Helliwell, who wrote regularly on a Sunday about both him and Hill without naming them in his column *Follow Me Around*. Indeed, it is Spot to whom Helliwell is referring in this piece. Note the 'in' references:

[4] Michael Ewing in *Evening Standard*, 6 January 1988.

In the last five years I have often spotlighted the Big Shot's activities. He walked into my office with two bodyguards and announced his intention of 'quitting the shady side of the street'.

No one knows who the next Big Shot will be but – gambling dens, racetracks etc. will be decidedly unhealthy spots.[5]

However, it is curious how little was generally known of Spot in Fleet Street even as late as 1953. A note to the *Daily Mirror* news desk in September that year read:

Comer is known as Jack Sprott. He is thought – almost certainly – to be the brains behind the London Airport bullion attempt in 1948 and the £250,000 mail van theft last year. Comer frequents most of the Soho betting clubs and does a lot of pavement betting in Gt Windmill Street, outside Jack Solomons's gym. I think there is a tie-up somewhere between Comer and Solomons. Comer is invariably attended by a bevy of smoothly dressed 'gorillas' and I have seen him in company of a very attractive dark-haired woman.[6]

The writer was correct about the dark-haired woman, who was Rita; wrong about the mail van; only possibly right about the Airport, and certainly correct about Spot's connections with Solomons.[7]

Indeed, one of Spot's allegedly finest hours came in 1950 when he was looking after the interests of Solomons. There were suggestions that Solomons, who was now promoting world title fights, might come under the control of the American Mafia who wanted fixed fights in Britain. Spot knew something of the art, having arranged such matters on a small basis from his haunt the Vienna Rooms in Paddington. A meeting was set up in Paris at the Scribe

[5] *People*, 13 October 1951.
[6] Quoted by Robert Murphy, *Smash and Grab*, p. 88.
[7] Israel Jacob Solomons was born on 10 December 1900 in a basement below a fish and chip shop at the corner of Frying Pan Alley in the East End. He had five fingers and a thumb on each hand and at birth already had two teeth. The fourth of a family of seven children of Polish parents, he was the first born in England and was educated at Old Castle Street School. He boxed professionally himself and promoted at the Devonshire Club in the East End. By the end of the war after he promoted Bruce Woodcock v Jack London he was Britain's foremost promoter. He handled the promotions for the world title fights in London of both Freddie Mills and Randolph Turpin.

hotel with Ralph 'Bottles' Capone, brother of the much more celebrated Al, and Frankie Carbo.[8] Spot claimed to have acted on his
own on behalf of Solomons, and according to his account he handled
himself so well that he was invited to go to America and work for
the Mob, an offer he declined. Again it is impossible to assess the
truth in the story. Certainly in the 1940s Carbo, who worked for
Murder Inc. and was named in numerous murder cases without
being convicted, became the Czar of boxing, retaining a personal
interest in fighters and also running a bookmaking operation.[9] Meyer
Lansky was an exception, but at the time the Mob generally was
not interested in placing Jewish figures in senior positions. When
they did so it had not always worked to their short-term advantage.
Bugsy Siegel, who on 20 June 1947 was shot after skimming them
over the development of the Flamingo hotel in Las Vegas, was a case
in point.

Whether Spot ever went to Paris, he was without doubt used as
a minder for Solomons and was particularly close to the Jewish boxer
Al Phillips, the Aldgate Tiger, near whose corner he could always
be found. The story is told that Spot, who was sitting with Tyrone
Power and Linda Christian at the Randolph Turpin v. Marcel Cerdan
fight at Earl's Court, was called over to help another boxing promoter
who was being insulted by some Covent Garden porters. He, Rosen
and Machin dealt severely with them and then saw the celebrities
leaving in alarm. It is cited as happening after his problems with
Duncan Webb in 1954, and is given as an instance when Spot
showed that he was still a man with whom to be reckoned.[10] Again
it is something of a good story. First, Turpin never fought Cerdan
who had been killed in 1948 in an air crash long before the

---

[8] Ralph Capone (1893–1974) acquired his nickname because he managed the syndicate's bottling plant. Although after Al Capone's conviction for tax evasion Ralph hosted
several Mob meetings at his brother's estate at Palm Island, Florida, he was never really
privy to Mob secrets.
[9] In 1958 Paul John 'Frankie' Carbo (1904–1976) was convicted of conspiracy and
extortion over his handling of the welterweight champion Don Jordan, and was sentenced
to 25 years. He was paroled early because of ill-health and died in Miami Beach.
[10] Wensley Clarkson, *Hit 'em Hard*, p. 126.

Leamington boy was championship material. Parker places the incident in 1948, in which case it would be either Mills v. Gus Lesnevich or Mills v. Joey Maxim which took place early the following year. However, it is possible that it occurred at the Turpin v. Charles Humez contest for the European Middleweight championship in 1952. If so, the guests may have fled the ringside but through boredom with the main event rather than fear. Parker has the story that the victim of the insults was a Jewish tailor whose inability to control his enthusiasm had annoyed the costermongers, who had spat all over him and added some anti-Semitic remarks. In turn, they were met by a fusillade of phlegm and left the arena. Spot, well satisfied, returned to his seat to find Power and Linda Christian gone and Solomons less than pleased.[11]

In general, however, this was Spot's peak. He and Hill were working together but often also in separate fields. Spot was regarded as the man to be seen over any racecourse problems. He was used as a debt-collecting agency by men in Leeds, Manchester and Birmingham who were taken by the smarter operators in London. His fee was fifty per cent of the money recovered – the standard tariff for such an operation.[12]

Things also went well for Spot on the racecourses themselves. Post-war, things may have been changing on racecourses – women were seen smoking in the enclosures at Ascot and, worse, placing bets, something thought to be likely to lose them their badges the next year[13] – but welshing by bookmakers was still rife. Bookmakers would turn up with barely enough money to pay out on the first race and would be quite prepared to scarper. A call of 'Not yet' would indicate that a bookmaker, knowing he had insufficient money, was not in a position to take a bet on a particular horse. According to Spot it was he who solved the problem at the request of the Chief Steward, the Duke of Norfolk. He would tell the tale

[11] In some versions of the story it is Frank Sinatra and Ava Gardner.
[12] See Gerald Byrne, 'Frightened men all over Britain' in *Empire News*, 2 October 1955.
[13] *Daily Express*, 21 June 1946.

that he had been recommended by the Northern racecourse inspectors he had helped at Doncaster – sometimes he would say it was a senior police officer – who had put his name forward. It has the same ring as his thoughts on his military career:

> 'Hello J-J-J-Jack,' the Duke stuttered. 'The police can do nothing about these bookies on the free side of the course who are giving racing a bad name but you might be able to help. You're not a crook, you're not a thief. You know everything. Why you haven't got a job in government I'll never know . . .'

Spot explained that organisation was needed. The Free Side had to be enclosed and a set number of pitches drawn up. These would only be allocated to bookmakers with a bank account with enough money to guarantee settlement. Altruistically, Spot would take it upon himself to make sure the allocations were fair and just.[14]

Whoever tells the tale, there is little doubt that Spot ousted Jimmy Wooder and the Islington Mob from Ascot. Spot tells the story that when the opposition was routed there was a frightened little man who was about to be evicted. 'Let him stay,' said Spot generously. The man was the once great Darby Sabini. Later Spot would receive unstinted praise for his work: 'You've made racing a pleasure, Jack. We no longer go in terror of our lives,' he was told.[15]

Another of Spot's stories is that he retrieved Lord Roseberry's binoculars for him after they had been stolen. The Earl generally wore them hanging round the back rather than the front, with their almost inevitable loss. According to Spot, he was summoned and told confidentially that the Earl's grandmother was Jewish, and on learning her pedigree he promised to do what he could to help. He was apparently rewarded with £300 – rather more than the cost of the binoculars – and a dinner with Roseberry and the Aga Khan who was roped in to meet the great man. How much of this is true is difficult to assess. The same story is told about the Sabinis. However,

---

[14] *Sunday Chronicle*, 23 January 1955.
[15] *Ibid.*, 30 January 1955.

there is no doubt that wallets, watches and binoculars did disappear frequently in those days. The firm advice was not to contact the police, on whom watch was kept by members of the gang of thieves. If the racegoer did nothing, by the end of the afternoon he would have been approached with a proposition which would ensure the return of his property in exchange for a compensatory gratuity.

9

On the Up

There were peaceful and highly profitable years for both Spot and Hill in 1950 and 1951. 'Visitors and strangers must have found the West End a rather dull place with no running gang-fights and feuds . . . The truth was that we cleared all the cheap racketeers out. There was no longer any blacking of club owners and restaurant keepers. In fact so peaceful did it all become that there was no gravy left for the small-timers,' wrote Hill.[1] So far as prostitution and the Messina brothers were concerned, on the face of it neither Hill nor Spot was interested. Under the surface, however, the Messinas paid a form of tax to them.

'Hill reigned almost with the blessing of the police,' says a solicitor's managing clerk from the period. 'He was a very likeable bloke, always paid his bills. If you overlooked his reputation you'd never have dreamed who he was. Whilst he was in control there was a peaceful scene. He kept discipline.' Others believe the peaceful reign was simply because Spot and Hill paid off the police. 'All top men, they work with the law to a certain degree,' recalls one Northern hardman. In the end

[1] Billy Hill, *Boss of Britain's Underworld*, p. 155.

his inability to do so was perhaps Spot's biggest failing. An even less charitable view comes from one of Hill's former friends. 'He kept control with the razor. People were paid a pound a stitch, so if you put twenty stitches in a man you got a score. You used to look in the evening papers next day to see how much you'd earned,' said the noted safebreaker, later man-about-Soho, Eddie Chapman.[2]

In fact, Hill along with Spot seems to have put an end to a quarrel between Ginger Randall from Shepherd's Bush and the remnants of the Whites following an altercation at the New Cross greyhound track. He also claims to have explained the facts of London life to Frank Fraser and Johnny Carter, who were beginning a long and involved feud which ran for years and ended in heavy prison sentences for some of Fraser's friends. Hill's intervention calmed things down, at least for the time being.

There were a few relatively minor problems to be dealt with, such as who had the lucrative concessions for the photographers and the bird-food vendors in Trafalgar Square at the time of the Festival of Britain, which Hill wanted for his brother Archie. And this brought another serious player into view – Billy Howard. In his biography it is suggested that the right to the concessions would be decided by a bare-knuckle fight, with Howard taking on all-comers and the last man standing to be the winner. It is difficult to see how Howard would have agreed to conditions such as this, particularly as he was by no means a young man. Nevertheless he continued to knock down or retire his opponents until at the end he came to face Tony Mella, a man with no great ability in the professional ring who was nevertheless one of the best street fighters of his era.[3] Mella duly won and the concession was claimed by Hill, who had backed him. Howard was not pleased and explained the rules of the game to him, whereupon Hill agreed that Howard would benefit from the pot over the period of the Festival.

[2] Conversation with author.
[3] Michael Connor, *The Soho Don*, pp. 60–1. Later Mella owned a number of clubs in Soho. He was shot and killed by his partner Alf Melvin, who in turn shot himself. See Frank Fraser, *Mad Frank's London*, pp. 58–9.

The first months of 1952 were not good for the forces of law and order or for the insurers of the Post Office. A GPO van was ambushed in Bruce Grove Road, Tottenham, in February, and later mail vans were stolen in Marylebone and the West End and registered letters taken. On 18 May came the theft of £11,000 in notes from sacks on the Brighton to London train.

Then three days later came the first really successful major post-war robbery. The Eastcastle Street Great Mailbag Robbery was undoubtedly a Billy Hill production, devised, arranged and orchestrated by him. A Post Officer worker who had been steadily losing in one of Hill's spielers came to his notice and was approached for useful information. This was supplied in return for the cancellation of his gaming debts, and Hill went to work.

The robbery was carried out with immaculate precision. A mail van was kept under observation and followed every night for months on its journey from Paddington station to the city. Rehearsals took place in the suburbs under the pretext of shooting a film. Cars were stolen specifically for the raid. On the night of the robbery, once the van left Paddington a call was made to the West End flat where Hill had lodged his men. Four men climbed into one of the stolen cars, a green Vanguard, and the other four into a stolen 2½-litre Riley.

Because of roadworks near Oxford Street there was a diversion, and as the van turned into Eastcastle Street one of the cars blocked the driver's path. Six men then attacked the three Post-Office workers and looted the vehicle. They drove off in the van, leaving two of the three unconscious on the pavement. It was driven to Augustus Street in the City where the cash was transferred into boxes on a fruit lorry belonging to Jack Gyp – who was minded by Sonny Sullivan, one of Hill's men – which had been left there earlier. Eighteen out of thirty-one bags were taken. 'The thieves were surprised', claimed the police. At first it was thought that £44,000 in old notes had been taken, but the full damage became known later in the week. The total was in the region of £287,000.

According to Hill, the remaining bags were left because there wasn't any more room in the lorry, which was driven to Spitalfields Market and parked there before being moved round to the Borough, Covent Garden, Stratford and back to Spitalfields where it was finally unloaded. The stolen cars were left in Rose Street in Covent Garden, where they were found over the next few days.

Immediate questions were raised in Parliament about security and the state of the van's alarm. It had been fitted with a siren which could be operated by the driver and could not be stopped until either the battery ran down or it was disconnected by an expert. What had happened was that in the early hours of Wednesday morning one of the team had disconnected the alarm system on the van while the staff were on their tea-break.

At the site of the robbery there were bolt cutters manufactured by a Sheffield firm and a trenchcoat with a mark ZD 662 C19, from which three buttons were missing. But these apparent clues led nowhere and in time it became apparent that they were simply false ones planted to divert the police. From the word go, Hill was seriously suspected of the robbery, and it is now accepted that he organised it. In his memoirs he wrote:

> Walk through Old Compton Street, or down Wardour Street or over the heath at Newmarket on any racing day, or along the promenade at Brighton any week and ask anyone who thinks they know. Ask them who planned the Big Mailbag Job. The one when £287,000 in freely negotiable currency notes, in hard cash, was nicked in May 1952, and they'll all tell you, 'We don't know who did it but we've got a good idea. In any case we do know that Billy Hill planned it. Only he could have done that.'[4]

This was the era of the new robber. The liability of the Post Office was only £5 for each of ninety packets, but rewards totalling £25,000 were put up by the insurance companies. Despite intense police activity for over a year – headed by Superintendent Bob Lee,

[4] Billy Hill, *Boss of Britain's Underworld*, p. 162.

then second-in-command of the Flying Squad – there were no charges.

According to Hill, the night before the robbery nine men – all of whom had been selected and warned of the raid the week before – were collected and taken to a flat in the West End where they were locked in before being fully briefed on the operation. Hill set a precedent on the necessity for keeping a tight hold on his men, one which was ignored by Bert Wickstead in October 1973 when he tried to arrest the Maltese pornographers in Soho, only to find they had been tipped off, but adopted by Nipper Read when he came to arrest the Krays in 1969.

Back in 1952 Hill found, as did Spot after the Airport robbery, that the police took reprisals. They might not have been able to pin the Eastcastle Street robbery on him, but they were able to raid his spielers on an almost nightly basis and eventually he handed them over to others. He was now also having domestic troubles. His wife Aggie was on his back, trying to persuade him that with the money from the robbery he could actually become legitimate. He maintained that he owed a loyalty to the men with whom he had worked over the years. According to his autobiography he was still providing money for the wives of the men such as the Wood brothers and Teddy Hughes who had gone down over the Airport robbery. With some of his earnings he invested in a legitimate toy business.

Just who was on the raid will never be fully established. It is highly likely that the brothers Slip and Sonny Sullivan were both participants, although Sonny Sullivan later denied Slip's involvement.[5] The housebreaker George 'Taters' Chatham is also likely to have been on the team. Chatham, a degenerate gambler as well as being one of the most skilled climbers of that and many another generation, was said to have received £15,000 for his efforts. He gambled it away within a matter of weeks in one of Hill's clubs and then had the misfortune to be found trying to blow Hill's safe in an

---

[5] Letter from Sonny Sullivan to author.

attempt to recoup his losses. Chatham claimed that an almost unknown South London thief Terry Hogan was the one who climbed into the cab.[6] Stories of the robbery surfaced over the years. One was that the man who had supplied one of the stolen vehicles used was paid £24,000. He hid the money in his flat and while he was serving a sentence for another matter members of his own team of car thieves dressed as police officers, called on his wife, searched the premises and confiscated the money.[7]

The previous year Hill had also become emotionally involved with 'Gypsy' Phyllis May Blanche Riley, who had had something of a chequered early career and was then working behind the bar in one of his clubs. She had by some accounts run away from home in East London, and had joined the Upton Park gypsies from where she had taken her soubriquet. She had also been on the game, minded by a Maltese pimp known as Tulip who took her from Hyde Park to Mayfair where she was then run by a pimp known as Belgian Johnny. In turn he passed her to Johnny Belan, with whom she remained until Hill fell for her charms and fiery temperament. Frank Fraser remembers her: 'She was a cracker, really good looking and real fire.' Gerry Parker describes her as, 'Not pretty but a good looking woman with jet-black hair and high cheekbones. She had a mouth on her but she was a fine-looking woman.' Brian Macdonald of the Elephant Boys recalls her: 'Gypsy? I think she attacked Hill once. She gave him a few good clouts one day and people had a good laugh. Billy Hill – and Bobby Ramsay as well – was keen to go with brasses.'[8]

In the September of 1951 Belgian Johnny had made further overtures to Gypsy who was offended; and so, in turn, was Hill. Ever handy with his knife, he cut the Belgian on the face and neck; then

[6] In early January 1995 Terry Hogan, who only served one short sentence, was killed in a fall from a window in Brentford. Aged 65, he had been suffering from depression. *Guardian*, 26 January 1995. Peter Scott, *Gentleman Thief*, pp. 2–3. Hogan had survived Fred Rogers, a victim of the coshing during the robbery, by 40 years. Rogers had died of a coronary thrombosis in 1955. *Empire News*, 29 May 1955.
[7] *People*, 13 June 1958.
[8] Conversations with author.

some hours later he telephoned Spot to beg him to go to Charing Cross Hospital, then near the station, to see if he could straighten things out. Spot was obliged at some personal expense to try to persuade the man not to name names, the difficulty being that the police were indicating they would deport him if he did not assist them. Money was handed over and Belgian Johnny returned home. Comer would later claim that the man had told him Hill hated him (Spot).

For the moment, however, the faithful Aggie was left with the club and the gift of a poodle, Chico. Hill went to Tangier and then toured North Africa: 'I ate food I had never heard of, met people who were actually kind as well as educated, who were friendly although they were loaded with gelt.' But the pull of London was too much for him. Aggie was still there running the club, and so was Spot.

Now there were offers of work of a different kind. Men were coming to ask Hill and Spot to collect debts for them. Spot wanted nothing to do with it at first. He might collect for his friends in the North, but now he maintained that they were not tallymen. Hill, ever the businessman, saw there was real money to be had. There was an initial fee and then a percentage for a successful collection.[9] Shortly after that Hill was offered money to undertake a contract killing. Again Spot was horrified, but Hill persuaded him that there would be no intention of actually carrying out the killing on behalf of a businessman who had been turned over by his partner. Money was paid up front by the aggrieved party and Hill then approached the potential victim, explained things to him in words of one syllable and, after claiming his expenses and an assurance that the troubles would be put right forthwith, walked away. From then on, he claims there was a steady stream of business.

Blackmail? Money by threat and extortion? Nothing of the kind. What, in fact, we were doing was preventing stupid idiots from

---

[9] Hill was, of course, right. Provided he avoided a charge of demanding money with menaces, a successful Underworld debt collector could expect to receive half the money recovered. Hill and Spot would therefore be collecting hundreds for each job.

doing desperate acts for which they would have been sorry afterwards. I don't know how many wives returned to their husbands as a result of our little excursions all over the country. There must have been dozens. For in the course of 1952–53 we undertook three hundred missions on our Murder Inc. business.[10]

Was it all so innocent? Frank Fraser, who worked with Hill a little later, maintains there were actual bodies. When touring promoting his books, he would tell the story of how Hill had a worker at a South London crematorium in his pay, and victims would be burned there in the early hours of a morning. Fraser would sometimes embroider the story by saying the ashes would be scattered at the front gate of Wandsworth prison, but there is little doubt that the basic details could have been true.

More often, however, the supposed victim was simply given a slapping. Jackie Collins, Parker's wife's uncle, employed Hill to have a man – with whom his wife was having an affair – cut. Frank Fraser gave him a 'slap or two' and told him to walk around Brighton in bandages. Jackie Collins paid £5,000 for the so-called cutting.[11]

Domestically, however, there were problems with Gypsy. Now Queen of the Underworld, she was unhappy to be reminded of her past. When in September 1953 she was approached by Tulip she persuaded Frederick 'Slip' Sullivan, a man who over the years suffered greatly at the hands of knives and women, to have him thrown out of a club known as French Henry's.[12] In turn Tulip was protected by the tearaway and all-time loser Tommy Smithson. Sullivan took a bad beating at his hands – Hill says his throat was cut – and reprisals were required to maintain the status quo.[13]

When it came to it Tommy Smithson suffered at just about everyone's hands during his own chequered and largely unsuccessful

---

[10] Billy Hill, *Boss of Britain's Underworld*, pp. 174–5.

[11] Frank Fraser, *Mad Frank's Friends*, p. 37.

[12] French Henry ran a number of clubs over the years, very often leasing out premises to other people to use as clubs. In the 1980s he let Parker have premises in Inverness Terrace.

[13] In his book Hill calls Smithson, Brownson, and claims that the cutting was over a girl whom Smithson fancied. Billy Hill, *Boss of Britain's Underworld*, p. 177.

career. Smithson, an ex-fairground fighter with a penchant for silk shirts and underwear, a man of immense courage and little stability or ability, was known as Mr Loser. Born in Liverpool in 1920 and brought to the East End two years later, he served in the Merchant Navy until his discharge in the 1950s. Back in Shoreditch he found things much changed. Maltese immigrants had assumed control of clubs and cafés, and Smithson decided to set up his own protection racket devoted to these Maltese businessmen as well as working a spinner[14] with Tony Mella around the dog tracks.

Parker remembers him as:

A nuisance. He was all right but if he had a couple of drinks he was trouble. He'd also go to people and say, 'I'll have a bit of this or a bit of that.' He did that to a friend of mine, Dennis, who had a fruit shop in Clipstone Street. Dennis gave him a right-hander and Smithson came looking for him with shooters. Dennis went to the States for a while after that. What can I say in Smithson's favour? He wasn't afraid.

Acting as minder and as a croupier, initially Smithson protected George Caruana – said to resemble Tony Curtis – whose gambling clubs included one in Batty Street, Stepney. At the time Caruana and the other Maltese were keen to avoid trouble, and Smithson soon extended his interest to a share of the takings in the clubs. A shilling in the £1 from the dice games earned him up to £100 an evening. He also moved into a series of drinking clubs in the West End.

Now after cutting Sullivan, Smithson went into hiding, only to be given up by the Maltese he had been protecting. It was, in fact, Caruana who betrayed him. Told there was a peace offer on the table, Smithson was asked – ordered is perhaps a better word – to attend a meeting at the Black Cat cigarette factory in Camden Town. He took with him the Paddington Club owner Dave Barry and at least one gun, a Luger. Arrayed against him were Hill, Spot, Slip

---

[14] A type of crooked roulette wheel used at fairs and greyhound tracks which was operated by a wire.

Sullivan's brother Sonny and Moishe Blueball. Spot explained to Smithson that they were simply there to talk and he handed over the gun. One version of the story is that it was not loaded anyway. Just as Spot was putting the gun away, Hill suddenly slashed the unprepared Smithson. The slashes on his face were in the form of the sides of the letter V down each cheek, meeting at his chin; it was a Hill trademark. In his book he wrote: 'Early in life I decided that the best stroke for chivving was the V for Victory sign, or a cross on the cheek. They remember that, and whenever you saw anyone wearing one you knew that it was Billy Hill who had done it.'[15]

Another version of the Smithson slashing is that Spot held the unfortunate man while Hill went to work. Why did he do that? Parker thinks that morally he had no alternative, since 'Hill was his partner.'

Whichever version is correct, Smithson was also slashed over his face, arms, legs and chest. Barry ran away and Hill, realising how badly Smithson was injured, turned white. This could have been a hanging matter. He was then thrown over a wall into Regent's Park, and it was left to Spot to send Moishe to call an ambulance and drive Hill back to his flat.

Fortunately for everyone, Smithson did not die. Somehow he survived, and forty-seven stitches were put in his face. Nor did he talk to the police. His reward for honouring the code of silence was a party, the soubriquet 'Scarface' and £500 or £1,000 with which he bought a share in a drinking club in Old Compton Street. According to some accounts it was Spot who paid the compensation. Smithson then bought another club, this time for illegal gaming; this was also closed down by the police, and he took up fencing as an occupation. For a time he was successful, but then word began to spread that he was a police informer. This time he received a further twenty-seven stitches.

Smithson retreated back to the East End to provide more protection

---

[15] Billy Hill, *Boss of Britain's Underworld*, pp. 27–8.

for the Maltese, but yet again he miscalculated. Now a new wave of Maltese club owners was becoming more powerful, and he was asking too much. They may not have wished for trouble, but they were readying themselves for a move into the recently vacated Messina territory and were not prepared to tolerate the likes of Smithson for long.[16]

By 1956, however, he had also contracted an unfortunate alliance. He fell in love with Fay Richardson (or Sadler), one-time prostitute, then prostitute's maid and seemingly bad luck for most of the men with whom she took up. Three of her lovers died early in their careers and others suffered bad beatings. Originally from Stockport, where she had been a mill girl, she was what could be described both as a gangster's moll and a *femme fatale*. She said of the handsome Smithson, '[He was] a dapper dresser, very fussy about having a clean shirt every day. He was a big gambler. He could have £400 on the nose.' Now she was on remand in Holloway prison on forged cheque allegations. Money was needed for her defence and Smithson set about raising it with a will. On 13 June 1956 he, together with Walter Downs and Christopher Thomas, went to a café in Berner Street, Stepney, and confronted his one-time employer Caruana and Philip Ellul, another Maltese who ran a second or third division string of prostitutes. Smithson said he wanted more than £50 from Caruana, and in the ensuing fight Caruana's fingers were slashed as he protected his face from a flick-knife. Other Maltese in the café were held off at gunpoint by Thomas. Thirty pounds was produced. In accordance with standard gangland practice, Ellul was told to start a collection for Fay and was provided with a book to record the contributions.

On 25 June Smithson was found in the gutter outside George Caruana's house in Carlton Vale; he had been shot in the arm and neck. His last words were said to be, 'Good morning, I'm dying.' Fay Sadler sent a wreath from Holloway: 'Till we meet again'.

[16] For a full account of Tommy Smithson and the repercussions and trials following his death, see James Morton, *Gangland*.

Smithson's death worked well in her favour, and she was placed on probation on condition that she returned to Lancashire and did not visit London for three years. Although there were reported sightings in the company of Australians and reports of a marriage to a club owner, over the years she faded into obscurity.

But three years earlier, the slashing of Smithson by Hill had in effect been the last joint enterprise of the now two rival Bosses of London's Underworld.

10

Sliding

The beginning of 1953 was not a good time for Spot. In the January when the police raided one of his favourite haunts – the Vienna Rooms, a spieler in Crawford Place, Marylebone – they found a dice game taking place on the billiard table. It was all pretty low key. Seven shillings was found in a box, and when the men were searched they had a total of £7.9s. between them. On 12 January at Marylebone Magistrates' Court, Louis Taylor was fined £75 along with costs and given three months imprisonment in default of payment for running a common gaming house. Spot was bound over in the sum of £10 not to frequent such places for two years.

There was undoubtedly a certain amount of low-level fixing of boxing in those days, and it was from the Vienna Rooms that Spot was said to operate. He may also have worked at a slightly higher level and, possibly, with those on a higher rung. Wensley Clarkson suggests that, unbeknown to a heavyweight champion, Spot arranged an early evening for him on one occasion when he defended his title.[1]

[1] John L. Gardner, the champion who is most usually named, however, is slightly off Spot's timescale, certainly later than his heyday. See Henry Ward and Tony Gray, *Buller*. Tony Mella is another who is said to have benefited from fixed contests. See Frank Fraser, *Mad Frank and Friends*, pp. 5–6.

Spot was back at Marylebone two months later when on 7 March he was fined £20 and Sonny Sullivan £5 more for being in the same club. This time Louis Taylor was fined £250, with £15 costs. How had they been so careless as to have the police raid them again? The answer was that they had a grass, Jacob Schenkman, under the carpet who tipped them off. Rather uncharitably he was prosecuted for being on the premises as well, but the magistrate accepted his evidence that he was there as an informer.[2]

Spot was now on the slide. The Jockey Club was helping the big credit bookmakers prepare for the legalisation of off-course betting and the smaller bookmakers were being squeezed. Now Spot's team was disintegrating and he lamented:

> At first little things went wrong. When a raid was carefully planned and schemed, something would go wrong at the last minute. The man detailed to steal the getaway car wouldn't be able to steal it or a bunch of skeleton keys that should have opened a door failed to do so at the crucial moment.
>
> The men who'd been responsible for these slip-ups had been bawled out. But they hadn't cried. Instead they'd walked straight out on me and got themselves a job with another organisation.[3]

Slowly he was losing both his gang and his reputation. The word was out in the Underworld that he was a grass. 'We'd had his sheet pulled from the Yard,' said the daredevil safebreaker Eddie Chapman, who had been released from prison during the war for work in German territory, 'and there it was for all to see.'[4] Spot was facing isolation and was not being helped by the mass defections of his troops to Hill.

The same month Spot was arrested by Detective Sergeant Careless for possessing an offensive weapon under the Prevention of Crime Act 1953 which had just come into force. He had received a telephone call that someone had a 'nice fur coat for sale – very cheap'.

---

[2] *Middlesex Independent*, 16 January, 13 March 1953.
[3] Hank Janson, *Jack Spot*, pp. 117–18.
[4] Conversation with author.

Spot, talking to Gerry Parker, would recall:

> Me, like a mug, I go and meet him. He gives me the fur coat and
> I paid him and walked away. Then out of a car come four detec-
> tives. One of them was known as Careless – he couldn't care less
> is right. And I'm taken to the station. They bring a knuckleduster
> round and they say, 'You're charged with carrying an offensive
> weapon.' It was all the work of that cunt Sparks who was the
> right-hand man of another bastard – Greeno – biggest thieves the
> world's ever known.

Curiously the receiving charge was dropped, and as for the offensive weapon there was no percentage in those days in alleging it had
been planted. That was a quick route to a conviction and imprisonment for defaming gallant officers.

So Comer said he was a commission agent in Camden Road.
Often he had three or four hundred pounds on him, and as he had
a feeling that people were getting to know this he had bought the
knife in a store in Holborn about two weeks before his arrest. The
explanation was accepted and he was perhaps lucky to be fined only
£20.[5] And the name of his partner in the betting office? None other
than Alf White.

'I don't believe it,' says Parker. 'Alf White hated Jews.' There may
have been a hint of sadism in Spot's behaviour. He obviously needed
an explanation for the weapon and, reminding him just who was
the master, he used his old enemy as he did White's son, Harry,
forcing him into giving evidence on his behalf at a later trial.

Spot was convinced the whole thing had been a set-up and he
blamed Herbert Sparks, head of the Flying Squad and the right-
hand man to Ted Greeno, thinking they had been acting for Billy
Hill. He was certainly right to regard them with suspicion. Greeno
had on the surface a glorious career. By the end, Sparks' was in
ruins.

Charles Sidney Careless was another curious officer whose career

---

[5] See *News of the World*, 26 June, 3 July, 10 July, 17 July 1960.

ended in tatters. In November 1958 he was a witness against seven people accused of conspiracy to help two men escape from Brixton. They were acquitted on the second day when the prosecution stopped the case. He resigned in August 1959 shortly before he was due to complete 25 years service.[6] Then he simply disappeared.

In May 1960 he was found in Toronto. Apparently he had disappeared the previous summer with Eileen Bergmann, a nightclub hostess, who was once the wife of the table-tennis player Richard Bergmann. Wanted for the offence of allegedly supplying false information to obtain Eileen's passport, he was returned to England in the safe hands of the *News of the World*, for their crime reporter Norman Rae stood bail for him at Bow Street when he was remanded.[7] He was defended by the former policeman William Hemming, who explained that Careless had done this for Eileen because there was something in her past which had prevented her from making a proper application. He was fined £25 with five guineas costs. Eileen had also been wanted for selling liquor after hours and she was fined £60 with 20 guineas costs at Thames Magistrates' Court on 30 June 1960, so proving that lying is cheaper than late-night drinking.

In his subsequent newspaper articles Careless told extraordinary stories of how he had been targeted by a syndicate of London criminals who had a contract on his head. He claimed £50,000 had been lodged with solicitors, and that he was the target of the seven biggest gangs in London who had sunk their differences. He spoke of secret courts before which crooks or even police officers could be put on trial and sentenced to receive a slashing or beating or death. Careless also claimed that before Solomon Lever, ex-Mayor of Stepney, had

[6] He was later sued by a Veronica Norris of Chauncey Street, Edmonton, whose husband along with Georgie Madsen was one of the men alleged to have been involved.
[7] Norman Rae was one of the great crime reporters of the period. In 1951 a Herbert Mills telephoned him to say he'd discovered a body and it seemed like murder. He went to see Rae and made a long confession which the newspaper passed to the police. Mills was telephoning the *News of the World* trying to get £250 for an exclusive when he was arrested in a telephone box. He was hanged at Lincoln prison on 11 December; his heart continued to beat for 20 minutes after the drop.

been abducted and brutally beaten, dying as a result, 'Members of The Syndicate' had met in Eileen's club. The story was in essence correct. On 19 July 1959 Lever, actually the Mayor of Hackney in 1951, received a call at his home in Victoria Park at 1.10 a.m. He was told there was a fire in the timberyard beside the Sylvester Path offices of the Workers' Circle Friendly Society of which he was the secretary, threatening the office which had £8,000 in the safe for holiday payouts.

Minutes later a bogus policeman arrived to collect Lever, who was pulled in a car and bound and gagged. The safe was emptied and Lever's body was later dumped some 100 yards from Rangers Road near the main London-Epping Road. He had suffered a coronary thrombosis. The coroner's verdict was one of manslaughter by persons unknown. No charges were ever brought.[8]

Careless later said that he had been offered money to say he was the father of Eileen's baby, which indeed he was. He received £2,700 for his series of articles in the *News of the World*. Eileen Bergmann received £9,000 for the exclusive rights to hers, but they were never published.

During his career Careless had on occasion been less than protective with his informants, including John 'Happy' Sambridge whom he took to Brighton races in order to point out Frank Fraser to him. When Fraser discovered this he shot Sambridge in the leg, which had to be amputated. Careless was also involved in the case of Dennis Stafford – later convicted of the murder in Newcastle of Angus Sibbett – when a gun was found in his car. Stafford claimed it had been planted by Sambridge, but his appeal to the Home Secretary was rejected. He had wanted to call Careless, now long gone, as a witness.[9]

On 21 October 1954 Spot committed a serious blunder, forgetting the cardinal rule which then prevailed that however tiresome a journalist might be, he – or then more rarely she – should not be

[8] See *inter alia*, *Daily Mirror*, 20 July 1959.
[9] *People*, 10 April 1960.

touched. Duncan Webb was writing Billy Hill's autobiography in serial form at the time, and was at a hotel in Kingston-on-Thames when he received a message to telephone a man named Nadel. He did so and found it was Spot, who said he had to see him right away in connection with the articles he was writing about Hill. Spot had previously threatened to break Webb's jaw.

At 10.30 that night Webb met him on the steps of the Dominion (then a cinema) in Tottenham Court Road. Spot greeted him by saying, 'Come on, it's bad.' He then took him into an alleyway where he knocked him down, and when he fell Webb broke his wrist.

Spot's private version was slightly different and in some respects bears scrutiny. In his account the meeting had been in the Horseshoe in Tottenham Court Road. Webb had told him that Spot was no longer the Guv'nor and that Hill had taken over. Then he had made the dangerous remark, 'How did Hitler miss you?' 'So I took him round the back of the Dominion and we had a nice talk and I gave him a right hook which I shouldn't have done.'

Spot was initially charged with grievous bodily harm. He may have lost much of his power in the West End, but he still had some contacts and Webb was straightened with £600. The blow which knocked him down had, on Webb's reflection, not been with a knuckleduster but had been more of a push. On 18 November 1954 at the Clerkenwell Magistrates' Court, Spot now pleaded guilty to a charge of actual bodily harm and was fined £50 with 20 guineas costs.

Webb may have been straightened so far as the criminal action was concerned, but he nevertheless brought a civil action for damages. On 5 March 1956 the case was heard at the Royal Courts of Justice, with Webb represented by R.F. Levy QC and Patrick Back. Another good time was had by all except Spot. Levy told the court his client was a journalist while: 'The defendant's occupation is perhaps a little indeterminate. Whatever his work is, it seems to bring him into contact with what is called the Underworld.'

Which was one way of putting it. Webb claimed that he had been working on a book and, since his wrist had been broken, he had been obliged to hire a typist to help him. He was awarded £732, a tidy little sum for the time which would have enabled him to buy a part-occupied house in Tottenham if he had ever so wished – and if he had received the money, which he never did.[10]

Worse, this one-time hardman was becoming something of a figure of fun. Spot and Rita had finally married, and the ceremony was an indication of how much she was trying to separate him from the Underworld. There was no Blueball, no Little Hymie, no Parker, no Bernie at the Marylebone Register Office on 8 July 1954 to give their leader a send-off. Instead the witnesses were a Mrs E. Flanagan and a Mrs P. Connor. Whatever is the correct position over Spot's earlier marriage, he is described on his marriage certificate with Rita as divorced. Now home life with Rita and the accompanying domesticity was suiting him. Later he was openly mocked that when the baby, Rachelle Alexis, cried he had to go home to look after her. To paraphrase the song, 'Big Bad John became Sweet Jackie now'. This was not the sort of behaviour required of a gang leader.

On the other hand Hill, as was often the case, had been thriving.

[10] *The Times*, 6 March 1956.

11

Smuggling

Billy Hill's last serious court appearance, at least in the dock, came in February 1954. The year before he had fallen out with his former friend, Freddy Andrews, whom he had known since childhood. According to Hill, Andrews thought he should have climbed a great deal higher up the criminal tree and resented the fact that he had not done so. He began drinking heavily and calling at Hill's club, challenging him. In December 1953 Andrews answered a knock on his front door and was slashed. He believed Hill was his attacker and, in a fit of uncharacteristic Underground behaviour, went to the police.

Andrews had had an interesting criminal career. In the war he served a long sentence for cutting an American soldier, and he was involved peripherally in the murder of George Alfred Ambridge, a coal merchant who was found dead at his home at 2 Hampton Road, Kilburn, on 12 April 1941. James O'Connor, known as Ginger, was charged with the robbery-murder and convicted. Almost on the morning of his execution, however, O'Connor was reprieved and, claiming he was not on the robbery, he blamed Freddy Andrews. There does not seem to have been any evidential basis for his claim.

Nevertheless, there was a considerable feeling in the Underworld that O'Connor had indeed been innocent.[1]

By the time Hill's trial came before Sir Gerald Dodson at the Central Criminal Court the deal had been done. Andrews had been paid and given assurances about any help he might need in the future. Now he failed to recognise Hill as his attacker. It was not a gesture which appealed to the Recorder, who was obliged to order Hill's release. After the hearing Andrews and Hill went together for a drink.

Hill was now casting about for something new. He had enjoyed his trip to Africa the previous year and now came the opportunity to combine business with pleasure. As he had discovered during his holidays there, Tangier was at the time a free city, governed by an international commission under licence from the Sultan of Morocco. It was also a home-from-home for smugglers. Cigarette smuggling was then, as it is now, capable of providing an enormous revenue. There was a great demand in France for what were known as *Les Blondes*, made with the light-coloured American tobacco. The export of cigarettes from Tangier was then perfectly legal, as was the transfer of the cargo to another vessel provided it was done outside territorial limits. It was the second boat which ran the gauntlet of Customs patrols and tried to land its cargo without interception.

Apart from the Customs, however, there was the risk of an attack by pirates and the Mediterranean at the time was a haven for them. One Corsican team which ran out of Marseilles was a group headed by Antoine Paolini, known as *Planche* or 'The Board', who as a distribution centre ran an illegal wholesale tobacco business from a bar in the Palmier quarter. His right-hand man was another Corsican, Dominique Muzziotti. One problem was that neither Muzziotti nor his crews were sailors, and Paolini put up the proposition of a part-

---

[1] Some years later Sir David Napley acted for O'Connor in his attempt to establish his innocence. The investigation on behalf of the police was carried out by Walter Virgo, who was later sentenced for corruption although his conviction was quashed on appeal. On his release O'Connor took up a career as a writer and had a number of plays produced on television. He married the barrister Nemone Lethbridge. See Jimmy O'Connor, *The Eleventh Commandment*.

nership to an American Elliott Forrest, hero of the Murmansk Russian convoy run and decorated four times in the Second World War. At first Forrest would not commit himself. Then at the end of September 1952 he was attending a bullfight in Tangier when, just before the last bull, he was contacted by another American, 'Nylon' Sid Paley, who said he had received a coded message that Paolini wanted to see Forrest urgently. This time the job was a big one. Forrest flew in a privately chartered plane to Marseilles and was told that the biggest ever load of *blondes* – twenty-seven tons in all – was to be smuggled on a Dutch vessel, the *Combinatie*, on 4 October. The job was sufficiently big that Forrest would be able to retire, if it was successful.

Now Forrest, together with Julio Renucci, hired a high-speed motor torpedo boat the *Esmé*, crewed by some unsuspecting British adventurers, and on 3 October left Tangier shortly before the *Combinatie*. Shortly before dawn the *Combinatie* was boarded; the Dutch captain was shot and seriously wounded, a grenade was exploded behind the vessel's control panel and the crew were locked below along with their injured captain. The cargo of stolen contraband cigarettes was now transferred to the *Esmé*, then in turn to a boat under the command of Muzziotti which came out of Marseilles. Stupidly Forrest went with them. The crew of the *Combinatie* managed to repair most of the damage and made for Marseilles. Forrest fled to Caviallon in the Luberon district. With an appalling accent there was no chance of his pretending to be a Frenchman and so he posed as a deaf and dumb American writer putting together a series of articles on smuggling and women.

In the meantime the British on the *Esmé* were then allowed to sail back to Tangier, where they were promptly arrested and held until an examining magistrate dismissed charges against them. Shortly afterwards Sid Paley was tried by an American court in Tangier over the affair, and he received three years' imprisonment from the consular judge, Judge Helnick. The other two judges sitting with him wished to return verdicts of not guilty, but the minority prevailed. This led to an automatic appeal and in May 1953 on appeal the sentence was changed to probation, to be served in America, and a modest fine.

A bloody struggle in the spirit of the pre-war French gangsters Spirito and Carbone began on the French mainland with Paolini's betrayal of Forrest to the police. The reasoning was simple. With Forrest gone, Paolini (apart from handing out a few small percentages) had the cargo for himself. Forrest, now in Les Baumettes prison awaiting trial, had powerful Corsican friends however. Paolini was shot in the lungs, pancreas and knee, in broad daylight outside his bar in the Panier district. His friends fought back and Jean Colonna was shot in Ajaccio, losing both legs to a cartridge which contained a dozen lead balls wired together through their centres.[2] Reprisal followed reprisal. Paolini's bodyguard Jacques Oliva was killed. In return Julio Renucci was murdered, followed by the death of Colonna on the Cours Napoléon in Ajaccio. Paolini's second bodyguard François Cassegrain was then shot and finally Paolini, who had survived the first attack, was shot and killed as he attended a funeral at the Saint-Julien cemetery in Marseilles.

Paolini's second-in-command Dominique Muzziotti, who apparently resembled Gregory Peck, had survived the slaughter mainly because he was serving time in Les Baumettes for carrying a gun of a greater calibre than that permitted to gangsters.[3] He was released shortly before Christmas 1955 and renounced a life of crime: in future he would carry religious *objets* rather than a gun. They did not avail him long, for on New Year's Eve 1955 he was machine-gunned as he stood in Mon Bar.

It was not until 1956 that Elliott Forrest and fifteen others involved

[2] Although this was the first recorded case of the technique in the twentieth century, it was a favourite of cannoneers in the Middle Ages. For more on the process and a more detailed account of the war see Derek Goodman, *Villainy Unlimited*, Ch. 8, Lawrence Wilkinson, *Behind the Face of Crime*, Ch. 9, and Michel Montarron, *Histoire du Milieu*.

[3] In fact imprisonment in Les Baumettes was not always a guarantee of survival in an Underworld struggle. In 1984 François Vanverberghe, 'François le Belge', was in the prison when his great rival Gaetan 'Tony' Zampa was brought in on tax evasion charges. A month after Vanverberghe's release Zampa was found hanging in his cell. See James Morton, *Gangland Today*, pp. 149–51.

in the *Combinatie* affair went on trial. Originally the authorities intended there should be thirty-eight defendants, but eight failed to appear and the other fifteen were dead. Forrest was convicted in Marseilles and sentenced to three years imprisonment, a sentence which was later increased to five years by the Court of Appeal in Aix. He was also fined a massive three milliard francs, and was then banned from living in France for five years after completing his sentence.[4]

There were also signs that American Mafia interests in the form of a right-hand man of 'Uncle' Frank Costello had taken up residence. He was thought to be trouble-shooting for Lucky Luciano, currently exiled in Italy and said to have an interest in the smuggling racket.[5] At one time in an eventful career, Forrest was believed to have been Luciano's bodyguard.

It was in this climate that Billy Hill bought a boat called the *Fourth Lady*, renamed it the *Flamingo* and, sailing under a Costa Rican flag, put together a crew who would well know how to deal with potential pirates.

The first Captain was Michael Henderson who had worked for George Dawson, the cockney financier later imprisoned for fraud. The crew itself was a motley one made up largely of Underworld friends of Hill, who obviously felt that he owed something to the unreliable Freddie Andrews. When Georgie Ball, with whom Hill had previously served sentences, asked if he could be brought along Hill unwisely agreed and Andrews was placed in charge of the engines. 'He's quiet. The type you'd rather have on your side than not,' wrote the daredevil Eddie Chapman of Ball sometime later. There were no such encomiums for Andrews. There was also Hill's old friend Franny Daniels, a successful escapee from the 1948 London Airport robbery, as well as another old friend Patsy Murphy. Also

[4] *The Times*, 20 December 1952; 5 May 1953; 16 February 1956. For an account of the case see Lawrence Wilkinson, *Behind the Face of Crime*, Ch. 9. (1 milliard = 1 thousand million.)

[5] In fact Luciano moved around the Mediterranean and even to Havana almost at will. See James Morton, *Gangland International*, p. 142. The connection between Hill and the Mafia is an interesting one. In the 1950s Frank Fraser was taken to Rome by Albert Dimes and introduced to Luciano. See Frank Fraser, *Mad Frank*, p. 133.

on the team was the former boxer George Walker – brother of Billy, the talented heavyweight. George's career had ended in a bloodbath with Dennis Powell for the British light-heavyweight title. When his boxing career was over he began to work for Hill and from time to time acted as his minder.[6]

Hill also engaged Eddie Chapman – a noted safebreaker and a man who had been a double agent in the Second World War – and it is easy to see why. After the war he had worked on the fringes of legality in both Tangier and West Africa. He was also fluent in French and German, and could turn his hand to more or less anything. Chapman's version is that he purchased a share in the boat for £2,000 from Hill, whom he describes as 'a fellow man-about-town'.[7] By now Hill had taken to drinking in the Star in Belgrave Mews, a favourite hangout of Chapman and a highly suitable place for him to find pigeons for plucking. Hill seems to have had the best of the deal; he only paid £2,900 for the boat.

Chapman was born in 1914, brought up in Sunderland and worked in the shipyards. Always a man of courage, he was awarded a certificate from the Humane Society when, at the age of eighteen, he saved a man who was drowning off Roker. He served in the Coldstream Guards until the mid-1930s when he turned his hand to a more profitable career, that of safebreaker. He had been on duty at the Tower of London and during a leave period a prostitute showed him some of the delights of the West End, so he bought himself a civilian suit and went AWOL. For his sins he received 112 days in the glasshouse and so to speak he never looked back. Next stop was Lewes prison where he met the man who would be his mentor and partner, Jimmy Hunt. Americans in London introduced him to the

[6] Paul Davidson, 'Shady Past of Tycoon George' in the *People*, 12 June 1988. Walker later, and very successfully, went into business, establishing Billy's Baked Potato – a fast-food chain which financed the purchase of the Hendon greyhound track which in turn metamorphosed into the shopping centre Brent Cross.
[7] *The Times*, 13 March 1939. Eddie Chapman, *Free Agent*, p.159. In the book pseudonyms are given to the crew. Franny Daniels becomes Dannie Lyons, George Walker is Jackie Dewer; George Ball becomes Gerald Bull, while Freddie Andrews is Ted Arthurs. The skipper of the boat is given as Will Kentish. The part of the book dealing with the *Flamingo* is largely an expansion of his articles in the *Sunday Chronicle*.

benefits of gelignite, and he and Hunt first stole 400 detonators and two packets of gelignite before putting the equipment to work on a weekly basis. Targets included the safe at Edgware Road underground station as well as Odeon cinemas. In the 1930s Chapman was living high off the hog in an hotel near Burlington Arcade. His downfall came in December 1938 when he and some others went to Edinburgh to rob the Co-op in Dundee Street. The safe, a half-ton Chubb, proved recalcitrant and they were interrupted by a passing policeman. One man was caught as he crashed into a pile of fruit tins but Chapman, giving the name Edward Edwards, made it as far as Newcastle Corner. The detective Edward Greeno travelled North to ask for Chapman's return to London, but in a turf dispute the magistrate ruled that he should stand trial in Scotland first. Later the Baillie gave Chapman bail and he repaid the kindness by breaking into another Odeon to raise the bail money for his friends. Then it was back down South.

According to legend he was in the Regent Palace Hotel behind Piccadilly Circus when he saw an advertisement on the menu for Jersey, and off he went with three others – Latt, Darry and Anson – with a view to travelling on to South America. They arrived with a girl sometime before 11 February, but unfortunately one of the other men sent a girlfriend a postcard. Even more unfortunately, her brother was in the CID. The Jersey police found them at the Hôtel de la Plage having their Sunday lunch and arrested his three companions, but Chapman walked through the winter garden of the hotel into a small lounge overlooking the sea, opened a window and climbed out onto the promenade. One elderly lady told the local reporter, 'I was petrified. I have never seen anything so thrilling in all my life.'

Chapman first broke into the R.E. Yard – stealing a quantity of tools 'prejudicial to His Majesty's War Department – and then the West Park Pavilion at St Helier, stealing £25 before going to a bed-and-breakfast for the night. His horizons had now shrunk to Dieppe, but his hopes were short-lived. He was arrested thirty-five hours later in a bed-and-breakfast and, described as a professional dancer, after confessing to breaking the safe was sent to the superior court for sentence. The Attorney-General asked for a minimum sentence of two years with hard labour and the court agreed. He was to serve his time on the island. The others had already been returned to England.[8] Chapman was still there when the war broke out and the Channel Islands were occupied in 1940. Now he began his third and most illustrious career.

He was first recruited by the Germans to carry out sabotage using his knowledge of explosives. Given the codename Fritzchen on 20 December 1942 he was dropped by parachute with a wireless, an automatic pistol, a suicide pill and currency worth £1,000. His mission was to blow up the De Havilland aircraft factory where the Mosquito fighter-bomber was being developed. The reward for a successful mission would be £15,000 and to be sent to America for further missions. The moment Chapman disentangled himself from his parachute he telephoned Wisbech police station, but he had a good deal of trouble making the station staff understand that he was a former safebreaker turned German spy who really wanted to work for MI5.

Now given the codename of Zig-Zag, on 29 January 1943 he and an MI5 officer climbed through the De Havilland fence and planted a series of dummy charges around the power plant. The operation was supervised by the great magician and illusionist Jasper Maskelyne, who carried out a controlled explosion and created the impression of much greater devastation.[9] It was duly reported in the newspapers and Chapman was told by the Abwehr to make his own way back to Germany from where he would be sent to America.

He was now given a second mission by the British, who put him on a ship bound for Lisbon. They had, perhaps surprisingly, declined

---

[8] Edward Greeno gives a slightly different version of the case when he names Chapman as Mike – in E.Greeno, *War on the Underworld*, pp. 90–97. *The Morning News* (St Helier) 13, 14 February, 6, 13 March 1939.
[9] Jasper Maskelyne was never given the credit he deserved for his illusions in wartime. His most spectacular was when he apparently destroyed a whole town. In a television series in 2003, the illusion was named the second greatest ever.

his offers to assassinate Hitler. In Portugal Chapman was given a piece of 'coal' by the Abwehr to put in the coalstore of the ship. It was in fact designed to detonate when put on a fire. The next year Chapman was sent by the Abwehr to Norway, then recalled to Germany and awarded the Iron Cross. He was sent back to England to be dropped again in East Anglia, this time near Newmarket on 27 June 1944 where he again had trouble persuading the local police exactly who he was. In recognition of his services he was allowed to keep money he had made while working for the Germans, and all outstanding charges against him were dropped. Over the next decade he became a man-about-Soho, living by his wits and some undetected safebreaking. He was also the putter-up of a number of thefts.[10] Frank Fraser remembers him: 'I liked Eddie. He was class . . . In a way Eddie was mixing with a different circle by then. He'd grown away from our life. He'd moved out of Soho and into Knightsbridge and Chelsea.'[11]

Whichever version of the elegant Chapman's recruitment is correct, in spring 1954 he and Hill flew to Tangier where the *Flamingo* was at anchor. Captain Henderson had marshalled his resources and his initially unseamanlike collection had made the journey safely. Once there, Henderson left the vessel and asked the British Consul for a passage home. He was replaced by Bill Beamish, a friend of Eddie Chapman who knew when to keep his mouth shut and was a fine sailor. When his mouth was open, he too had the advantage of speaking a number of languages.

Unlike many former prisoners, Billy Hill retained an affection for prison food. He was not averse to porridge and Eddie Chapman thought that if he had the opportunity he would eat bully beef – which in the 1930s and 1940s was served in prisons on a Sunday

---

[10] Chapman first published his story in a French newspaper and was prosecuted under the Official Secrets Act at Bow Street where on 29 March 1946 he was fined £50 and ordered to pay £25 costs. In 1948, when he appeared on currency charges, he was described by a senior officer from the War Office as 'one of the bravest men who served in the last war'. See Frank Owen, *The Eddie Chapman Story*. The book was made into the film *Triple Cross* starring Christopher Plummer and Romy Schneider.
[11] Frank Fraser, *Mad Frank's Britain*, pp. 177–9.

– every day of his life. Accordingly the *Flamingo* was stocked with four sacks of potatoes and 156 tins of corned beef.

There was no question of Jack Spot being invited, or of accepting even if he had been. Parker remembers:

> He said he wasn't a fucking pirate. It wasn't his game going on boats. He liked it in London too much. He liked to walk about the West End. I remember one time walking with him and Sonny the Yank, the length of Oxford Street, and the barrow boys on the fruit stalls was giving him two quid here, three quid there. It wasn't protection. They was all licensed by this time. They didn't have to give; it was more a mark of respect. He loved all that. Jack couldn't drive and I don't think he ever paid for a cab. He'd just jump in one and he was never charged. He was a real West End Face.

It was now that – to the annoyance of Hill – Spot would hold court in an hotel near Marble Arch where the barman had named a cocktail 'Jack Boss', made with Scotch and French vermouth, after him. The joke was that woe betide anyone who expected Italian vermouth.[12]

Nipper Read recalled him:

> By the 1950s he was one of the two self-styled 'Kings of the Underworld' and was something of a grand old man . . . he had mellowed since his early days . . . and now was well groomed with well-tailored – usually brown – suits, a brown fedora hat and handmade shoes. He would leave his flat, walk across the road to his barber's and then down to the Cumberland Hotel, where at a corner table in the Bear Garden he would hold court, offering advice and wisdom to anyone who sought it. He looked like a successful businessman. He seemed to have modelled himself on the American *mafioso*, Frank Costello, but he had neither that man's intellectual power nor his political connections.[13]

Hill tried to establish a similar court in the Royal Garden, Hyde Park, where he would sit accompanied by Bobby Ramsey and

---

[12] Brian McDonald, *Elephant Boys*, pp. 248–9.
[13] Leonard Read, *Nipper Read*, p. 74.

Franny Daniels, but it was not an arrangement which appealed to the management in the way Spot did.

Spot was well out of the trip. Just about everything which could go wrong eventually did so. Chapman says that he and Hill put up at a small and inconspicuous hotel, but their arrival had been noted by the police already and they were promptly hauled downtown to be interviewed by the Sûreté.[14]

Nor did their appearance in Tangier go unremarked by the locals. There were rumours that they were there to rob a bank or burn the ships of the other contrabandoliers. There was also the story that they had been hired to kill. There were visits to bars and brothels by some of the crew; there were fights and offers of work. Chapman established a company, Anglo-American Fidelity, which would guarantee employees would not abscond with the takings of the insured. 'This to me was a splendid idea. Who better than us to investigate thefts? It seemed too, like a legalised protection racket which, after all, is what insurance companies really are!'[15] Then there was an offer to kill a man's brother, for which Chapman took a deposit of $1,500; it was the usual scam, with the brother paying £500 not to be murdered. There was at least one successful smuggling run.

While in London, Hill had been approached with the offer of a truly hare-brained scheme. It was nothing less than the effective kidnap of the Sultan of Morocco, then in detention in Madagascar. The aim was to return him to his supporters and so force the French to restore him to his throne. Hill thought that a spot of smuggling would mask the true intention behind the voyage. This was where Chapman would be so useful. With his charm and command of French he would persuade the Sultan and his sons that freedom lay aboard the *Flamingo*, from where he would be taken to a seaplane and then flown back home.

Now, in Tangier, negotiations were satisfactorily concluded. A

[14] Eddie Chapman, *Free Agent*, Part Three.
[15] *Ibid.*, p. 168.

down payment of £3,000 was made against a fee of £100,000 for successful completion, and an arrangement was made to take on two Arab men to be part of the crew. The final arrangements were to be concluded in Barcelona, where the ship could draw arms and provisions. However, the rendezvous never took place because of a fight in the brothel quarter of Tangier. The Queen and the Duke of Edinburgh were due to visit Gibraltar and there were anti-British cries from the Tangier residents. A Spaniard was knocked about and the reprisal came in the form of an attack on the *Flamingo*. This was repelled, but it was followed by another trip to the Sûreté when Chapman and the others were given their sailing orders.

They sailed first for Ceuta and then disappeared. Indications had been given that they were making for Beirut. 'La Motovedetto Fantasma,' said the Italian papers enthusiastically when the boat appeared in Savona near Genoa, and soon there was a *Sunday Chronicle* reporter in tow. By now Hill, Chapman and the others also had their own detectives following them quite openly. Hill thought this was both because they were suspected of gold running and because some of them were suspected of involvement in the mailbag robbery. A warrant was issued in Tangier for a Belgian member of the crew who had joined the *Flamingo* in Ceuta. In turn Patrick Murphy left the boat and flew to Nice. Now they were ordered out of Savona but before the boat was allowed to sail Beamish, as captain, was fined a modest 25/- because 400 cigarettes had disappeared from the packages sealed by Customs officials. It was thought to be preferable to pay the fine rather than to argue. During their stay the crew had been the object of much speculation and interest as they sat around playing the Guy Mitchell song, 'She wears red feathers'. It was not the sort of caper which would have appealed to the by-now thoroughly domesticated Spot.

Before they sailed Chapman told a reporter, 'This time we are planning a dangerous and exciting – but not a suspicious – mission in the Far East. It is going to shake a few people when they know the truth.' Hill, who denied a crew member had been shanghaied, and said that he had chartered the yacht so that Eddie Chapman could write a series of articles about adventurous places, added his few pence-worth: 'We intend to make for Singapore and the Far East. We will be away for two or three years.'[16]

By the end of the trip the enmity between Hill and Andrews had resurfaced, and it became clear that Hill had poorly disguised intentions to deal with him: 'Often when I was alone, working and doing some repairs with Arthur [Andrews] I looked at him and tried to picture what he would look like with his throat cut.'[17] Chapman was no longer into this sort of aggravation and it was arranged that he should stay in Corsica and so avoid the forthcoming troubles. However, once on shore he was again ordered by the authorities to leave. It was then arranged that he would rejoin the ship in Barcelona for the run to rescue the Sultan, but by then the voyage had ended. Meanwhile he rejoined his pregnant wife, Betty, in England.

The *Flamingo* had put in to the civil port at Toulon allegedly to shelter from bad weather, and never left. Her arrival was not auspicious. Initially, she had sailed into the naval port and promptly been escorted out. In the early hours of 22 July the boat caught fire and, according to Bill Beamish, who was badly burned, the fire was deliberate. He claimed that three people had set the engine room alight and had thrown him onto the flames, saying he knew too much, but he survived to tell the tale. The police put an armed guard on deck and halted repairs.

Eddie Chapman says the culprit was Andrews who, when drunk, had fired the vessel; sprinkling petrol over the engine, after climbing the ladder he had tossed down a lighted match setting the engine-room alight. He had been seen and challenged by Beamish, whom he threw into the flames. When, in turn, he was interviewed he turned things around by saying it was Beamish who had fired the boat. Freddie Andrews promptly disappeared, and it

[16] *Sunday Chronicle*, 4, 11, 18, 25 July, 1 August 1954; *Daily Express*, 5, 6, 9, 10 July 1954.
[17] Eddie Chapman, *Free Agent*, p. 203.

was thought he might again have fallen foul of his old Underworld connections.[18]

Chapman thought the boat might be re-fitted, but as time went by the dock fees mounted and remained unpaid. Now Hill decided the boat was jinxed, and it was while sunning himself in Nice that he prematurely announced his retirement to the faithful Duncan Webb. Within a matter of weeks, however, he would pull off his last great coup.

It was another robbery which produced his second major triumph. On 21 September 1954 his team robbed a bullion lorry in Lincoln's Inn Fields, clearing £45,000.[19] It was another meticulously planned job and is an interesting example of Hill's methods both in planning the robbery and ensuring he was never charged. Less than a fortnight earlier he had announced his retirement to Duncan Webb: 'I've made my pile so I'm quitting.'[20] Aged 43, he was now sitting peacefully in the sun in the South of France spouting pabulum to the ever-faithful journalist. The spielers were bringing in a good sum each week, everybody was behaving themselves. If there was any trouble he would be told in his daily telephone call and would catch the next plane back to deal with things, but as far as he was concerned:

> I'm willing to bet half my bank roll – and believe me, that's plenty – that if you could see me today, sunning myself on the Riviera, among the millionaires, you would never guess who I am.
>
> I know I can't expect to reign for ever as the boss of gangland, any more than Rocky Marciano can hold the heavyweight title all his life.
>
> There are plenty of young crooks who would like to step into my shoes! The pickings are rich and they know it.
>
> At the moment they all fear me. My reputation alone – built

---

[18] Duncan Webb, 'Yacht fire was Murder Plot' in *People*, 29 August 1959.
[19] A suitably immodest account can be found in Billy Hill, *Boss of Britain's Underworld*, Ch. 16. For an admiring but slightly more dispassionate one see Duncan Webb, *Line up for Crime*, Ch. 7.
[20] William Hill said to Duncan Webb, 'I've made my pile so I'm quitting' in *People*, 12 September 1954.

up in scores of gang fights – is enough to keep order in the Underworld. One day it might be a different story.[21]

The Lincoln's Inn snatch had all the hallmarks of a Hill robbery, but because he was believed to be in the South of France – after all, that was what had appeared in the *People* – at first it was not thought he was involved. Respectively he was not and he was.

At 4.30 p.m. on the day of the robbery a man and a woman sat in a black Austin outside Rothschild's watching a Reginald Crane load two white boxes into a lorry owned by his employers, Higgs Transport. Each box contained about a hundredweight of gold bullion. Crane was then joined by John Levy as his escort and the lorry was driven to Jockey's Fields, a narrow mews-type street off Theobald's Road. Twenty minutes later the bullion was unloaded and placed in the freight room of the airline KLM which had offices there. Just before 6 p.m. another Higgs Transport vehicle was backed into the road to collect the load by the driver, James Kent. The moment it stopped outside the KLM offices the black Austin drove in and parked diagonally across the road, blocking the exit to Theobald's Road. The driver locked the car and walked to a nearby public lavatory, leaving by another exit. As the bullion was being transferred a small blue lorry began to back down the road, crashing into Kent's vehicle. As it did so, a man leaned out and snatched the bullion and the blue van accelerated away. The whole operation took less than a minute.

A man's felt hat, a transparent wrapping and a mophead were found in the Austin, along with two sets of fingerprints which could not be matched. The next day the van in which the gold had been taken was found in Ormond Place, a quarter of a mile away. In it were a green tweed coat, a light trilby with a dark band and a blue scarf with white spots. These were disregarded because they were thought to be false clues left by the robbers.

Once again Hill's old adversary Chief Superintendent Robert Lee

[21] *People*, 12 September 1954.

took part in the inquiry, this time rather by accident. By this time, in promotional terms, he had rather paid for his failure to deal with the Eastcastle Street robbery and had been transferred to No. 3 District which covered Holborn. His place on the Flying Squad was taken by Chief Superintendent Guy Mahon, who quickly joined him. Now it was a question of rounding up the usual suspects. Most of those involved with the Airport robbery had now been released and there were, of course, the suspects from the successful Eastcastle Street job still out and about. Within 48 hours there had been police raids on five houses in North London and another twenty-seven homes in South and East London. Fifty arrests were made and five men were held for identification.

Alibis were securely in place. Two men had fortunately reported a lost dog to a police station at the moment of the robbery. Another had genuinely been in a Soho drinking club at the time. Two suspects were stripped and hoovered to try to find gold particles. It was not a success. Next came tips that the gold was to leave the country from Southampton in a private yacht. It was not. Then came another tip that it would be smuggled out of the Surrey docks. It was not. A raid was now organised on a warehouse in the Whitechapel Road owned by Hill, who retained offices there and at one time had his legitimate partnership distributing toys.

On the morning of the raid on his premises Hill was followed by a plain-clothes police officer. He lost the tail at Aldgate tube station by leaping out when the doors began to close, leaving the officer stranded. He telephoned his warehouse and received no reply although his staff should have been there; telephoned again and, when a man answered, asked to speak to the senior officer. The receiver was replaced. Hill took a taxi to his solicitor and made a statement saying he believed his warehouse was being raided and that nothing would be found there. Meanwhile the police were having a fine time examining some 50,000 dolls which called out 'Mama' when they were turned upside down and Teddy Bears which went, 'A-a-h'.

It was then that Hill arrived with his solicitor. Some wood shavings had been found in an upstairs room and he was asked where they had come from. He replied that he had never seen them before. Shown a carpet on which the police suggested there was an imprint of the boxes of bullion, Hill said that he could not see any marks and wanted the carpet and the wood photographed. A photographer was found and the photographs taken, but Hill was not satisfied; he wanted them photographed all over again, and reluctantly Mahon acceded. Now Hill wanted a ten shilling note which he produced and placed on the carpet to be photographed so that the numbers showed on the print. He said he did not want to leave any chance that, euphemistically speaking, the photographs might be mixed up with others back at Scotland Yard. The note was then handed to his solicitor.[22]

Now he was asked for his alibi and produced the perfect response. He knew exactly where he had been. It was at the offices of the *People* where he had seen the old and respected journalist Hannen Swaffer; he had been there for hours. And who else was there? None other than Duncan Webb. That, so far as Hill was concerned, was the end of the case. He affected surprise about the whole thing when the newspapers found him in his shirtsleeves at his 'luxurious retreat':

> I thought I had finished with all this sort of thing. But just because someone has pulled a big job back they come to me again. Why they searched my place I don't know. Perhaps they expected to find gold bars. Anyway they left without finding a thing. I'm retired now and want to live quietly without upsetting the cops.[23]

In April 1955 Reginald Crane, the driver of the lorry, pleaded guilty to conspiracy to steal and receiving, along with another man named Albert Beech who had at one time worked for KLM. Crane had been paid £1,000 to allow the robbery to take place. Beech had received £200 of the money. It appears the men had been approached in a public house where they had been heard talking about their jobs.

[22] Duncan Webb, 'Yard told bullion secrets' in *People*, 3 October 1954.
[23] *Daily Express*, 29 September 1954.

The gold was never recovered. Webb, no doubt on very good authority, believed that it had been smelted on the night of the robbery and buried in a garden north of London. No more arrests were made.

Webb, again theorising, wrote that the idea had come from the crash of a KLM flight on 5 September 1954 when a plane had gone down on the mud flats of the River Shannon, killing 28 passengers. Hill had learned that the flight had also been carrying diamonds, and he sent men to find out where the jewels were with instructions to follow their path when they were recovered by the airline. The trail led back to London. 'Mr X has a lot of men working for him all over the world. As the genius behind some of the biggest crimes in Britain this century, he needs to have', wrote the completely impartial Webb.[24]

[24] Duncan Webb, *'Spot in a Spot'* in *People*, 17 June 1956.

Sabinis and the former friends the Cortesis. Darby Sabini is standing in the flat cap
he right of Enrico Cortesi in the boater. Harryboy is in the front row with dark trilby.
t Marsh is second from the left in the back row, in the flat cap.

k Spot gets a trim.

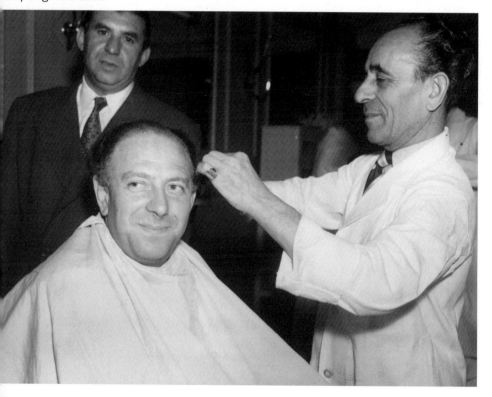

The barbers, normally the province of Albert Dimes, where Spot collapsed.

Gerry Parker and his wife Shirley in Paris.

ot with Rita (right) and her sister Marion Cooney at the ill-fated Highball Club.

day at the races. Parker is on the right. Jack Spot is almost out of the picture on the
. George Wood is in the trilby and James Wood is standing beneath him. (William Hill
idon has no connection to the bookmakers so widely known today.)

Spot, Rita and the children.

Eddie Chapman, Billy Hill and George Walker discuss the wreck of the Flamingo in July 1954.

Spot and Rita after his acquittal for the wounding of Tommy Falco.

ck Kid Berg and Spot in one of the last photographs of the gang leader.

The corner of Frith and Old Compton Streets where the fight that never was took place.

Billy Hill interviewed by the press on his abortive trip to Australia.

Sir Bernard and Lady Docker play marbles.

Rose Heilbron QC.

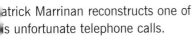

Patrick Marrinan reconstructs one of his unfortunate telephone calls.

Billy Hill attends Billy Blythe's funeral.

Rita Comer boards the plane back to England to face the perjury charge.

Jack Spot holding court in his heyday (c. 1954).

Battles Rossi (far left) and Frank Fraser (far right) at the Italian Festival in Clerkenwell.

12

Hill's Angels

One ability possessed by Hill, and lacking to an extent in Darby Sabini and certainly in the case of Jack Spot, was that of keeping the troops loyal. Not only that, but he was able to recruit troops who fulfilled significant extra-curricular roles. One of the many supporting actors in Billy Hill's cast of players – and someone who was used both to improve the gangleader's own image and damage that of Jack Spot – was the very curious crime reporter from the *People*, Thomas Duncan 'Tommy' Webb. In fact Webb did not like the title of crime reporter, preferring to be referred to as a crime investigator.

Webb began his career with the *South London Press* in the 1930s, always displaying an interest in crime. He served in the war in West Africa before he was invalided out in 1944, after which he went to the *Daily Express* working under the legendary editor Arthur Christiansen. From there it was a move to the sister paper the *Evening Standard*.

He claimed that one of the reasons he left was:

. . . my superiors claimed it was not the business of a newspaper to go prying into the affairs of corpses with no arms. Lady So and

So [Lady Beaverbrook], the wife of the proprietor, would not like it, I was told. They pooh-poohed the idea. 'We are a respectable newspaper,' they said. 'After all murders are so vulgar.'

In fact Webb was sacked following a very curious incident. Shortly after his discharge from the Navy in 1944, he managed to acquire a conviction at Plymouth Magistrates' Court for communicating the movements of His Majesty's ships. He had telephoned the *Daily Express* and spoken so loudly that he had been overheard. He pleaded not guilty but was convicted. The magistrates took the view that Webb had been acting carelessly rather than maliciously and he was fined £50.[1]

That may be ascribed to a relatively young reporter's zeal, but his next appearance in the dock was altogether more damaging. This time he appeared at Marlborough Street Magistrates' Court on charges of grievous bodily harm and impersonating a police officer. He had, so the court was told by prostitute Jean Crews, agreed to have intercourse with her for £2. They had gone to her flat at 52 Langham Street where they had what she delicately described as 'connections', and he went to the bathroom to 'cleanse himself'. It was after this that he refused to leave the flat; when she said she would call the police, he left with her. In the street they encountered a Herbert Gardner Wadham and Webb showed him his press card, masking it so it appeared to be a police warrant card. He seems to have 'arrested' Wadham and then hit him in the face, splitting his lip which had to be stitched. As they marched along Tottenham Court Road Wadham approached a temporary reserve policeman and asked for help. At the police station Webb denied ever having seen Wadham. The grievous bodily harm charge was reduced to one of common assault, to which he pleaded guilty, and he was bound over in the sum of two guineas under the Prosecution of Offences Act. He was also ordered to pay fifteen guineas to Wadham. The charge of impersonating a police officer was dismissed. And, back at the paper, so was Webb. It is not clear from

---

[1] *The Times*, 27 January 1944.

the records whether Wadham knew Crews or if this was genuinely a chance encounter.[2] The former is the more probable.

It was then that he moved to the *People*, a broadsheet in name but a tabloid in spirit, where he worked for the editor Sam Campbell. He really was a hero of the gutter press; he was quite prepared to put himself physically at risk and to assume disguises to obtain his information. It is he who, after being offered what were described as 'vice services', is said to have coined the phrase 'I made my excuses and left'.

Webb made his name with the case of John George Haigh, the so-called acid bath murderer, who was hanged on 6 August 1949. Haigh had a wife living in a bigamous marriage in Cornwall and, with himself as best man and also giving the bride away, Webb arranged a remarriage for the benefit of readers of the *People* the week after Haigh's execution.[3] Two months later he followed up the story with that of the murder of Stanley Setty by Donald Hume in October 1949.[4] On 21 January 1950 he faced a contempt of court charge over his conduct in the trial; he had approached Hume's wife and sent her a telegram which could have been interpreted as trying to persuade her not to give evidence. After Hume's conviction and a subsequent divorce Webb married his wife Cynthia, who had worked as a nightclub hostess.

Frank Fraser recalls him:

> Billy could do what he wanted with Webb. I think Duncan was frightened he'd get a hiding because of Donald Hume's wife. Hume

---

[2] Nat. Arch. MEPO 3 3037.

[3] *People*, 21 August 1949. For further information on Haigh, see Douglas Browne, *Sir Travers Humphreys*, Ch.19.

[4] It was never clear exactly for what reason – possibly a quarrel over black market dealing – Stanley Setty was killed and his body dismembered at Hume's flat in the Finchley Road in October 1949. Hume then hired a light aircraft and dropped the parts in parcels over the Essex marshes where they were found. At his trial he claimed that he had been hired to dispose of the parcels for the actual killers. After a disagreement in his trial when the verdict had to be unanimous, he agreed to plead guilty to a charge of being an accessory after the fact. He expected a short sentence but received one of twelve years. On his release he killed a taxi driver during a bank robbery in Switzerland. James Morton, *A Calendar of Killing*.

had been convicted after a retrial for the murder of Stanley Setty. On the second go round the prosecution was in a mess, because it wasn't popular to hang someone when the jury had disagreed; so Hume was offered a plea to being an accessory. He thought he'd get 2–3 years; he never dreamed he'd get twelve. That's when his wife divorced him – she was a nightclub hostess – and married Webb. He'd gone to interview her and wound up marrying her. By now Webb was shit scared. Hume's time was getting on and he was up for remission. Duncan wanted protection and Hilly was intelligent enough to know that he could feed Webb with information and Webb could be useful to him.

Bill used to wind Webb up something rotten. We'd be sitting in Peter Mario's restaurant in Gerrard Street and Billy would say about Hume, 'What's he like, Frank? You've done bird with him.' And I would nod and say, 'He never forgets, Bill, he never forgets.' And you'd see Duncan literally cringe and shrivel.[5]

It was, however, through his investigation into the Messinas who – with the tacit approval of Hill and Spot – controlled vice in the West End over two decades, that Webb became involved with Billy Hill and his entourage. In September 1950 he published his exposé of the brothers under the banner headline 'Arrest These Four Men':

> On the night of 30 June 1950 I performed one of the most distasteful duties I have ever carried out in my career as a crime reporter – something I never want to do again. I went to the West End of London and picked up a woman of the streets.

His earlier escapade with Mrs Crews had conveniently been forgotten.

According to Robert Murphy, the brothers came looking for him and found him with Hill in the Brunswick Arms, Bloomsbury.[6] That may have saved him from a beating but it did not stop the Messinas' top girl Marthe Marie Watts from attempting on 21 November that year to have him prosecuted for blackmail. She alleged that he had

[5] Frank Fraser, *Mad Frank*, pp. 88–9.
[6] *People*, 3 September 1950; Robert Murphy, *Smash and Grab*.

demanded £50 each from her and another prostitute not to have their photographs published. She had, so she said, offered him £7 which he had contemptuously declined. The stories of the two girls contradicted each other and no charge was brought.

Without doubt, Webb had a dark side. He overstepped the role of investigative journalist and became a confidant and effectively a tool of Billy Hill and his friends, meeting and eating with them in Peter Mario's restaurant at the Leicester Square end of Gerrard Street.[7]

Webb would become Hill's Boswell, describing the gangleader as 'a crook, a villain, a thief, a thug' and 'a genius and a kind and tolerant man'. He would also become a close associate of Frank Fraser and Bert Rossi, to be used both to promote their stories such as the escape by Peter Fleming and Alfie Hinds and to denigrate Spot.[8]

After Webb, at times a devout Roman Catholic, had exposed the Messinas he put an advertisement in *The Times* offering his thanks to St Jude. Once he had triumphed over that family, he turned his attention to the lesser vice lights of the West End including the madam Jessie Featherstonehaugh and the Paddington brothel keeper, Maurice Conley. 'A hateful little bastard,' says Parker. 'Conley was very friendly with Hubby Distleman. He had a couple of clubs in the West End and Jack would get a few quid from him for looking after them.' Here was Webb as crusading journalist. The tenor of his articles can be judged by one on the Club Americana off Piccadilly where, 'For jazz-crazy negroes and their white imitators this basement club is paradise.'[9]

Another of Hill's acolytes was the barrister Patrick Aloysius Marrinan, a large, dark-haired, jovial Irishman who advised and appeared for him and his entourage in the 1950s. Frank Fraser remembers Marrinan:

He was a brief who seemed to come from out of nowhere. When I got the three years for the cigarettes no one had even heard of

[7] Peter Mario's has now become the Chinese restaurant, Harbour City.
[8] 'I broke out for love' in *People*, 11 December 1955.
[9] *People*, 18 December 1955.

him. But from 1952 onwards his name came into focus. I heard his name time and again whilst I was away and when I came out from Broadmoor in 1955 he was the predominant figure. I had many drinks with him at Bill's flat over at Barnes. He was a good drinker. He'd start with Guinness and go on to Irish whiskey.[10]

Marrinan's father had been an officer in the Royal Irish Constabulary before becoming a barrister. Marrinan himself had read law at Queen's University, Belfast, and became the Irish Universities' heavyweight champion. He had one brother who became a professional boxer and later a trainer in Quebec, and another who also went into the law. After his graduation Marrinan was a well-known frequenter of the Belfast clubs and greyhound tracks. Fraser saw him through rose-coloured spectacles: 'I think Marrinan was a rebel. It was the unfairness and corruptness of the legal profession he fought against.' Robert Murphy takes a different, less charitable, view: '[He] was greedy, ambitious and unscrupulous.' Murphy may well be right. While still a law student Marrinan had started badly with a court appearance in Liverpool.

He was arrested by the senior Liverpool policeman Herbert Balmer in the Washington Hotel at 10.15 a.m. on 15 May 1942. The police were looking into a ring smuggling watches and jewellery from the Irish Free State. When questioned, at first Marrinan denied he had any uncustomed goods and had, he said, pulling back his shirt cuffs, only his wristwatch. Balmer did not believe him and began a search. Marrinan then said he would find what he wanted if he looked in his suitcase. In it were 202 watches, 234 gold crosses, 109 bracelets, 12 rings and £126 cash. There was also an order form in code. 'Having a good time' meant more watches were to be sent to him; 'I wish I were home' called for 10–15 rings with stones, and 'Nothing to do but go to the pictures' meant he wanted 50–60 rings. 'Very bored' indicated there was nothing doing. He was remanded in custody for a week.

[10] Frank Fraser, *Mad Frank*, p. 95.

The next week he pleaded guilty, and it was explained to the court that he was a 'totally innocent dupe . . . totally unaware that in disposing of this jewellery he was doing something against the law'. He had met a man in a public house in Dublin at Christmas time and, on telling him he was going to London, he learned there was a chance to earn a few pounds. In fact he had travelled to Glasgow, selling the jewellery there as well. Balmer thought rather worse of him. As far as he was concerned, Marrinan was part and parcel of a well-planned scheme and was near to the top if not the top man. Marrinan was fined £4,500 with the alternative of three months' hard labour. He was not given time to pay.[11]

This kept him out of the profession for nearly ten years and it was only after he had been rejected by the Bar Council that he appealed successfully to the High Court. He was then in his early thirties. In November 1951 he joined the chambers at 2 Harcourt Building in Middle Temple Lane of which F. Ashe Lincoln – the brother of solicitor Ellis, who later represented Spot – was a member. Marrinan had not undergone formal pupillage – the practice in which a young barrister pays a senior to school him – because he had insufficient money. In his first year he earned £80 and described himself as often being faint with hunger. The next year was better; he earned £400. But after only three years at the bar Marrinan made a name defending two of the great London burglars of the time, first George 'Taters' Chatham, and then another of Hill's burglar friends Billy Benstead. It was something of a mutual admiration society. Webb wrote of his defence of Chatham:

> With his record coupled with an escape while on remand – on top of a gigantic number of crimes – it would seem that Chatham would get the full 14 years' sentence prescribed by the law. But Marrinan's eloquence brought the sentence down to 10 years.

Webb was equally gushing over the defence of Benstead:

[11] *Liverpool Echo*, 16, 22 May 1942.

Generations of Scotland Yard chiefs knew all about Billy. All his
life he had been a burglar.

Yet when he appeared in the magistrate's court on a string of
new charges of burglary and safebreaking, Marrinan actually
persuaded the bench to grant him bail!

Frank Fraser does not remember him as a great advocate:

> If he defended you, he defended you. But he hadn't a good appear-
> ance. He had the brain but not the talk. Marrinan had it up there
> but a very poor speaking voice. In his enthusiasm to do his best
> he stuttered. A barrister has to have a lot of the actor in him
> which helps to carry the day. If he gets overheated he loses a lot
> of the punch and that's what was wrong with him.

Marrinan also became far too close to Billy Hill for his own good.
They both had flats in the same block in Barnes and, despite his
later protestations to the contrary, Marrinan would visit Hill to drink
with him. One reason for his popularity was that he was dishonest;
he was used to pass messages to criminals and if necessary take a
hand in things himself.

Fraser recalls:

> My alibi for the slashing of Spot was that I was in the office of a
> bookmaker who was taking bets over the phone for an evening
> at a dog meeting. They were called SP offices in those days. Sammy
> Bellson was to be a witness, along with another man who worked
> in the office. When Reginald Seaton, who was leading counsel for
> the Crown, was cross-examining me he asked how many phones
> there were and what colours they were. I'd been to the office but
> I'd never worked there and I was in a bit of a quandary. I hadn't
> squared this with my witnesses at all and whatever I said they
> was stuck with. They would have to answer correctly and it could
> be fatal.
>
> I see Patrick looking at me very intently and instinct told me
> that I could say whatever I wanted and somehow he would see
> it was conveyed to my witnesses. It was proved correct. I said
> there were three phones, one green, one red and one black or

whatever. Marrinan stood up and bowed to the judge, rather indicating he wished to go to the lavatory. Out he went – security was not the same in those days – and he saw my two witnesses and told them what I said. He came back and looked at me again. It told me he'd done it. Both witnesses gave exactly the same evidence as I had done. Not that it did me any good.[12]

Over the years Marrinan would become the nearest thing England had then known to in-house counsel for a criminal gang.

[12] Frank Fraser, *Mad Frank*, pp. 96–7.

13

The Fight That Never Was

Depending on one's point of view, the year 1955 was an *annus horri-bilis* or *annus mirabilis* for the various participating members of the London Underworld. It started very badly indeed for Alfred Charles Ady and Countess Thelma Madeleine Noad-Johnston, known both as Black Maria and the Black Orchid, who died in a suicide pact at the Pack Horse Hotel, Staines, where they had registered as Mr and Mrs A.H. Lewis from Cambridge. They were both wanted for a big jewel robbery in Hatton Garden for which the 22-year-old American Hubert Edward Clark had received three years at the Old Bailey the day before.

The well-planned robbery had taken place at the offices of Abraham Cobden on 20 November 1954. The trio had gone to the premises, which they had previously reconnoitred, and chloroformed the jeweller who unfortunately for them had recovered sufficiently to see them pouring the contents of the safe and some jewellery into a sack. They had rushed out onto the pavement where Clark had knocked over and out a passer-by who tried to stop them. Since then the Countess and Ady had been on the run, living on their wits, robberies and the proceeds of dud cheques. Before she died she wrote a letter to her son, 'Alfred and I think there is some sort of explanation due to you.' Ady had killed her, gone down to the hotel lobby where he had himself written a letter saying she had died in his arms, and then returned to their room and poisoned himself.

The Countess had had a very interesting career. She was reputed to have 'killed' three men, something on which she remarked, 'I didn't kill any man. Any man who died just couldn't stand the pace.' She had been sent to a convent school in Sheffield and, despite intending to become a nursery school teacher with Madam Montessori, had then gone to her aunt's hotel in Torquay. There she had been seduced by 'a handsome chauffeur' who had both impregnated her and duplicitously failed to tell her he was already married. Her savings went on the necessary abortion, and she modelled at the Central School of Art as a nude at 15 shillings a day until she was told of the riches available as a hostess at 'Ma of Soho', Madame Coletta's Queen's Hotel, Leicester Square. There she had fallen in love with an Irishman and, despite Ma's best efforts to dissuade her, she had married him, moving to the Cosmopolitan Artistes Club in Wardour Street. From there it was on to run a club owned by someone she described as 'a celebrated Frenchman'.

In 1938 she married a thoroughly shady solicitor with a practice in Berwick Street, Count J.E. Noad-Johnston who was related to the royal family of Montenegro. He had had a number of scrapes including an assault, a conviction quashed on appeal and a conviction for being a party to the continued use of premises as a brothel. He appealed again and told the court that he knew the women frequenting the place were 'of a certain class', but he lived there with Thelma and took no notice of the other tenants. As for the management, he was merely the solicitor to L & A Business Enterprises who leased part of the premises. His £25 fine was returned to him.

In 1940 he was struck off the rolls for his general bad behaviour, and in the early 1950s the Countess had been the brains behind selling non-existent flats with him at Howard's Estate Agency, Brompton Road. He fled to France where she supported him for a year before his extradition. In turn he had protected her when he received ten years in 1952. Two years later she met Ady, and with him had embarked on a career of professional crime.[1]

The year had started badly enough for Billy Hill with the death of his long-standing henchman, Frederick 'Slip' Sullivan, at the hands of Sullivan's girlfriend at their flat in Greville Place, St John's Wood. A father of seven, Sullivan had left his wife behind in Crossley Street, Islington, and had set up light housekeeping with Mary Cooper. Impossibly jealous, he had already served 21 months for throwing a man from a taxi in which he had been with Mary. At first it was suggested that Sullivan's death might result in a leadership fight between gangs, but in fact he was a capable lieutenant rather than a captain. It was also clear that Mary was in deep trouble, and after the stabbing she stayed at Albany Street police station. She then disappeared and now, thought the newspapers dramatically, since she was believed to know the truth behind the Eastcastle Mailbag Robbery she was in danger. Rival gangs were said to be looking for her.[2]

What is clear is that things had been sorted out by the time the 23-year-old beautiful blonde Mary Cooper, also known as Kustanci, appeared at the inquest. Fears that she had been debriefed during her 24-hour stay at Albany Street police station – even if she did know anything – proved unjustified. Now she told the coroner that Sullivan had beaten her both before and after his prison sentence from which he had been released on 11 December the previous year. On the evening of their fight she refused to make him another meal after he had thrown the first plate of stew on the fire. She was in her dressing gown at the kitchen sink when he held her head under

---

[1] *The Times*, 18 October 1935, 16, 17 August 1939, 21 September 1940, 2 April, 3 May 1952, 8, 11, 26, 29 January 1955; *Daily Mirror*, 8 January 1955; *Empire News*, 9 January 1955; *Sunday Chronicle*, 9 January 1955; Norman Rae, 'Death waited upstairs for a crook on the run' in *News of the World*, 9 January 1955.
[2] 'Murder breaks a £280,000 secret' in *Empire News*, 30 January 1955.

the cold tap. He picked up a knife but she managed to turn it on him. He died in hospital a week later.

At the opening of the inquest, Hill's house counsel, Patrick Marrinan, appeared for Sullivan's widow and alleged that Mary Cooper had murdered him. The inquest was then adjourned because of the absence of Sullivan's brother Alexander, known as Sonny, who had sent in a doctor's certificate. Sonny Sullivan was still absent when the inquest reopened, and now the police went looking for him. The inquest was again adjourned, this time until the middle of March. He was still not around, but the police believed that his family knew where he was. In his absence a statement was read that he had been to see his brother in hospital and had been told the incident was an accident, something Slip Sullivan had repeated to the police, prefacing it with the remark, 'I'm too old to talk.'

'There is not the slightest evidence of murder', the coroner told the jury, which returned an open verdict. The credit for orchestrating the inquest is given to Billy Hill, who is said to have arranged that Sonny should make the exculpatory statement for his brother and then disappear so that he could not be questioned. Hill's employment of Marrinan showed his solidarity with family life and also possibly served as a warning to Ms Cooper.

As for the funeral, it was a suitably grand one. There were over 600 wreaths and it took the 21 limousines more than an hour to leave Lough Road, Islington. One of the floral tributes was a three-and-a-half-foot-long billiard table with a pair of dice on it.

Now Hill was very much in the ascendancy while Spot was in serious decline. What had begun as a partnership if not a friendship turned to enmity. One of the reasons was their mutual love of publicity. The second and probably equally potent cause was that Hill had taken up with Gypsy Riley, leaving behind his wife Aggie Hill who ran the Modernaires Club in Greek Court off the Charing Cross Road (which once belonged to Spot) as well as the Cabinet Club in Gerrard Street. According to Underworld legend they went on holiday to the South of France in September 1951 with Spot and his beautiful Irish wife, Rita, and the women did not hit it off at all.

Perhaps at first, 1955 seemed the brightest for Spot. First there was the birth of his second daughter, Marion Margaret, on 8 January. Then he achieved his long-held ambition with the publication of his memoirs in the *Sunday Chronicle*. Now, in terms of newsprint at least, he was again the equal of Hill. The first two Sundays of the year were taken up with previewing them. For example: 'He is Britain's nearest approach to the American gangster chief. He knows all the rackets and the people who run them. He is known in London's Underworld as "The Big Shot".'

The next week came a justification for the series from J.L. Mellor, the news editor: 'This is no crime story, though crime comes into it. It is a factual real-life documentary. You might call it sensational but only because the facts speak for themselves and the facts themselves are sensational.'

The puff carried endorsements of authenticity by both the celebrated Fabian of the Yard and ex-Chief Superintendent John Sands, 'one of Scotland Yard's Big Five'. Sir Harold Scott, the retired Commissioner of Scotland Yard, had 'read the story and given helpful criticism'.[3]

The series itself began on 16 January and continued for some weeks. When it came to it there was nothing very much in it: his early life, Spot's trademark story of his clubbing the wrestler Roughneck during the Mosley marches, his times in Leeds during the war where there were four big gaming clubs, one called appropriately the Economic Club, the routing of the Whites when he claimed he had an army of 1,000 behind him. As always with Spot's stories, the characters were Liverpool Mike, Edgware Road Sam and so forth.

In a later edition there was also a gushing account of the celebrities he had met – Billy Daniels, 'A great singer, a great chap and a

---

[3] *Sunday Chronicle*, 2, 9 January 1955. The paper, very much a poor man's version of the *People* or the *Empire News*, did not survive the year.

very good friend of mine. He always looks me up when he is over'; the comedians Abbott and Costello; the boxer Jersey Joe Walcott who gave him a tip on an outsider which won at 100–7 and on which Spot had placed a £250 bet; the story of how he was with Tyrone Power and Linda Christian at Earl's Court when he had thrown some thugs out of the arena because they had been tormenting a Jewish refugee at the Turpin-Cerdan fight – this last being a little difficult because Randolph Turpin never fought Marcel Cerdan; what a good family man he was, and stories about great burglars he had known.

Much was made of Spot's six-guinea silk ties, his twenty suits at £40 a piece and his hand-made shoes. It is, however, a curious fact about the English gangleaders of the period that they never seemed to aspire to the trappings of wealth sported by their admittedly grander-scale American counterparts. True Hill had a boat, but that was used for business purposes – well, for the smuggling of ciga-rettes. He lived in a modest flat in Moscow Road. Spot, the devoted family man, lived in a slightly larger rented flat in Hyde Park Mansions. 'If they went to the Astor Club a couple of nights a week that was a big deal,' says Nipper Read. Albert Dimes seems to have been in that mould as well. 'Of course he never had to pay for a meal anywhere, never had to spend any real money,' says Read. 'He held court in the Italian Café in Frith Street and would have his suits made for free, free haircuts, and tributes like chickens and meat brought to him. But he was never a man who, whilst he was always well dressed, ever threw money about.'

From then on, however, the year was downhill for Spot. For a start, he was coming under increasing pressure from the Italians over his control of the point-to-point pitches. Once splits occur in Underworld factions even the slightest quarrel or perceived insult can trigger a string of repercussions. One such incident occurred in Manzi's restau-rant off Leicester Square when one of Spot's men, Bill Diamond, gave Johnny Jackson, a man more aligned to Hill, a backhander. Such a public display caused both a loss of face and loss of patience.

Hill's relationship with Aggie was now very strained. She had been begging him to give up crime. Instead he gave her up, although they remained close friends for years afterwards. Hill had always dallied with women, often prostitutes, but he always returned back home. Now, with Gypsy, he appeared to have genuinely fallen in love.

In April that year Hill decided to set sail on the maiden voyage of the *Southern Cross* for a new life with her in Australia, leaving Spot in effective if uneasy control of things. Aggie was to be consoled by the gift of a new black poodle, Chico, and the Modernaires Club. What was Hill like, she was asked. He had a kind heart. Indeed he had just bought her a tea-making machine to put beside the bedside in case he wasn't around in the morning. 'He is a proper sucker with money.' She did not believe Gypsy would last:

> You have read an awful lot of rubbish about Billy in the papers but his friends know him better. He is just a great big playboy. He'll come back to me, he always does and quick enough when he finds himself in trouble. This Gypsy's just a novelty that will soon wear off.[4]

Meanwhile, Hill had sent £10,000 to a bank in Sydney and he and Ms Riley made friends on board: 'My wife – call her Gypsy.' Then, when they reached Wellington the New Zealand police came aboard with a message from Scotland Yard and told him he would not be allowed to land. It was the same in Sydney; Hill was not permitted to disembark. Instead out came the New South Wales detective Ray Kelly to explain the facts of life down under to him.[5] And out came sightseers in their dozens. Hill gave interviews to reporters, made a radio broadcast and showed some city councillors over the boat, now nicknamed the *Suffering Cross*. He claimed 10,000 spectators

---

[4] John Watney, 'He's Just A Big Playboy To Me' in *Sunday Dispatch*, 22 May 1955.
[5] Kelly's intervention was ironic. A good friend of many of the top criminals of the period, he was regarded as one of the most able but also one of the most corrupt detectives of his era. Perhaps Hill was fortunate because it was said that Kelly's speciality was setting up criminals to be killed. He also ran an abortion racket. See David Hickie, *The Prince and the Premier*.

were on the quay to see him off. In South Africa he once again had to remain on board. Disembarkation would have led to his arrest over the 1948 attack on Neville. The detention had not pleased Gypsy: 'It makes you sick when you think we have come so far and then for this to happen. If only we had known sooner we could have got off at one of the other places we called at. Even at Tahiti – wouldn't we, Billy?'[6]

The perhaps more worldly-wise Aggie was not surprised: 'The only thing about this trip that has made me mad is that he has made it public. I knew he was going to Australia; I told him he was a fool to try, it was plain as anything they would never let him stay. He should have gone as a tourist, that's what I told him'.[7]

One consolation was that he made the ship's owners pay for his return passage. As a reprisal, he was moved from his cabin and was put in another situated below some refrigerators. On 13 June 1955, 102 days after he first sailed, Hill, 'in trenchcoat, dove-coloured sombrero and gripping two fat briefcases', was back in England, the mink-clad Gypsy and the newspapers in close attendance. Now he would make some television films to show young people that crime did not pay.[8]

Meanwhile, however, Spot's career was almost completely in ruins. According to the story told to John Pearson, things had deteriorated so much that he feared for his pitches on the course at the Epsom Spring Meeting. Frank Fraser and another hardman, the diminutive and bald Billy Blythe, were now more closely aligned with Hill than he was. They would be at the meeting, and Spot called on the Kray Twins in their billiard hall in the East End to seek help. The Krays were never keen on Spot; nor, it seems, he on them. However, there was no trouble. They had their day at the races, their first outing into the upper echelons of Underworld society; at the end of the meeting they took their money and drove off.

[6] Bertram Jones, 'Billy Hill sighs for a beer garden' in *Daily Express*, 5 May 1955.
[7] John Watney, 'He's Just A Big Playboy To Me' in *Sunday Dispatch*, 22 May 1955.
[8] *Daily Express*, 14 June 1955; Duncan Webb, 'Billy Hill speaks' in *People*, 19 June 1955.

After the Spring Meeting, so the story goes, Fraser and Blythe wished to meet the Krays at a pub in Islington to sort things out. The Krays spent time arming themselves and assembling a team but Hill, having got word of the challenge issued by Fraser and Blythe, was strong enough to have the meeting called off. 'The last thing he wanted was to have bloodshed,' says Pearson. The Krays waited around at the pub and then drove home, no doubt satisfied that Fraser did not dare to enter their manor.

Unfortunately the story is another of those self-perpetuating Underworld myths. Fraser was still in Broadmoor at the time, and certainly had not been given day leave to go to the races and run around Islington for the evening. Nor is there any record of his escaping for the day.

It would be seven years before the Twins reached the apotheosis of their careers:

Local businessmen Reggie and Ronnie Kray of the Kentucky Club, Mile End Road seem to have a winner with their latest venture, the Barn Twist Club opened just recently in Wilton Place, Knightsbridge. Attractively decorated, the club is open seven days a week from 8 pm. until two in the morning.[9]

In due course they remembered their appearance at the races:

It wasn't that we liked him [Spot]. We despised him really. We just turned out with Spotty to show everyone that *we* was the up-and-coming firm and didn't give a fuck for anyone. Old Spotty understood. Whatever else he may have been he wasn't stupid. He knew quite well that though we were there in theory as his friends, we meant to end up taking over from him.[10]

Spot still had friends if not supporters, and was trying to realign his position by recruiting the fearsome Frank Fraser to his side. At Brighton races he asked George Wood to approach Fraser, now

[9] *East London Advertiser*, 28 September 1962.
[10] John Pearson, *The Profession of Violence*, p. 87.

out of Broadmoor, who was handing out change on Albert Dimes'
pitch – or, more likely, minding it with Billy Blythe – with an offer
to go into a drinking club which Spot would back. Fraser declined.
It was on that occasion that DS Careless had Fraser pointed out
to him.[11]

Overall, the summer had not been a good one. Spot's friends in
Manchester could normally call on him for help, but now when he
was summoned and took five men up with him he found that a
Scunthorpe bookmaker had organised a large and unwelcoming
reception committee for him. He and his men retreated in some
disorder.[12]

It was around that time that Rita Smith, a cousin of the Twins,
met him:

> As I walked in the door and stood looking round, this man sitting
> with my cousin said, 'Hello green eyes. Come over here a minute.'
> As I walked over I heard Reg say, 'That's my cousin', and Spotty's
> manner changed because until then I think he had ideas of chat-
> ting me up. Mind you, he was good-looking in a film tough guy
> sort of way, especially with the scar all down one cheek. On top
> of that he wore a grey trilby hat, which he took off when he spoke
> to me (I thought that was very polite) and in his hand a very long
> cigar.[13]

Then at the Epsom August Meeting when the Apprentices' Derby
was run, Dimes actually dared to move one of his bookmakers onto
the pitch of a Spot incumbent. Spot promptly moved him out and
according to him there was a run-in with Bert Marsh. Marsh
demanded Spot hand over control of the pitches on the free course.
The police had intervened to prevent any trouble. Now Spot's relationship with the Italian bookmakers, who had the ability to see the
coming of the betting shop and who were far better prepared than
he, was worsening exponentially. He determined on action and

---

[11] Frank Fraser, *Mad Frank*, p. 75.
[12] *Empire News*, 16 October 1955.
[13] Joe Lee and Rita Smith, *Inside the Kray Family*, p. 114.

sought out the man whom he saw as the leader – Albert Dimes. This was an almost fatal error.

The effective end of Spot's reign came on 11 August 1955 in his drinking club, the Galahad in Charlotte Street, which he controlled if not owned. There he was told that 'Big Albert' Dimes wanted to see him. This must have been the crowning insult. His temper up, he went to find Dimes and caught up with him on the corner of Frith Street in Soho.

Spot had now ventured into Italian – and so foreign – territory. It was here that a good deal of street bookmaking as well as prostitution was conducted. Spot went after Dimes with a knife and Dimes ran away. Now came Spot's big mistake when he chased after him. Apart from the fact that there would have been no court case if he had let him run, Spot's status in Soho would have soared. Dimes' flight was watched by the Italians and it would have been a tremendous feather in Spot's cap to be able to say that the great Albert had fled from him. Instead he went after him and now they fought almost to the death on the street and inside a green-grocery shop where ironically a Jewish lady Bertha Hyams, a large lady fruiterer, broke up the fight by banging Spot with a brass weighing-pan.

'If she hadn't intervened Spot would have done him,' says a bystander who never gave evidence. 'Once she hit him, Albert got the knife away and did him.' Both men were badly injured. Dimes got away with Bert Marsh in a taxi. Spot picked himself off the pavement, staggered into a nearby barber's shop, said, 'Fix me up' and fainted.

Dimes went to the Charing Cross Hospital and Spot to the nearby Middlesex. Spot had been stabbed over the left eye and in the left cheek as well as the neck and ear; he also had four stab wounds in the left arm and two in the chest, one of which had penetrated the lung. Dimes had his forehead cut to the bone requiring twenty stitches, a wound in the thigh and one in the stomach which, as prosecutor Reginald Seaton later said, 'mercifully just failed to penetrate the abdominal cavity'.

The press coverage was of Spot. Flowers and telegrams of good wishes were sent to the hospital. Breath was held until the great man had something to say to the waiting public. No doubt unconsciously echoing Neville Chamberlain, he commented in time for the Sunday editions, 'There ain't gonna be no war.' And the *Sunday Chronicle* for one breathed a sigh of relief: 'The pronouncement was passed along the grapevine. The effect was an immediate lessening of tension in Soho.'[14]

Both must have had iron constitutions because it was only a matter of days later that the pair were arrested shortly after leaving their respective beds. When questioned Spot said, 'It is between me and Albert Dimes – between us, and nothing to do with you.' Asked who had attacked him, Dimes replied, 'You know as well as I do. It was Jackie Spot. I'm not prossing.' When asked to make a formal statement, he said he had been attacked 'by a tall man . . . I don't know his name'. When they were charged Spot replied, 'Why me? Albert did me and I get knocked off.' Dimes commented, 'Spotty does me up and I get pinched. That don't seem fair.'

The police were certainly not pleased with what had happened in broad daylight in a crowded shopping area. Brian McDonald, who had been with Spot immediately before the incident, recalls that he was interviewed at Tottenham Court Road police station after the fight:

> They were really looking for witnesses but I told them I was taking care of myself. I didn't even tell them I was walking with Spot. Johnny Rice lived up near Albany Police Station and they had him in there. We were both slightly knocked about and I was given a talking to and a warning to stay out of things. In fact both Spot and Dimes looked as if it could be a hanging matter. They were both white [with the loss of blood]. I got out of there pretty quickly. Spot never asked me to be a witness and that was the last thing I'd have wanted to be. I was good at disappearing and

[14] *Sunday Chronicle*, 14 August 1955.

that's what I did. I wasn't a knife-happy gangster. I was more in things for fun.[15]

Once the news of the fight broke there was a flurry of activity. Parker remembers he was in Sussex at the time:

I got a call on my number, Hove 3375 it was, and I came up to town straight away. I stayed with my Uncle Judah in Ossulton Way, Finchley. I went to see Jack in hospital and I talked to Bernie and Hymie. Sonny was now more or less in charge and he'd sit in Lyons Corner House in Coventry Street and keep saying, 'We've got to declare war.' It didn't help. Things were very tight with Old Bill at the time. They were determined to clear things up one way or the other. Even if they weren't, who was going to fight on Jack's side? There was no general, no captains. There was still George and Jimmy Wood and there was Porky Bennett from Millwall; he was still around, but that was about it. When I went back to Brighton to mind the club Jack had with Sammy Bellson, Sammy told me to stay away from London. 'They'll fit you up,' was what Sammy said.

For the opposition, Frank Fraser was in Billy Howard's club the Beehive near Brixton. Fraser recalls:

Me and Eva's husband, Jimmy Brindle, and Tony Nappi went up Albert's house at 22 River Street in Clerkenwell where he lived at that time to see how he was getting on and we went downstairs, opened the street door and there were the police come to arrest Albert. I wouldn't let them in and Jimmy and Tony stood straight behind me. They were trying to push in but then Albert heard what was going on and said it was all right, let them in. I asked what he wanted me to do and he said I was to see Bert Marsh and then see Bill.
    Jimmy had a motor and I went straight to see Marsh. At the time he had an illegal bookmaker's pitch in Frith and Old Compton with his partner, a man called Vesta. I told him on me own and Bert just said 'Leave it to me.' That's when the police conveniently

[15] Conversation with author.

found the knife just off Soho Square, the very knife Spot had used. Bert had picked it up just after the fight. It was very important in Albert's favour. I'd went with Bert when he put it in the square and then went with Hilly. There was then an anonymous phone call and the knife was found. It was a moody of course.[16]

Spot claimed he was discharging himself from hospital because Rita had been threatened. Now he instructed the solicitor Bernie Perkoff, whose father had run the Windmill public house in the East End which Spot had used and which, before the war, had once been wrecked by the Sabinis on the rampage.

Perkoff had qualified as a solicitor and had opened a small office in Aldgate. He was immensely popular with the locals. One East London face recalls him:

The first time I saw Bernie Perkoff was over forty years ago; he was in the Twins' billiard hall, the Regal, talking to Reggie. He dressed in a typical Jewish manner, sharp suits and colourful ties. I never had any reason to use him in criminal cases but I did use him over an accident in the docks and he got me £280 something. It was fair money in those days considering I didn't do any work in the docks. I thought it was a very good result.

I remember going to see him. I left a phone number where he could get me because we didn't have a phone at home and I went up there and had a drink with him in the Seven Stars near enough next door. He'd had the cheque cashed in a bank. I never used him after that and I don't know why not. I was satisfied, in fact more than happy.

In court Perkoff was the antithesis of his local rival, the urbane George Young. A short, stubby man, he was actually prone to wearing a brown suit, but in the days when solicitors had no formal advocacy training and everything was taught by experience and word of mouth he was always willing to take the time to advise beginners on etiquette and tactics. Then in the 1950s he went up-market and

---

[16] Frank Fraser, *Mad Frank and Friends*, pp. 61–2.

opened a practice in the West End with his partner Monty Raphael, using the name Peters & Peters. It was there that Spot found him on this occasion.

Almost miraculously, the wounds of both Spot and Dimes had sufficiently healed eleven days later for their appearance on 22 August before Clyde Wilson at Marlborough Street Magistrates' Court, charged with wounding with intent to commit grievous bodily harm and affray. Bernie Perkoff appeared for Spot and E.H. Bestford for Dimes.[17]

In those days it was not usual to have solicitors or counsel appear for the police at remand hearings, and on that first hearing the objections to bail were given by the dubious officer Herbert Sparks who gave Bestford the run-around. He had objected to Spot's bail on the grounds that Spot had said he would flee to Ireland and that witnesses would be interfered with. Nothing had been said at this stage about Dimes interfering with witnesses, and Bestford unwisely brought up the subject. 'There is a possibility of anything in this case,' replied Sparks. When Bestford suggested that Dimes had indicated he had acted in self-defence, Sparks again showed who was master of the exchanges, saying that Dimes had 'made a subsequent communication' to him.

The way Reggie Seaton – later to become Chairman of the Inner London Quarter Sessions – put the case for the Crown was that Spot had started the attack, and that Dimes had at some time in the struggle wrested the knife from him and had struck back, going far beyond the limits of self-defence.

Clearly the abiding and increasingly broken tradition of the Underworld that one member should not give evidence against another did not apply to their defending lawyers at the committal proceedings. Patrick Marrinan, later appearing for Dimes, said his client had acted completely in self-defence after being attacked by

---

[17] Although they themselves kept a low profile, Bellamy, Bestford & Co., who had offices in Mortimer Street, were instructed in a considerable number of major criminal cases of the period including the Great Train Robbery.

'this other murderous, treacherous rascal'. Bert Marsh, who just happened to have been in Frith Street at the time, and who could not now abide his former friend Spot, loyally gave evidence favouring Dimes and was roundly attacked for his pains. Perkoff objected to the secrecy of two witnesses being allowed to write down their names and addresses but Marrinan, for once reading the cards right, said he had no objection.

There was clearly a case to answer, said the magistrate. Spot and Dimes were committed for trial at the Old Bailey. Spot was committed in custody, but Dimes was given bail in his own recognisance of £250 and two sureties of the same amount. Parker recalls that Spot would say of his prison experience that he was in for a haircut and a shave, and he'd laugh about it. The reality was that Spot did not like imprisonment. Isolated and in some despair, on 30 August he was found in his cell at Brixton with his wrists slashed. He was now moved to a special cell.[18]

Meanwhile Hill was working on the further estrangement of Spot from his supporters, and he sent Frank Fraser to the South Coast to mark Sammy Bellson's card.

I went to Brighton with Billy Hill who was now collecting money for Albert's defence. Bill could easily have paid for it himself, but he deliberately did this to let Spot see how popular Albert was in contrast with what Spot would get. We went to all the people who Spot had been very thick with so they would elbow him and only contribute to Albert. Sammy Bellson was one of them and, yes, he knew Albert very well and he put up quite a good sum, around £500. Billy suggested that I should stay there in Brighton with him to keep Spot's men away from him. Sam agreed and a few days later he had a very nice flat for me, which normally Spot would have had, in Marine Parade going up towards Rottingdean.[19]

[18] *The Times*, 31 August 1955.
[19] Frank Fraser, *Mad Frank*, p. 82.

The trials which followed were genuinely sensational. At first Mr Justice Glyn-Jones refused an application for separate trials, which on the face of it was reasonable. The defendants were charged with making an affray. One of the tenets of prosecuting is to have as many people in the dock as possible so, with luck, they will run what is known as a cut-throat defence and blame each other, which will result in convictions for all. Unfortunately the judge had what would be described, in the world of Spot and Dimes, as a touch of the seconds. The next day he asked counsel for Spot, Rose Heilbron – who was later to become the second woman High Court judge – and doyen of the Bar G.D. 'Khaki' Roberts, for Dimes, what they had to say about making an affray in a public place. The junior in the case for Dimes was Patrick Marrinan.

Roberts argued that the reactions of a man fighting for his life could never be described as making an affray. Reggie Seaton, for the Crown, accepting that view, then tried to argue that the affray was in the greengrocery shop itself where the fight had ended. If, he argued, it was a public place then Dimes' excessive conduct after he had wrested the knife from Spot was capable of being an affray. This was not a view accepted by the judge, who withdrew from the jury the charge of affray against both Spot and Dimes and told them that, if they wished, they could acquit Dimes on the charge of wounding Spot: 'It is not for Dimes to prove that he was acting in self-defence. It is for the prosecution to prove that he was not.'

The jury was not convinced and in the circumstances Glyn-Jones discharged them, saying that, 'A joint trial without the first charge would not be lawful.' He then directed that Dimes be acquitted of possessing an offensive weapon, gave him bail and remanded Spot in custody. The separate trial of Spot was fixed to take place forty-eight hours later.

Spot's trial began on Thursday 22 September 1955 at the Old Bailey. Now Reggie Seaton and E.J.P. Cussen appeared for the Crown, with Rose Heilbron QC and Sebag Shaw defending. Rose Heilbron, the first woman to have been appointed Queen's Counsel, had the advantage from Spot's point of view of being Jewish – as was Sebag Shaw, a man who also later became a judge but who in the meantime could be found in card clubs and spielers throughout the West End. Rose Heilbron had made her name in the North in 1950 appearing (albeit unsuccessfully) for George Kelly in the celebrated Liverpool Cameo Murder case.[20] Earlier in 1955 she had appeared for Dennis Murtagh, whose conviction for murder had been quashed on appeal.[21] Miss Heilbron had three other advantages. First, she was very good-looking, something which would appeal to the predominantly male jury, and secondly she was an out-and-out battler. Most importantly, she was immensely talented and would not lie down under an attack by a trial judge. A potential disadvantage was that she was not part of the coterie of the London Bar and the camaraderie of the Old Bailey. This showed up early in the trial when she got across the Recorder of London who had taken over the case:

> *Heilbron:* In addition to the people there are many cars parked, like all London streets?
> *The Recorder:* You may assume that the jury know Frith Street.
> *Heilbron:* I am grateful to your Lordship. I do not want to assume anything in this case that is not evidence.
> *The Recorder:* It is a very well known London street.

The first of the witnesses (apart from a plan drawer and a forensic officer) was the bookmaker Sebastian Buonacore, known as Vesta, who described himself rather grandly as a commission agent. He had been sitting on the wing of a car in Frith Street with Dimes talking at about 11.30 a.m. on 11 August. Spot had come across the road and had said, 'I want to talk to you, Albert.' Buonacore

[20] George Kelly was convicted of the shooting of the manager in a robbery at the Cameo Cinema in Wavertree. The evidence at the trial, which lasted thirteen days, was principally that of informers and a prison grass. Kelly was hanged on 28 March 1950. After years of campaigning on his behalf his conviction was quashed on 10 June 2003. It transpired that the prison informer had earlier made another statement naming another man, which had not been disclosed to the defence. *The Times*, 11 June 2003.
[21] *The Times*, 25 May 1955.

had sensibly moved away and then he heard a shout and there in the middle of the road was Spot with what seemed to him to be a dagger or a knife. Dimes ran towards the Hyams' fruit shop, the Continental Fruit Store on the corner, and was chased by Spot. Albert went into the shop and Comer followed. That was the signal for Buonacore to go to the Caterer's Club to report to Bert Marsh who promptly left the club.

Now Heilbron struck. Buonacore had been a street bookmaker working Frith Street for something like fourteen years with Bert Marsh as his partner. The barber's shop into which Spot staggered was about fifty yards from the corner and the Caterer's Club about thirty yards. Buonacore accepted that he was friendly – but not that friendly – with Dimes, and had known him for twenty years. In fact he didn't really know if Dimes went racing at all. Wasn't all this a quarrel about rival betting pitches? No, not in the least. Didn't Bert and he employ Dimes? Utter nonsense. He certainly didn't employ Dimes as a paid servant and he couldn't even remember getting him to put money on a horse for him. Comer had said, 'I'm not going to stand for it. I've been going racing for the last twenty years.' Dimes had said, 'You needn't go any more, because you haven't got any more pitches.' Not conversation that Buonacore had heard.

In English cases it is essential to put details of the defence case to witnesses for the prosecution. Comer's defence, as outlined by Rose Heilbron, was that Dimes was the first one to shove him before Comer pushed him into the road, and Dimes charged back at him pushing him into a pile of boxes at the Continental Fruit Store. Then Dimes produced a knife and slashed at Spot. But Buonacore would not be shifted. Spot was the man who had the knife; he hadn't, however, seen either of them use it.

Hyman Hyams, who owned the greengrocery, was sure that Dimes was bleeding by the time he got into the shop and that Comer had a blade and was stabbing him in the shop. There was blood all over the place.

They got to the girder part right at the beginning of the shop; Albert got onto the girder and held on to one side of it, and he must have got hold of the sleeve where the knife was and I do not know how he done it, but he got the knife out.

The Recorder: Out of what?

A: Out of the other chappie's hand, sir. He was holding onto this girder. Then he started digging back, sir.

It had ended in Bert Marsh running into the shop calling out 'Albert', and Dimes had run out with the knife. As for blood, there was 'pails of it all over the place – blood on everything'. But what he hadn't seen was blood on Comer.

Heilbron elicited the fact that no knife was found in his shop. No, Hyams hadn't seen his wife bang either Comer or Dimes with the scale pan.

Q: Mr Hyams, you are not nervous about giving evidence implicating Dimes, are you?

A: No.

Q: Not at all?

A: I was nervous of 'Spot' at the beginning, and would not talk but the police reassured me.

His wife, Bertha Hyams, confirmed that, contrary to newspaper reports, she had not hit the pair over their heads with the scoop. She said she had been using it to push Spot from the shop.

As for their son Alec who had been in the shop, he recalled that during the fight Comer said, 'Tearaway, are you?' Alec had said to Dimes, 'Be careful.' He accepted he had once said hitting with the scale pan, but he had meant pushing.

Bert Marsh (under the name of Pasquale Papa) was not about when he was called first time around; but despite the Recorder rather hopefully suggesting he added nothing to the previous evidence, Miss Heilbron wanted him nevertheless. The quarrel over betting pitches, originated by Dimes and Marsh, was the crux of her case.

When he did give evidence, Marsh said he had taken Dimes to

Charing Cross Hospital. He thought he was a good friend of Dimes and also a friend of Comer. It was a fairy tale that he resented Spot's monopoly of racecourse pitches. He had not told him so at Epsom. He had never had a bad word with Comer in his life. So far as he was concerned, he hadn't seen Dimes with a knife.

Now the police officer Herbert Sparks told how he had received an anonymous message and found a knife wrapped in brown paper in the bushes in Soho Square. According to Frankie Fraser, this was the knife planted there by him and Bert Marsh. That particular piece of evidence was not something the court heard. And that was the case for the prosecution and clearly one for Spot to answer.

Jack Comer told the court that he lived at 12F Hyde Park Mansions and was a bookmaker, mainly at point-to-point meetings and tracks in the South where there were free enclosures. He bought the ground for the day for which he would pay £300 and charged £30 to ten bookmakers, clearly making no profit for himself. He'd been doing it for twenty years and Bert Marsh, Vesta and Italian Albert were very jealous. Dimes was a strong-arm man for Marsh.

The trouble had started in August at the Epsom meeting when the so-called Apprentices' Derby was run. Marsh had told him, 'You've been going racing a long time, and you have all the best pitches. I think it's about time you were finished.' According to Spot, 'I took no notice but later I got a note.'

The reason he had gone to Frith Street was that he wanted to make clear why Marsh wanted him to leave. He had asked, 'What's this all about?' And Dimes had replied, 'This is your final warning. I don't want you to go racing no more.'

'But why?'

'I'm telling you, you have had your day. You've been going away all these years and it's about time someone else had your pitches.'

'What about Brighton?' Spot had asked, almost as if he was conceding defeat but wanting to cling on to one track. Brighton races were the week following the fight.

'You've lost that too.'

He accepted that he pushed Dimes, who then drew a knife and stabbed him. In fact it was he who had managed to wrest the knife from Dimes and stabbed him in self-defence.

Cross-examined by Seaton, he maintained that there had been no bad blood on his part. He hadn't thought it unwise to go and talk to Italian Albert, a strong-arm man, on his own patch. He certainly hadn't had a knife.

Then came the witnesses. Christopher Glinski was a man who happened to have been in Soho that day. He lived at 46 Kendall Street, Paddington, and was an interpreter. He had served in the Polish Air Force and had received the Croix de Guerre as well as a Polish decoration. He had been in Soho seeing a friend who had an office in Sherwood House. He hadn't known either of the men, but he had seen the newspaper report of 29 August. He realised it was wrong but he hadn't gone to the police: 'There was no necessity for it.' He preferred to go to the solicitor and the solicitor would inform the police.

In the 1950s and for a decade afterwards there was no need for an alibi to be given to the prosecution before the trial. The practice was to put a witness in the box and get through his evidence as soon as possible. Once the prosecution began their cross-examination the opening question would be to ask the witness his date of birth. A police officer would then leave court and telephone Scotland Yard to try to find out whether the person had a criminal record and get the result back into court before the cross-examination had finished. Adjournments even for the prosecution were not readily granted in an era when trials were over in a matter of hours or days, not weeks and months. Although Glinski was not an alibi witness, the same rules applied, but this time Seaton asked for and was granted an adjournment. Would Glinski be available the next morning? Certainly.

The next day Seaton wanted to talk to him about textiles and, obliquely, long firm frauds. Yes, Glinski apart from being an interpreter was employed as a salesman. Yes, he had been convicted at

County of London Sessions in December 1951. He had received two years probation for receiving – 'minding things for a friend', he said. It was certainly enough to damage his evidence.

Then came the clincher in the form of the Reverend Basil Claude Hudson Andrews of 44 Inverness Terrace, Bayswater, who had held an appointment at Kensal Green for thirty-nine years. In the days before the country lost a large proportion of its faith in religion generally and the Church of England in particular, the evidence of the clergy was highly regarded by the courts.

14

Perjury and the Vicar

The 88-year-old vicar was admittedly shabby, but there again unde-
niably a gent. A man with an upper-class accent in this world of
Cockney, Italian and East European voices was something to which
the jury could relate.

He had, it seems, read newspaper reports of the trial and realised
something was seriously wrong. It had astonished him because, quite
by chance, he had been in Frith Street at the time and it was the
darker man (Dimes) who had attacked the fairer man (Spot).
Although many would have thought the fairer man was indeed
Dimes. He had deliberated for some time about involving himself
and it had preyed on his mind. 'Ultimately I decided I had better
do something.'

According to the reporter Arthur Tietjen, five minutes into
Andrews' evidence a detective in the court leaned over to him and
commented, 'Arthur, the old villain's bent.'[1]

But, at a time when rogue vicars were rarer than today, the jury
did not see him in that light and it was enough to tilt things in

---

[1] Arthur Tietjen, *Soho*, p. 40.

favour of Spot. The jury retired at 2.46 p.m. and returned to acquit him at 3.50 p.m. Spot leaped up and down in the dock, his hands raised like a successful boxer, and was first admonished and then discharged by the Recorder:

> *Heilbron:* May he be discharged, my Lord?
> *The Recorder:* Yes. Behave yourself, Comer.
> *Spot:* Thank you. I have suffered enough.

It was, of course, a field day for the newspapers, mainly at Spot's expense. The taunt was out that unlike a real crook such as Billy Hill, 'Jack Spot had never tasted porridge'. Allen Andrews wrote: 'There is not a tearaway gangster in town now who would give a throw of the dice in a spieler – or illegal gambling joint – for his chances in the future. Mobsters maintain he is NOT a crook in the sense of being a criminal who is a master of his craft.'[2]

For the moment things were good. Garlanded with flowers and reading telegrams from well-wishers, Spot spent the first night at home since his arrest, said the supportive *Sunday Chronicle*. His first words on waking had been to ask for the racing papers but Rita had reproached him, reminding him he had promised to give up the turf. He told a reporter:

> First I'm going to take a holiday possibly in the South of France with the wife and kids. I've had lots of offers from various people including one from the Kabaka of Buganda who wants to hire me as a bodyguard. But I think textiles is the game for me. I intend to do some more writing possibly about the racing game.[3]

A week later the Home Secretary announced that the situation with regard to the control of bookmakers must never be allowed to

---

[2] Allen Andrews, 'An Empty Throne in Gangland' in *Daily Herald*, 1 October 1955.
[3] *Sunday Chronicle*, 25 September 1955. King Freddie, the Kabaka of Buganda and a notorious womaniser, was about to return home after two years' exile in England. He did so on 16 October 1955.

reoccur.[4] In fact nothing really happened until the Betting and Gaming Act was passed in 1960. The Whites merely resumed interim control.

Harry White was also fairly smartly out of the traps with the story of Spot's threats and attacks on him back in 1947, along with a cowardly attack on an elderly bookmaker Newcastle Fred at Pontefract races.[5]

However, the *Daily Sketch* had beaten everyone to the line. Not only did they have the Parson under wraps but, in a great example of a journalistic each-way bet, they had editorials blazing: 'The threat is that if the gangster Spot is again put on trial and sent to prison the Underworld will "blow the top off" about the police and their methods in the West End.'[6] Whether the Underworld would do this simply to protect Spot was doubtful, but there were certainly some stories which its members could tell to the disadvantage of certain officers at West End Central.[7]

In November that year the *Daily Mail* reported that Detective Superintendent Bert Hannam had led an inquiry which revealed that there was extensive corruption amongst West End officers, with uniformed officers receiving up to £60 a week in bribes. This was promptly and vociferously denied by the Commissioner Sir John Nott-Bower, but the controversy raged for some time with other newspapers weighing in on the side of the *Mail*.[8] Had the Commissioner been willing to listen, a great deal of trouble for the Metropolitan Police in the 1960s and 1970s might have been avoided.

The *Sketch* also had Jack Spot giving his story, something they

[4] 'Spot – The Last Gangster' in *Sunday Chronicle*, 2 October 1955.
[5] Sidney Williams, 'The Case of the Frightened Bookmaker' in *Daily Herald*, 8 October 1955.
[6] *Daily Sketch*, 1 October 1955.
[7] They included Inspector Charles Jacobs who, it was alleged, tipped off Joseph Grech when brothels were about to be raided, and Detective Sergeant Robertson who provided a key to enable a burglary to be executed at Grech's home. Robertson received two years' imprisonment. Jacobs was dismissed from the force. See James Morton, *Gangland*, pp. 234–5.
[8] *Daily Mail*, 17, 18, 19, 24 November 1955.

justified with, 'When the facts are known the public will realise why at the moment the *Sketch* is giving publicity to Jack Spot's own life story.' Over the next few issues it railed at the police and the Director of Public Prosecutions, asking why nothing was being done.

Duncan Webb was also up and running. Unsurprisingly he lost no time in downgrading Spot: 'Before him Billy Hill had earned his position as London's gangster boss and by the sheer force of his personality had kept the peace in the Underworld and seen fair play.'[9]

Albert Dimes was on parade too to give his version. 'When Hill went away he started demanding protection from all us small book-makers.' He had also been going into clubs and demanding a share, and his men were eating on the arm in restaurants telling waiters, 'Charge it up to Jack Spot.' His downfall had been inevitable. Worse, he had behaved in such a cowardly fashion during the fight, calling out, 'Police, police! Ring the police. Don't let him hurt me.' Spot had pleaded, 'Don't cut me, Albert. Please don't cut me.'[10]

According to Webb, Spot had been tried by his own gang and found wanting. Only Blueball and Schack were remaining staunch. The Woods and the others had seen the light. Spot was nothing but a tinpot tyrant.[11] Next, as the unofficial press agent for Billy Hill and with the help of Albert Dimes, Webb did not even have to dig very deep in the soil to find out about the Reverend Andrews. In fact a flip through *The Times' Index* would have shown that back in the 1920s he had been made bankrupt when, he said, he had gone to the moneylenders on behalf of a friend who promptly defaulted. That may have seemed bad luck, but there was something about a wine merchant's account as well. Far from being a respectable old gent, the Reverend was also keen on the horses and didn't pay his debts.

---

[9] Duncan Webb, 'Tinpot Tyrant' in *People*, 25 September 1955.
[10] 'The Strange life of the "Jack Spot" Parson' in *Sunday Dispatch*, 2 October 1955. 'Soho – Albert Dimes takes the lid off' in *People*, 2 October 1955.
[11] Duncan Webb, 'Tinpot Tyrant Jack Spot was "tried" by his own Mob' in *People*, 25 September 1955.

For a time he tried to brazen things out. Protected by the naïve
or opportunist – depending upon how you look at it – but certainly
pro-Spot *Daily Sketch*, he set out his stall:

> I am fully aware that cowardly people who dare not come forward
> into the light of day are suggesting that I am a fraudulent witness
> and that I hoodwinked Mr Comer's legal advisers.
>
> I would recall to you that when I gave evidence last week I
> gave it on my solemn oath, and I need not remind you that I am
> a clerk in Holy Orders also. I therefore wish to affirm in the most
> solemn terms that what I said in the witness-box was the whole
> truth and nothing but the truth. I wish to deny that I have
> committed perjury. I wish to deny that I have any hopes of ma-
> terial gain from having come forward as a witness. I did so only
> in the interests of truth and I am willing to tell the police that if
> they come to me. Any financial difficulties due to my change of
> address and my harmless flutters in the sporting world are only
> temporary, due to my age and inexperience.

All things considered, he might have left or been allowed to leave
it there, but indeed added that his desire was to: 'Bring about a
reconciliation between the parties in strife who seem to have
forgotten that, by what they have done, they are debasing the sacred
Brotherhood of Man.'

What he did bring about was a series of fights, attacks, prosecutions and prison sentences which but for his interference would
never have happened.

That same day the prosecution conceded that given the acquittal
of Spot and the subsequent revelations it would not be safe to proceed
against Dimes, and accordingly Sir Gerald Dodson recorded a verdict
of 'Not Guilty'. The newspapers were overjoyed. Here was 'The fight
that never was'.

The *Sketch* turned the Parson over soon enough: 'I am beginning
to remember things which had slipped my memory. I shall be able
to tell the police all about them. It is strange how one's memory fades.'
The newspaper pointed out that he had been warned by his Bishop

about his financial affairs, and there was a potentially doubtful marriage between a woman friend of Andrews and a man from whom he had borrowed money. Andrews seemingly had a niece, Sybil Owens, and there had been a bit of trouble over an unpaid taxi fare of nine shillings. One of the passengers was apparently a 'Lady' Owens.[12]

Other papers painted him as quaint. He was a great frequenter of the prostitutes in the Bayswater Road but not, at his age, for carnal reasons. One offered, 'He knew many girls like me to speak to. He never tried to reform us or preach sermons. We regarded him as a nice old man with a bit of a bee in his bonnet.'[13]

Investigations were put into the hands of Chief Superintendent Edward Greeno and his deputy the doubtful Superintendent Herbert Sparks, the so-called Iron Man of Soho, and both of them Hill men to the core. It did not take them long to uncover the sins and peccadilloes of the Reverend, who had been ordained in 1890 and had wandered off to the Kimberley goldfields before moving to Toronto where he had been secretary to the Bishop. He had then returned to London with a Canadian wife, but it was not exactly clear what had happened to her.

Much of the information available to the police came through Gertrude Adelaide Vizard, who had been the caretaker at 89 Elgin Avenue since 1910. Andrews was there when she arrived. Then he had been living with a woman whom he claimed to have married but had not actually bothered. She was Ruby Young and had been a witness in the celebrated Rising Sun case when Robert Ward was prosecuted for the murder of Phyllis Dimmock on 12 December 1907.[14] Although they appeared to be in reduced circumstances they had a maid, Annie Morton. Ruby left Andrews after twenty years

[12] *Daily Sketch*, 29 September 1955.
[13] *Empire News*, 2 October 1955.
[14] Nat. Arch. Crim 1 2659.
   The prostitute, Phyllis Dimmock, was found with her throat cut by Bert Shaw, her common-law husband, when he returned from work to their two-room lodgings in Camden Town. It seems incredible that Shaw, who apparently had a cast-iron alibi, did not know she was plying her trade while he was working as a dining-car attendant on the London to Sheffield run. In her flat was a letter inviting her to meet a named Bert.

together. He had, so she said, met her on a train journey from Beckenham. She then married a journalist who worked for the *Sketch*, and Gertrude Vizard attended the wedding.

After that Andrews married a widow named Edith Henderson. In turn she died on 17 February 1952 and was cremated at Kensal Green. She left £9,000; much to Andrews' disappointment it all went to her brother, Seymour.

Then in February 1953 he brought a woman and her young daughter, Barbara, to the flat, saying it was his niece Sybil Owens. Mrs Owens said that her husband was the secretary of the Bishop of Oxford, and that she had left him in order to keep her uncle company. She had a beautiful fur coat and £1,000. Certainly Sybil called him 'Uncle Claude'. On many occasions Vizard saw Andrews and Owens kissing and cuddling, and the young daughter would sit watching. She said she liked to see Mummy with her boyfriends.

Vizard was shown the £1,000 cash and she was told the fur coat had been sold, but she was not to tell Andrews as he would want it. Mrs Owens was always being sent to borrow money. They left on 14 June 1953 and went to live in a block of flats near Baker Street. He tried to let the Elgin Mansions flat at £8 a week, but could not do so and gave it up.

Mrs Owens had also said that Andrews had the benefit of the Vicarage at Stoney Stratford, but had had to leave after being caught in bed with a local doctor's wife. A month before Andrews left, Vizard took a call from a woman at the Dorchester who said her

---

There was also a postcard with a drawing of a rising sun, suggesting a rendezvous at that public house. Robert Wood, a young artist, came forward to identify the card as his. He asked Ruby Young, another prostitute, to give him an alibi but instead she went first to a journalist friend and then the police. The evidence against him was mainly identification evidence, but it was quite strong because he had a distinctive walk. He was a good-looking man who gave his evidence well, and Dimmock had another client named Bert. There was also resentment about the betrayal by Ruby Young. Wood was acquitted and went to Australia. The case had caused much speculation. Wood's detractors say he was fortunate to have Marshall Hall instructed by the talented if dishonest solicitor Arthur Newton to defend him. His supporters suggest that Shaw could have jumped off the train as it approached St Pancras and made his way to Camden Town to kill Dimmock. See e.g. Sir John Hall (ed.), *Notable British Trials*; L. Gribble, *They Got Away with Murder*.

'darling boy' wanted £1,000 and in turn she wanted to know what this was for. Andrews was furious when Vizard told him.

A solicitor then let him premises at 31 De Walden Street, and later took him to court over the unpaid rent. The Church Commissioners sent part of his pension to pay this after judgement had been obtained.

Now it was said that Greeno wished to interview three men and a woman. Meanwhile the *Sunday Pictorial* had already done some interviewing of its own. 'A frightened mother of two lovely children' had come forward to say she had been shopping in Old Compton Street at the time of the fight. 'I am ashamed I did not tell the truth. I was afraid. I was about 12 yards away and a man sidled up; "You've seen nothing. If you want to keep healthy keep your trap shut".'[15]

There was, of course, human interest in Spot's domestic circumstances, and a curious item appeared in the *Sketch* in which Rita told the reporter, 'My youngest baby Marion aged seven months has teething troubles and when he managed to drop off to sleep people kept knocking at the door into the early hours of the morning. The poor little fellow had no rest.'[16] Which was odd because according to her birth certificate – and everyone else for that matter – Marion Margaret was certainly a girl.

Spot was still of enormous interest to the readers. The children had been sent to Ireland to a 'dingy block of council flats off Townsend Street' in Dublin, but he was no longer at his flat. 'Where is Jack Spot?' asked the *Daily Mail*. The question was partially answered on 5 October when dressed in a brown overcoat, muffled up with a scarf and with a cap pulled well down he and Rita disembarked from the SS *Cambria* and took a taxi, asking for the Shelborne. There they alighted but, instead of going inside, wandered off across St Stephen's Green and vanished once more.

As the days went by, and with the Director of Public Prosecutions apparently dragging his heels, the Spot episodes grew smaller. Soon

---

[15] *Sunday Pictorial*, 2 October 1955.
[16] Rosalie Macrae, 'My Life is absolute hell' in *Daily Sketch*, 4 October 1955.

the pair, who had knocked the runaway spies Burgess and Maclean out of the headlines, were themselves replaced on the front pages by the travails of the love affair between Princess Margaret and Group Captain Peter Townsend.

The wheels of the law were, however, grinding and the story now emerged that before the trial Andrews had been in Spot's old haunt the Cumberland Hotel, looking for someone to touch for his breakfast, when he met Peter MacDonough, another friend of Spot who had rented the parson a room a year earlier. When MacDonough told him he could earn some money if he cared to say six words, Andrews leaped like a trout at a mayfly. He was taken to Hyde Park Mansions, vetted by Rita and then taken to see Perkoff. Presumably the six words were, 'It was Dimes who attacked Spot'. For this service he would receive £65, and if Spot were to be acquitted he would 'never want'. There was some corroboration from the doorman of the Cumberland Hotel who placed the vicar with MacDonough, and someone who had seen him at Hyde Park Mansions. There were also the obligatory 1950s verbals, but it was a thin case. Arrests followed.

Rita Comer was retrieved from Dublin on 21 October when she was arrested at 1 a.m. in the small flat in Pierce House, Townsend Street. Reporters were there to comment on her immaculate make-up and listen as her high heels 'clacked down the forty-nine steps to the waiting car'. The day before she had told reporters she had come to Ireland because her daughter Rachelle had had a fall and had had concussion for three days. Where was Jack? Certainly not hiding. He might have been in London but he certainly wasn't hiding. All that talk about him and protection was lies, lies, lies. 'He wouldn't hurt a fly. He never passes a beggar without giving something,' she said in a fine non-sequitur.[17]

She was not best pleased to find herself collected from the Bridewell the next day. 'I suppose I shall have to go to the Old Bailey and it will be the same thing over again with me instead of Jack. Moisha

---

[17] *Daily Mail*, 7, 20, 22 October 1955.

said the old man would give evidence for a few quid,' she is alleged to have told the officers. She travelled back with Detective Inspector E. Shepphard and a Detective Sergeant Shirley Beck under assumed names, but by the time the aeroplane reached Heath Row at 9.30 a.m. a crowd of newspapermen was waiting.[18] Into the dock with her went MacDonough, Moisha Blueball and Bernard Schack. They could not say they had not been warned. If the arrest of Rita Comer had not been sufficient, the ever-useful Hubby Distleman had already told Bernard Schack, 'If I was you, Sonny, I would get a ship and get out of the country.' When Neville Coleman, applying for bail, asked Sparkes, 'Do you know that she has two small children, one aged three and a half and the other one aged two and a half?' the wily detective replied, 'Yes, being well cared for by her relatives in Ireland.' And it was off to prison to await her trial. In Holloway she lost two stone in weight despite a daily diet of 'roast chicken, duckling, rare delicacies, fruit and flowers' which Spot had delivered to her.[19] Crowds gathered outside Holloway prison to see Spot arrive for a visit. According to reports, Rita was well but missing her family.[20]

In theory it should not have been difficult to destroy Andrews in the witness box, but theory and practice are two completely different things. The difficulty for the defending counsel was that here was a sanctimonious old sinner who was playing the age, deafness, memory, sympathy and repentance cards and playing them with some skill:

> It was very wicked of me. I was very hard up and I was tempted and I fell. It is rather humiliating for me to have to tell you. I was desperately hungry. I had had what is called Continental breakfasts and nothing in between. I was very poor and hungry and I should not have yielded but I did. Thank God, I have asked to be forgiven!

[18] *Irish Press*, 22 October 1955.
[19] Rita Comer, 'They call me a Gangster's Moll' in *Sunday Pictorial*, 11 December 1955.
[20] *Sunday Chronicle*, 23 October 1955.

And:

> I have not come here to tell lies. I have come here to try and undo
> the lies I did tell at the trial. Your object is to damn me. I was deter-
> mined then and there, not because I was influenced by any indi-
> vidual to tell the truth at all costs, although I should have to confess
> to the public that I had been a most dreadful liar. But I have done
> it, and I am very glad I have. I feel much happier about it.

Even the experienced silks could do nothing with him. Appearing
for Schack, Anthony Marlowe QC asked Andrews how long it was
after the Comer trial that he repented: 'You mean when did I come
to my real senses? I cannot tell you the time. Have you never heard
of a sudden conversion?'

To add to the discomfort of the defence, Andrews decided his life
was in danger. As for being in court before, no, that was not correct.
What about those county court proceedings? Well, he hadn't understood that was a court in this sense of the word. Nor presumably
would the Bankruptcy Court have counted either if anyone had
mentioned it. That had been back in 1925 when he admitted debts
of £6,000 and assets of a mere £300. His problem, he said then,
was that he had backed a friend who borrowed £500 from the
moneylenders, but even with their extortionate rates it is difficult
to see how he had run up that sort of debt. It is much more likely
that the Reverend had been doing a spot of high living for himself.
To put the money in context, on the day *The Times* reported his
bankruptcy there were advertisements in the paper for a five-
bedroom, two-bathroom house in South Kensington on sale for
£4,200, and a freehold house and factory in Acton bringing in £234
a year on offer at £1,550. A house in the Brompton Road was to let
at seven guineas a week.[21]

Everyone gave evidence. So far as the 45-year-old MacDonough
was concerned, he suffered from ill-health and could not even attend
prison chapel because of the steps he would have to climb. He

[21] *The Times*, 6 January 1925.

certainly had not mentioned the possibility of earning £25 to Andrews. Indeed, apart from seeing him in the Cumberland Hotel he had not seen him until four days after the Spot trial. Goldstein and Schack had only acted out of the goodness of their hearts. Goldstein said that although he suffered from a Jewish persecution complex he was a respectable East Ender whose interest was in his family. He was a bookmaker who had known Spot for twenty-eight years, and when he was arrested he went to see Rita. 'There was not a soul who would help her because she has two babies.' Schack had been similarly minded. He had known Spot since he was a boy: 'I had heard most of his friends had deserted him. They were fair-weather friends.' He had always believed Andrews' story. Indeed he would take an oath on his children on it. Goldstein had first seen Andrews at Mr Perkoff's office. The next day he had been to see Rita and had found the kindly old gentleman there. He had been surprised but reassured when Andrews told him, 'I have come to cheer the good lady up.' Not a single word had been uttered by him or anyone else about perjured evidence.

Goldstein as the ringleader received two years, and MacDonough and Schack a year apiece. Rita Comer, as the downtrodden wife fighting valiantly for her husband, was fined £50. The betting had been 4–1 on an acquittal. Spot had been in tears when he heard of his wife's conviction, but was now quite happy with British justice. Schack's wife was not so happy; he also had persisted with the fiction that his earlier conviction came from fighting Fascists and no one seemed to mind. Now Spot comforted the wife of his fallen soldier: 'I'm so sorry, dear.' She said two words in reply and hurried away. As Spot left with his wife – 'Love, let's go' – people outside the Old Bailey shouted, 'Good luck, Rita.'[22]

The next day Spot went out with a *Mail* reporter in tow to detail the shopping list. Rita had lost nearly two stone in weight and needed feeding up. Spot bought half-a-dozen new-laid eggs, two tins of soup

[22] *Daily Mail*, 8 December 1955.

and one of pickled onions, four large chump chops and some lamb's liver. The cost was 'nearly fifteen shillings.'[23]

The parson was in action again in early November, this time giving evidence against Christopher Glinski who was defended by the very hard-working, fearless and extremely dubious solicitor Norman Beach who wanted to know of his relationship with the *Daily Sketch*. He was still under their wing and they were protecting their investment although the Crown – in the form once more of Reggie Seaton – did not quite see it that way. Beach forced Andrews into answering the question of who had been paying his living expenses. He agreed the *Sketch* had been paying his bills and moving him from place to place: 'I have been very kindly treated by the *Daily Sketch*.'

> *Beach:* Your articles would be useless to the *Daily Sketch* unless the people going to be defamed in those articles were convicted?
> *Andrews:* I don't think so.
> *Seaton:* He cannot know to what use people are going to put articles he has not written.

The Reverend was also starting to over-egg the pudding. 'I am told if I am seen by some of the gang I shall have my throat cut,' he said in evidence. He had, it is true, received a letter: 'You dirty beast. Since Dimes has been released why should you poke your nose in where it is not wanted. Let me tell you if this case comes up you will not be alive for long.' Indeed, the *Daily Sketch* reporter had seen Andrews' hand tremble as he read it.[24]

In December at the trial itself Andrews had to face the bruising and mercurial Billy Rees-Davies, known as the One Arm Bandit following the loss of his right arm during the war. This time the parson was supported by Barbara Smythe whose father was a Hyde Park Mansions resident. One day when visiting him she had, she said, seen Glinski with Andrews and Rita Comer. There was also

---

[23] *Daily Mail*, 9 December 1955.
[24] *The Times*, 5 November 1955; *Daily Sketch*, 1 October 1955.

another comprehensive verbal. According to the police Glinski, on being arrested, had said:

> Look, the trial is over. We had advice and now you can do nothing about it. I never talked about the evidence of the parson and nobody can prove that I did. If Hubby Distleman has been talking about me going to the flat, I will do him. It must be him because he is the only one who knows about me going to Comer's flat. Moisha and Sonny won't squeal and Mrs Comer isn't there. I will still beat you.

Rees-Davies was not always a barrister with great finesse but, unlike many of his colleagues at the time, he did not shirk from making a full-frontal attack when it was required – and sometimes when it was not. On this occasion to an extent he was fortunate. Glinski was a Polish Air Force officer who had won the Polish Military Cross and the Croix de Guerre. This did not necessarily make him above suspicion. Doubtful RAF officers such as Neville Heath were two a penny in the clubs and pubs of London during the 1940s and '50s, but what it meant was that Rees-Davies could attack the police and have his client's record – two war medals against only a minor conviction for receiving – put in evidence. He suggested that the apparent confession was a 'miracle of admission', adding that the language used was 'more appropriate to one of the thugs of the East End than to a middle-class Pole'. As for the parson and the witness Mrs Smythe, Rees-Davies was always good at confusing supposed eye-witnesses.

When it came to it Mr Justice Ormerod put things squarely:

> There is no mincing of words in this case. The attitude of the defence is that those two police officers [Sparks and Chief Inspector John Manning] invented this conversation, that it is a tissue of lies from beginning to end. The defence say that not one word was ever said by Glinski and that it is sheer imagination by the police officers for the purpose of bolstering up the evidence of Andrews and Mrs Smythe. It is not suggested, as it

is sometimes, that the police have been mistaken in hearing what was said or that the recollection of the police is at fault. It is suggested that the police officers were deliberately lying when they gave their evidence.

Glinski was acquitted in less than an hour. It was not, however, the end of his career in the courts. He sued for malicious prosecution and, with Rees-Davies making one of his rare appearances in a civil case, was awarded £250 damages. There were also libel actions against various newspapers. A decade later he was back giving evidence against Charlie and Eddie Richardson in the so-called Torture Trial.

Gerry Parker remembers Glinski:

He was a box of tricks. If he said today's Tuesday you'd have to nail him to the floor whilst you checked it out. He tried to cut up the Richardsons over a long firm. It was foolish. Here you have heavy people putting money in for you and you're making a good living. At the end of the day when there's the bust out you stand to make ten or fifteen grand and there's the prospect of more work. It's penny wise, pound foolish to try and turn them over but that's what he did.

Meanwhile the freed Rita gave her story to a newspaper, telling of her life and hopes:

I am simply a wife and mother. If my husband is in trouble – it is my trouble too . . . We shall rent a house somewhere quiet – maybe in the Sussex countryside. There I feel we shall be safer if any threats are made to kill us.
I know Jack is Rough
I know Jack is TOUGH
But HE IS MY KIND OF MAN.[25]

The Reverend Basil changed his name, stopped wearing his dog-collar and went to live in Oxford. He was existing on a Church

[25] Rita Comer, 'They call me a Gangster's Moll' in *Sunday Pictorial*, 11 December 1955.

pension of £5 per week, having beer and cheese for lunch and a hot meal in the evening, when the papers interviewed him again a little before his death in 1958.

15

The Slashing That Was

Spot himself may have been acquitted following the Dimes fight, but he was a worried man. A week after his trial, on 30 September, he contacted an old police acquaintance from the East End, a Detective Inspector John Kirby. Spot had known him in Aldgate days up to 1947, but Kirby had seen him only once since then when he was in Old Compton Street seeking information about a Post Office breaking that had occurred at Eldon Street in the City in July 1954. Now Spot wanted a drink, but instead they went to the ABC at 40 Cannon Street. Spot was apparently extremely nervous and distraught, claiming that no one in the West End would talk to him and the law was against him. Kirby suggested he go to Brighton for a few days.

The problem with that idea was that Spot no longer held control of Brighton. True there was the faithful Parker but the Guv'nor, Sammy Bellson, was now safely locked away in Hill's pockets.

So after the trial, in accordance with Rita's wishes, Spot announced that he was quitting Soho and the racecourses. He would, he said, open a small café. It would have been fortunate for him had he done so. Soho was up for grabs once more. Dimes does not appear to have been too interested; he simply took over Spot's point-to-point interests.

Despite the pronouncement by the Home Secretary that there must never be another Underworld King, and threats to close racecourses at least temporarily if they were found to be frequented by criminals, newspapers reported that there were five major gangs each seeking to put their top man into the position vacated by Spot. After his bullion coup, Hill was indeed semi-retired.

> One man who has been boosted as the new Guv'nor is a morose psychopathic personality who has been a Broadmoor 'patient'. He was once a member of the Elephant and Castle Gang, 'The Elephant Boys'.
> For the last two weeks this man has been staying at a Brighton hotel with one of the bookmakers who are supporting him. He was due to have returned to London this weekend but the hue and cry raised as a result of the Spot case decided him to remain where he is for the present.[1]

This was something of a reprise of the story which had followed the death of Slip Sullivan in the January. Curiously, however, the outbreak of gang violence anticipated with some relish by sections of the press never quite reached all-out war.

Although some of the details were incorrect, this was a clear reference to Frank Fraser who had indeed been down in Brighton, generally making sure that there was scant local support for Spot from bookmakers. In fact Francis Fraser, financed to an extent by Billy Hill, was – along with Robert Warren – hard at work establishing his business, putting gaming machines into Soho clubs.

The article went on to suggest that there would be a challenge from a Greek Cypriot gang or possibly from a junior gang who went under the title of the Hammersmith Boys – in homage to a once formidable but long-defunct gang of that name. It was all newspaper talk.

[1] 'Spot – the Last Gangster' in *Sunday Chronicle*, 2 October 1955.

At the end of November, Hill's autobiography, ghosted by Webb, was launched at a party in Gennaro's, a restaurant with a warren of rooms in Romilly Street. Fake telegrams were read out: 'Sorry I can't be here, I'm in a Spot'. 'Have a topping time. Britain's No. 1 hangman'. Guests included Lady Docker, who was initially said to be nervous about the occasion and asked for police protection. Instead she was provided with a minder, Ted Bushell. Afterwards she was quoted in the *Daily Mirror* as saying, 'I didn't know Mr Hill before, but now I think he's a charming person.' She then claimed she had been misled into attending the party and issued libel proceedings against both Webb and Odhams Press alleging fraudulent misrepresentation. She had been photographed being kissed by Hill as Sir Bernard stood smiling beside her.[2]

In her autobiography she recalled:

It was a very crowded party in a cramped room. I found myself blocked in by some frightening-looking faces whom I could not conceive of as being policemen. Some had stitched scars on their cheekbones, others had cauliflower ears, and there was quite a variety with blunt noses. Nevertheless the first gentleman I was introduced to was Chief Inspector Dimes, and as he was one of them I told myself they were all policemen.[3]

In 1959 when her jewels valued at £150,000 were stolen, she summoned Hill to her flat to ask if he could retrieve them. The meeting lasted four hours and ended in mutual admiration. 'I promised her I would not leave a stone unturned until I got those jewels back for her. She knows I am a respectable man now.' 'Billy once

[2] Edward Hart, *True Detective*, September 1993.
[3] Lady Docker, *Norah*, pp. 194–5. The flamboyant society hostess Norah Docker was born on 23 June 1906 in Derby and grew up in Birmingham. She worked as a dance partner and later teacher at the Café de Paris. She had the fortune to marry three millionaires, each of whom she survived. Partly because of her extravagance and lack of judgement, her third husband Sir Bernard Docker was ousted from his position as chairman of B.S.A. Their meeting with Hill took place when he was under extreme pressure and cannot have helped his position in any way. Later she was expelled from Monaco for destroying a paper Monegasque flag in a nightclub. She died in December 1983.

gave me a flower from his buttonhole at a party – I'll never forget that. Oh, it's so rare that I come up against a gentleman like Billy Hill, and I mean a gentleman,' she simpered.[4]

The jewels were lost in most peculiar circumstances. After a row with Sir Bernard, Lady Docker allowed herself to be picked up by a 'yachting man', whom she does not name, on a train and took him to her home near Stockbridge. She 'befriended a complete stranger', was how she put the encounter. According to her autobiography he took no advantage of her distress and she was quickly reconciled with her husband. Nevertheless the man was introduced into the family and some days later he travelled with Sir Bernard and the jewels (in her husband's briefcase) in a Rolls-Royce. They disappeared while the Dockers and the man were having lunch in Southampton. The briefcase was found in the River Itchen. The jewels were not. Apparently Hill told her that the work was that of an amateur opportunist, otherwise he would have been able to help.[5]

If Fraser is correct Billy had given her more than a flower, or perhaps she was speaking in euphemisms:

> . . . when Albert and I were wandering about looking for Bill [at the launch party] we opened a door and there was Hilly giving her Ladyship one. Albert gave her a slap; he thought it was disrespectful because her husband was at the party. I just burst out laughing.[6]

A variety of people attended, including the journalist 'The Pope of Fleet Street' Hannen Swaffer, who had earlier alibied Hill, and of course Duncan Webb was there along with Henry Sherek the theatrical impresario, one of the partygoers to wear a policeman's helmet. Swaffer gave a speech: 'I have no doubt that if I had come from the same environment as Billy Hill I could easily have become what he was. Don't kid yourselves. We all could.'

[4] *Daily Express*, 13, 14 March 1959.
[5] Lady Docker, *Norah*, p. 196.
[6] Frank Fraser, *Mad Frank*, p. 90.

Overall the party did not go down well in the newspapers, who generally adopted a holier than thou attitude, and there were right-eously disapproving comments. The *Daily Sketch* noted the book was published by a subsidiary of William Heinemann: 'A firm that does not normally go in for the publication of viciousness'.[7] Journalists had forced themselves to go and drink the champagne on behalf of their readers. William Hickey in the *Daily Express* wondered whether he was being priggish and thought it was '. . . all so stupid . . . They are not heroic characters. They are sad, little men who have lost their way.' Simon Ward in the *Daily Sketch* thought there had been nothing like it since the days of Al Capone in Chicago: 'It was the most insolent gesture the Underworld has ever made.'[8]

Swaffer, castigating his brother journalists for their hypocrisy, later wrote that sixty invitations had been sent out and 226 people accepted. The detective Robert Fabian was one of them, before turning it down at the last minute because he had to go to Doncaster. However he sent a genuine telegram: 'Sorry not to be with you. But as Billy Hill used to say, "Job first and fun and games afterwards".'[9]

Nor did the criminal fraternity wholly approve of the book. In particular Ginger Randall from Shepherd's Bush (referred to as Rumble in the text) took umbrage, and challenges were put out. Hill took his men with him and effectively sealed off local streets, but in the end the matter was settled for £500. This was a pattern in Hill's later life. Any criminal wishing to confront him would find the master 'mobbed-up', very often in the Star in Belgrave Mews.

It was around the time of the party that Spot made a seriously bad decision. If he had done nothing, in all probability the whole affair

---

[7] *Daily Sketch*, 17 November 1955. Until then the Naldrett Press had made something of a speciality of publishing policemen's memoirs such as those of Robert Fabian, *Fabian of the Yard*. Robert Fabian had a long and distinguished career with Scotland Yard at a time when it was fashionable to have star detectives on whose every word the news-papers relied. His cases included the so-called and unsolved witchcraft murder at Meon Hill in 1945, the de Antiquis murder in Charlotte Street in 1947 and the Wrotham Hill murder in the same year. A television series was made of his cases.

[8] Quoted in 'That ex-Gangster Party' in *Picture Post*, 3 December 1955.

[9] Hannen Swaffer, 'Swaffer says . . .' in *World's Press News*, 25 November 1955.

would have died down and he would have been allowed to open his club or public house. Hill was not interested in the racecourse pitches. Marsh and Dimes had what they wanted. Unfortunately, just after Christmas 1955 Spot decided to employ the up-and-coming Joe Cannon from the Notting Hill family – another, if later, graduate of Portland Borstal and a minder at the Miramar, a smartish supper club in Paddington where Spot sometimes drank. At first Cannon was to be his minder at the theoretically decent wage of £50 a week. Cannon saw it as a step up in the world. This was an opportunity to see how the top men lived:

> There was only one fly in the ointment. Jack was the most tight-fisted geezer I had ever come across. He would be sitting in a pub, with everybody buying rounds, but he never put his hand in his pocket. At times the situation became so embarrassing that I would go to the bar and get them. When we got back to the flat he would make no effort to pay me what I laid out, but would say 'Here's a present for you, Joe' and bung me a silk tie. . . . I reckon that Jack had bought up a job lot of these ties to give away as tips.[10]

So far so good, but then Spot decided to pay Cannon to shoot Hill and Dimes, possibly when Hill went to have his regular Sunday lunch with the estranged Aggie. It was not a wise move. Cannon says that he took a few pot-shots but missed. Albert Dimes then had a quiet word with him and the whole episode blew over.

Fraser, who confirms the story in the round, does not agree with the details:

> The Joe Cannon story in his book *Tough Guys Don't Cry* about taking a pop at Albert and Billy is mostly complete rubbish. It's right though that him and three other kids were given guns by Spot to shoot Bill and Albert. Every Sunday Bill used to have Sunday dinner in Kentish Town with Aggie, and the kids were supposed to do him then but they had no intention of trying.

[10] Ellen Cannon, *Gangster's Lady*, pp. 53–4.

Instead of doing the sensible thing and forgetting it, they boasted about it. Bill got to hear and so him and Albert and I got hold of them, gave them a slap, and explained the facts of life to them over in Bayswater where they came from. Joe and the other kids went and gave the guns back to Spot.[11]

Now so far as Spot and Hill were concerned, things were different. This sort of behaviour could not be allowed to go unpunished. It was agreed in a meeting at Hill's flat in Barnes High Street that Spot must be dealt with, a decision which would have long-term repercussions for many people.

For his part Spot, who knew from rumours in the Underworld that he was due for retribution, repeatedly went to Paddington police station seeking protection.

Nipper Read, who was then a First Class Sergeant at Paddington, recalls:

He started by talking to Peter Beveridge, the Detective Chief Superintendent of the District, and worked his way down through the Detective Inspector and various sergeants until he ended up with me. He told me on numerous occasions that the other mob was going to do him, and he often pleaded with me to do something about it, but as I pointed out unless there was more direct evidence there was nothing we could do. As a betting man Jack must have known that it was 6/4 on that he would become a victim eventually, but it would have been impossible to offer him any sort of protection against a situation he had manufactured himself.

When the police could not help, Spot continued to put his misplaced trust in Joe Cannon. He had thought seriously about buying a pub in Paddington. It was inconceivable that he would have been granted a licence himself and it would, of course, have had to be run by a nominee; not that that would have been any sort of a problem.

[11] Some time later there was wind of the Cannon story in the press, when it was reported that a young prisoner told the police he had been offered £4,000 and given a gun to kill Billy Hill. Nothing came of the inquiry. *Daily Mail*, 5 November 1956.

On 2 May 1956 he and Rita went to look at the Little Weston, a public house off Praed Street which they were thinking of buying. When on their way home about 9 p.m. they were attacked by a number of armed men. Spot was knocked to the ground with a shillelagh – recognised by his wife as one which, in happier days, she had given Billy Hill – kicked and viciously slashed.

Ten years later Spot retold his story with slight embellishments:

> It would be about nine months [after the Soho fight and I was just nicely walking about again when this other mob got me. They reckoned I might rise up again, see. Thirty men with razors and choppers and bars of iron.
>
> I should have known they'd get me some day. Once they get you, you've had it. You're on your own. You suddenly realise that all your right-hand men aren't about anymore.[12]

But where was Joe Cannon? Spot had told him that he was taking Rita out for a meal in the Edgware Road, and to meet him back at the flat. Cannon had taken his girlfriend Ellen out for the night and had forgotten the time:

> . . . . when I looked at my watch it was one o'clock in the morning, long past the time when I was due to meet Jack and Rita. Still, there was no use crying over spilt milk, so I spent the rest of the night with Ellen.
>
> In a way I was lucky. If I had been with Jack when he made his way home I would have been dead or, at best, seriously injured. . . .[13]

At first Spot made a statement giving the names of his attackers, but later retracted it. Rita was made of sterner stuff. She named Billy Hill as wielder of the shillelagh and Albert Dimes, Frank Fraser and Bobby Warren as other leaders of the attack. Nipper Read was sent to collect Hill:

---

[12] Pauline Peters, 'Jack Spot' in *Sunday Times Magazine*, 6 August 1965.
[13] Joe Cannon, *Tough Guys Don't Cry*, p. 39.

Billy Hill, short, slim, and with his hair greased and pasted back, looking every inch a spiv of the 1950s, was unconcerned. It was just as if he expected a pull. He took his time getting dressed and smartening himself up. Just before we left his small flat in a nonde-script block in Moscow Road, Bayswater, he went to a sideboard, opened a cupboard and took out a roll of notes that would have choked a pig. 'I suppose I'd better bring a few quid, just in case', he said as we took him away.[14]

After the attack, and once it was realised this was a police matter, there were the usual out-of-court negotiations. It was arranged that Cannon should go to Hill's office at Warren Street, just off Tottenham Court Road. According to his memoirs, Cannon took the precau-tion of taking a .45 revolver with him to the rendezvous where he met Hill and Albert Dimes. The message he was to convey was that Hill knew Rita was set on going to court but that he, Jack, would talk her out of it. The *quid pro quo* was that Hill would stop the escalating aggravation between them. Hill was not pleased, telling Cannon that Spot was a wrong 'un and that he would get the same treatment if he remained his man. Indeed it was only the kindly intervention of Frank Fraser, who put in a good word for Cannon, which had kept him unmarked so far.

As was often the case, Dimes appears to have been the peace-maker. All that mattered now was that no one was charged. Could Cannon fix it so that a couple of the Hill boys could get in to Spot's bedside so things could be agreed in person? One problem was the police sitting by the bed. The negotiator Jimmy Wood, one of the few who had remained loyal to Spot, went with Cannon to the hospital and in whispers it was agreed that there was no point in nicking Fraser and the rest. Spot now said he would persuade Rita not to go ahead. So far as he knew, it was a genuine settlement negotiated by interested but not involved parties. But his antennae were still tuned in. As he was leaving, Wood was asked by the ever-percipient Spot whether he had seen Hill recently. 'Haven't seen him for months,'

[14] Nipper Read, *The Man Who Nicked the Krays*, p. 55.

was the reply. Unfortunately, instead of waiting for Cannon and Wood at the Fifty One club as arranged, Hill had come to the hospital where he was photographed with them. Cannon and Spot realised they had been set up. Now it was a question of *sauve qui peut*.

As for the attackers, Fraser first went to Brighton. He was already wanted on a warrant for attacking his long-time South London rival, Johnny Carter. Meanwhile Hill was directing operations. Then Fraser returned to London and it was arranged for him and some of the others to go to Ireland. Fraser and Hill went in one car and Ray Rosa and Dido Frett – involved in the Carter matter – went to Manchester to be looked after by the great Manchester villain, Bobby McDermott. Billy Blythe and Battles Rossi also went to Ireland independently. Hill had rented a doctor's house on the outskirts of Dublin and Fraser remained there for the next ten days. Unfortunately on the way to Manchester, along with Patsy Lyons who was driving them, Blythe and Rossi were arrested over a jewellery theft. They were not picked out on an identification parade, but were returned to London for another one regarding Carter. Fraser heard the news and, feeling it was his responsibility, returned to England. Unfortunately Hill's telephone was being tapped at the time and Fraser was promptly arrested at Heathrow: 'I came off the plane like any ordinary traveller and half a minute later I was surrounded.'[15] He would hardly have recognised himself, let alone be recognised by Rita Comer, from one of the descriptions of this small Cockney in a newspaper: 'Medium height, fair wavy hair and speaks with a Scottish accent'.[16]

He was alleged to have said to the police, 'Look here, you know I was in it, but you have got to prove it, and I am not saying anything more.' It was the standard sort of verbal at the time.

The week before, Bobby Warren had also been charged and despite Marrinan's best efforts, describing Rita Comer as having 'a pawn-

---

[15] For an account of Fraser's troubles with the Carter family see *Mad Frank*, Ch. 5.
[16] *Sunday Dispatch*, 13 May 1956.

broker's valuation of the truth', bail was refused. The police said there had already been interference with witnesses.[17]

In court Spot did what he could to restore the Underworld tradition of *omerta*, but it was too little and far too late. The prosecution had his statement made two days after the attack in which he named seven or eight people including Fraser and Warren. Now he said he was unable to identify his attackers but he was quite sure that they were neither Warren nor Fraser. Once the trial began Spot elaborated a little. 'I do not recognise these men,' he told the court. 'I know that these men did not attack me.'

Curiously the prosecution did not ask the judge Mr Justice Donovan to make Spot a hostile witness, something which would have meant he could have been shown his original statement and cross-examined. However, the matter came up during the cross-examination of a police officer. The problem had been with Rita Comer, who had not been so reticent. In a backhand way to discredit her evidence, Marrinan asked the officer whether she had not named other people who had taken part in the attack but who had provided alibis. The policeman replied, 'No, it was Mr Comer who indicated such persons', and the cat was out of the bag. Donovan sent for the statement and he cross-examined Spot himself. It was, said Lord Goddard later when hearing the application by Warren and Fraser for leave to appeal, 'just one of those things that fortunately happen in the interests of justice.'

But Rita was quite prepared to go through with it. She named Billy Hill as wielding the shillelagh and stuck to her story. She was cross-examined vigorously by Patrick Marrinan on behalf of Warren, who put it to her that she was giving evidence to get rid of Hill, Dimes and friends in order to re-establish her husband as 'King of the Underworld'.

'I don't care about the other people. I just want to be left alone with my husband and children,' she replied after earlier saying, 'I

[17] *Sunday Dispatch*, 20 May 1956.

would be very happy if they let my husband and me alone. I'd like him to get just a small job.'

Was it right, Marrinan asked her, that on the day after the attack she had telephoned a Mrs Harry White and said, 'I'm going to get your husband ten years. I saw him with a knife in his hand stab my husband last night.' No, she replied, she had said, 'I suppose you and your husband are pleased now.'

Harry White certainly must have been pleased with the attack. After the Spot–Dimes fight he had given an interview to his old friend Sidney Williams, spitting on the floor as he said, 'That's how frightened we are of Jack Spot and his men now. He hasn't got five men he can rely on to stand at his back.'

It was easy to see the way the trial was going. One essential in a major criminal trial at the Old Bailey or any Assize in the 1950s and 1960s was to have a barrister who was on good terms with the judge or was talented enough to overcome the handicap of the judge's interruptions and asides. Marrinan was not popular with the hierarchy and, by all accounts, while he stood up to the judicial heckling he was always on the butt end of what passed as judicial humour. Certainly everybody in court laughed dutifully.

Trying to discredit Rita Comer, Marrinan first asked whether she had been living with Spot before their marriage and then passed on to the question of publicity:

Q: Do you shun publicity?
A: I do not like it.
Q: Did you receive a cheque for £300 from the *Daily Express* recently?
A: Yes.
Q: Was that for posing with your husband?
A: Yes.
Q: £300 for showing a number of injuries your husband had received?
A: I can explain it, if you want me to.

Now was the time for judicial intervention:

> *Judge:* I don't think that is relevant.
> *Marrinan:* If the witness is prepared to commercialise her husband's injuries and she says she shuns publicity . . .
> *Judge:* The fact that the *Daily Express* paid her £300 for a photograph is not relevant. I wish they would pay £300 for mine.

Game, set and match.

When it came to it the case against Warren and Fraser was not that strong. Basically it was the convicted perjuress Rita Comer on whom the Crown now had to rely, just as it had done on the good Reverend in an earlier trial. Needs must.

Fraser ran an alibi defence; he was always a perky if not necessarily a good witness. He had been working in Brighton in a bookmaker's office on the night of the attack and that same night had asked for a week's leave. He had not paid income tax for some time, if ever. He had been in hospital, but now he earned £1 or £2 a night. He thought he might make a bit more money than that by smuggling cigarette lighters, and 'other people' had bought him a ticket to Ireland. It had not worked out and so he had returned. Bellson duly gave his telephone colour evidence.[18]

Fraser's other witness was Patrick Carney, who had been with the Comers on the night of the attack and who came from the same part of Dublin as Rita. He was convinced that neither Fraser nor Warren had been in the group who had attacked them. There was, however, more trouble for Rita. During the luncheon interval she apparently went and spoke with Carney, who was still in the middle of his evidence, saying, 'That was a very unkind thing to do.' Called into the witness box to explain her conduct, she said that it was Carney who had approached her asking if she would like a drink. She said she was going down to the basement to get some refreshments, but then a policeman had walked over and told Carney he

[18] See Ch. 12, p. 162.

had to leave. The judge was by no means convinced, but he was not prepared to do more than issue a warning: 'If this case should have to be retried or if you are in any other criminal proceedings, you had better understand very clearly that you must not talk to witnesses on the other side during the case. Will you remember that for your own good?'

Warren called no evidence and Marrinan was in full flow in his closing speech. Spot was, he said: 'That vile, cut-throat gangster, that corner boy of the lowest ilk, that man who went into court and swore lies'. As for Rita, what an actress:

> This is a woman prepared to go and live with a gangster and have a voluntary association with him. It is not a case of a woman marrying an honest man for better or worse and then sticking to her man. We have seen in the box the sweetest little person . . . a tearful little woman crying up to God Almighty that he was going to punish these men. All acting, members of the jury.

The judge, summing up, clearly indicated the way for the jury to think about things. Disregard Spot but as for Rita, well, she might almost have been as fragrant as Mary Archer decades later:

> You will probably ask yourselves what Mrs Comer has to gain by inventing the story? If that story were false, what repercussions has she got to expect in this world of violence in which she and her children have been living for some time past and which she told us she would give anything to escape?

Could the jury see any motive for lying? Many non-jurors could but the jury, correctly in Fraser's case, could not. Fraser, who by then had fifteen convictions and who had twice been certified 'insane', had – said his counsel John Ritchie in full barristerial flow – to be 'one of the weaker vessels of mankind' who had been 'made use of by other persons for a foul purpose'. On 15 June 1956 Warren, with no convictions for violence, received the same seven-years sentence as Fraser.

The result of the trial was signalled by tic-tac men to Billy Hill who, dressed in a grey slouch hat and a brown linen suit, was sitting in St Sepulchre's churchyard on a seat marked 'Remembrance'. Surrounded by a dozen bodyguards, he had divided his time at the trial between the churchyard bench and the Rex café opposite the court. Spot and his wife were driven home in a police car where Spot said, 'I ain't afraid of anyone but I want a quiet life now.' Rita said over her shoulder that, 'The boys were used.'

Applications by Fraser and Warren for leave to appeal against their convictions were heard by Lord Goddard, the Lord Chief Justice, on 5 November 1956 and were a foregone conclusion. Lord Goddard had little time for professional criminals and less for those accused of having 'razor fights in the streets of London or any other city'. Alfred Hinds, the master escaper, said that the moment Goddard was seen to begin picking his nose a case was lost, and he cannot have wasted much time on the pair.

After dismissing the appeals, there was a box on the ears all round and a statement of general importance to be made. When a Crown witness gave evidence on oath in direct contradiction of a previous statement made by him which was in the possession of the prosecution, it was the duty of the prosecuting counsel to show the statement to the judge and ask for permission to cross-examine the witness.[19]

By then, however, the Underworld had been in turmoil. Immediately after the trial the Hill machine went into action. First he and Johnny Rice – another named by Rita but not charged – issued writs for libel. Billy Hill's was against Comer and Rita, and Rice's against Rita alone over the allegations that they had been involved in the attack. Then Marrinan claimed that he had received death threats. One man with an Irish brogue had said, 'There was plenty of lead in Whitechapel waiting for me'.

Meanwhile Duncan Webb was doing his bit for the party: 'Jack

[19] [1956] Crim App R 160.

Spot, so-called King of London's Underworld, was fined £50 when he waylaid and attacked me in the street. For doing the same thing two men have been sent to prison for seven years.'[20]

He went on to recount a conversation he had happened to have the previous day with 'former gangster chief' Billy Hill, who told him, 'One reason he's unpopular in the Underworld is because crooks are convinced he's a stool pigeon for the police.' Spot had apparently been making overtures to his former partner: 'About three months ago Spot rang me up. He talked about owing me £500 and asked if he could call and pay it. He said that he wanted to be allowed to operate in the Underworld again. He called at one of my offices with the money.' Now that their old friend Sammy Ross from the Airport robbery was out and about there had been talk of joining forces to form a protection racket in the North, but Hill had turned this down. 'So Spot gave a few quid to Edgware Road Teddy Boys and got them to put out feelers about what he called peace talks. When the youngsters threatened to break up a few clubs the Underworld began to get annoyed with Spot. But no one would have anything to do with him.'[21] All in all a bit rich from a man who was a 'former gangster chief'.

On 29 June 1956 Billy Blythe and Bert Rossi were arrested in a public house in Morehampton Road, in the Donnybrook district of Dublin. Now Patrick Marrinan, demonstrating just how much he was in Hill's pocket, put his feet straight into it. Dimes had heard of the arrest and, in a club along with Franny Daniels and a *Daily Express* reporter Frederick MacGarry, he said he needed to get in touch with Marrinan. MacGarry then telephoned Marrinan and the barrister hot-footed it to Old Compton Street. Once he heard of the arrests Marrinan was anxious to go to Dublin as soon as possible because, it seems, he feared that Rossi and Blythe were going to be verballed by the English officers who came to collect them. The so-called verbal, common in England until the passing of the Police

[20] Duncan Webb, 'Spot in a Spot' in *People*, 17 June 1956.
[21] *Ibid.*

and Criminal Evidence Act 1984 put something of a stop to the
practice, was the false attribution by police officers of incriminating
statements made by the suspect. The presence of a legal representative should prevent this. Dimes said that Hill must be consulted
and they all took a taxi to Hill's flat in Barnes where he handed over
banknotes to Marrinan and a plane ticket was booked. Dimes gave
him a further £20.

Without being instructed and accompanied by a solicitor, as was
the required practice, Marrinan then went alone to Dublin to see
what could be done, arriving about four in the morning. In fact he
need not have bothered. Hill had already been on the telephone,
and an immediate application for a writ of *habeas corpus* had been
issued by local solicitors on the grounds that the English warrants
were deficient. On the Saturday morning a decision on the application was deferred until a hearing on the following Monday.

That day the men were ordered to be released, with Mr Justice
Murnaghan commenting that there were about ten men in the court
to whom the descriptions on the warrants could apply. The fact that
they were good in England was immaterial, nor did it matter that
he thought they were the correct men. An application for costs was
refused. But the weekend had given the English police enough time
to tidy up their paperwork. There were now new and improved
descriptions on the warrants.

It is not clear just what part Marrinan played in the next few
minutes when the men were served with the new warrants and rearrested. Nor is it really clear whether they were actually released.
Tommy Butler would later allege that Marrinan had tried to block
officers, so giving Blythe and Rossi a chance to escape from the
Bridewell. Later, he told the Benchers of Lincoln's Inn that he had
heard Marrinan say to Blythe, 'They are all outside and are going to
nick you again. If I were you I should make a dive for it.' Blythe
had replied, 'Too fucking true' and Butler had seen him button up
his overcoat. DI Philip MacMahon of the Dublin police had tried to
step past Marrinan but could not initially do so. MacMahon would

later say that he believed Marrinan had acted deliberately. In turn Marrinan would say that he thought MacMahon's conduct was disgraceful and he had told the Inspector somewhat enigmatically, 'I am as good an Irishman as you are.' He had also remarked to Butler that he was not in London now. Later, after telephoning Hill, he paid over £75 to the Irish solicitors. Hill repaid him a week later.

Billy Blythe struggled violently before being put into a car by MacMahon, and along with Rossi he was driven to a London-bound plane at Nutts Corner aerodrome to avoid any further attempt at *habeas corpus* proceedings by them. An application later that day to have Sergeant James Bell committed for not releasing the men properly in accordance with the order of Mr Justice Murnaghan was rejected by the same judge.[22] Now Marrinan rang Hill to report on the fiasco.

---

[22] *Irish Press*, 30 June 1956.

16

The Slashing That Never Was

Meanwhile Jack Spot himself had been arrested again. This time it was for the slashing of a Hill man, Tommy Falco, in Fitzmaurice Place outside the Astor Club in Mayfair on the night of 20 June. This was big news indeed and Geoffrey Dowling in the *Daily Express* gave a minute-by-minute account of the affair under the heading:

Charged with Mayfair slashing

WIFE WEEPS:

1.10 p.m. FALCO leaves St George's Hospital by a disused exit in Grosvenor Crescent-mews.

1.20 HE arrives with detectives at Savile-row.

2.15 OFF to Bow-street court go Detective Chief Inspector Jack Mannings and Detective Inspector John du Rose. With them are Falco and the man who was with him before the attack, Johnny Rice.

At the court they are seen by Mr R.H. Blundell, a magistrate, who signs two arrest warrants. One is for Jack Comer. The other is for a man at present unknown to the police except for his description.

And so on until:

> 3 p.m. FROM Savile-row Chief Inspector Mannings drives to
> Paddington.
>   He goes to Comer's flat in Hyde Park Mansions and speaks to
> Mrs Comer. Then he drives to Paddington Green police station.
> 3.30 COMER walks into the police station making 'a social call'
> on Chief Inspector Fred Cornish. The West End detectives read
> him the warrant and detain him.

After that Mrs Comer arrived at the station in a taxi and was told
Spot had been arrested. He was charged at 4.43 and at:

> 8 p.m. MRS COMER, in blue suit with a white nylon blouse, goes
> back to Hyde Park Mansions in a police car. Detectives bar the
> doors.[1]

Spot was brought up at Bow Street the next day when, appearing
on his behalf, James Dunlop told the magistrate: 'There is a complete
answer to this offence and it will reveal a vile and treacherous
conspiracy on the part of certain people to wreak vengeance for
some reason or another upon Mr Comer.'[2]

At the committal proceedings James Dunlop continued where he
had left off, saying of the allegation that 'it is a complete and utter
fabrication from start to finish'. He would, he added, be calling a
witness who had volunteered first-hand information. Meanwhile Big
Tommy Falco gave evidence, admitting, 'I work for Albert Dimes
when we go to the races . . . When he wins, I get wages.'

In the completely unjustified attack, he had acquired cuts needing
47 stitches as a result, claiming that as Spot had slashed him he had
said, 'This is one for Albert . . .'

Ex-boxer Johnny Rice, the 6'4" Hill man who had already issued
writs against the Comers, had been with Falco when the attack
took place. He remembered the words slightly differently as, 'This

---

[1] *Daily Express*, 22 June 1956.
[2] *Irish Press*, 30 June 1956.

is one for Albert Dimes'. He was photographed a few days later at
Brighton races. The newspapers must already have thought there
was a smell to the whole affair because the *Daily Express* published
a fairly hostile account of the day out. There he was with Tommy
Falco, who was wearing a green tweed suit, and curiously Harry
White, with whom there had obviously been a rapprochement.
White had two pitches. Archie Hill, Billy's brother, had another and
Rice a fourth. White told the reporter, 'It's wrong for people to say
that some gang leader controls these pitches. Talk about racecourse
gangs is making things difficult. It's affecting our business. The big
boys don't come out.' Falco explained that the pitch 'was given to
me by an old partner of Jack Spot. Nobody runs us. We pay our
own ground rent. There's no gangster business up here. There's been
some nasty things said about people. Look what they said about
Albert Dimes. Now Albert is a quiet fellow, never touched anybody
for anything. He pays five shillings for a shave – generous he is.
Nothing wrong with Albert.' Rice explained he had bought his pitch
from Jack Spot four years previously.[3]

The criminal process moved much faster half a century ago.
There were no year-long waits between arrest and trial as there are
today. Just under a month later Spot's trial began at the Old Bailey
in front of Mr Justice Streatfield, and for once it was genuinely a
sensational one.

Reginald Seaton was once again prosecuting. The case against
Spot was that at about 2.15 a.m. on 20 June Tommy Falco and
Johnny Rice had just left the Astor Club when Falco was approached
by Spot. Falco had seen something shining and now felt a sting in
his arm; looking down, he saw a bad cut. Rice, who had been a few
yards away, ran up to see what was the matter and both men heard
Comer say, 'This one is for Albert' or 'This one is for Albert Dimes'.
They were not sure. Comer was then seen to run up Fitzmaurice
Place and they heard a car starting. The question of the second man

[3] *Daily Express*, 3 July 1956.

seemed to have been forgotten. Falco and Rice went back to the Astor where the sleeve of the jacket was cut off and Falco was taken to hospital.

When Spot was seen later that morning he gave the somewhat unoriginal alibi that he had been home all night and that the whole story was a frame-up. There was no blood on Spot's clothes because, said Seaton, it had been absorbed in Falco's own jacket.

Defending him Spot now had Victor Durand, a man regarded as possibly the best of a very fine crop of barristers of the time and tipped for judicial honours. He was straight into the attack in his cross-examination of Falco:

> *Q:* Where is Billy Hill at this moment, in Marylebone Magistrates' Court or at this court?
> *A:* I have no idea where Billy Hill is. I am not his keeper.
> *Q:* He is your governor?
> *A:* He is not my governor.
> *Q:* Who is?
> *A:* Mr Dimes. I work for Mr Dimes. He goes to the races. He is a commission agent.

Next, Rice was in all sorts of difficulties. He was, he said, a steel merchant, but unfortunately he had been photographed at Brighton races a fortnight earlier taking bets under the banner of William Hill. He had, he said, bought the pitch from Jack Spot.

> *Judge:* Is that a sideline from the steel business?
> *A:* Yes.

The key point, so far as Durand was concerned, was why Falco had not immediately called the police. The reasoning was that he dared not do so in case Spot had a watertight alibi. If he was merely at his flat, that was not thought to be good enough. They would arrange for the police informer Sid Mercado – who bet as Sid Kiki and who lived in the same block as Spot – to tell them when Spot would be home. Mercado was useful; he was the one who had told Hill of

Spot's whereabouts when he was attacked by Fraser and the others. Apparently Falco could not read, and his wife had not read out an article on Spot by Duncan Webb the weekend before the attack as it would have upset him.

Very much as Bert Marsh had found a knife in the Spot–Dimes case, so a cut-throat razor was found outside the door of the home of Princess Marie Louise near Fitzmaurice Place.

There was one other hurdle for the prosecution to jump. There had been threats to Rita Comer, and she was under a police watch if not guard. Detective Chief Inspector John Mannings told the court that there had been an irregular patrol by uniformed officers, and CID officers also kept a watch on Hyde Park Mansions. If Comer had been out and about then, on his return, he might have run into the patrol or indeed the block's porters sniffing the night air. The judge was not desperately impressed: 'The porters cannot say whether Comer came home at 2 a.m. They were in their room. Probably gambling as well.'[4]

Spot gave evidence and, given that he was telling the truth, he told it well. There were some minor hiccoughs. His 1939 conviction was brushed off as fighting Fascists. Did he protect the Astor Club? 'No, the police protect the clubs.' The grievous bodily harm on Webb became 'Just pushing a man'.

The whole shabby story was revealed when Spot's old friend – the Glasgow hardman Victor 'Scarface Jock' Russo – came to give evidence. Accepting that he had twenty-four previous convictions and had been in prison nine times, he said he had been offered £500 by Albert Dimes to allow himself to be slashed so that Spot could be framed. The idea was that he would be cut on the face, on the arm and have substantial cuts to his stomach. He had gone to Peter Mario's restaurant in Gerrard Street, Soho, and there met Dimes, Hill, Franny Daniels and Johnny Rice in a back-room meeting. Also present was Duncan Webb to whom Hill had said, 'I

---

[4] *Daily Telegraph*, 17 July 1956.

want you to have a go at Spot this week', and Webb had agreed to write up something to Spot's detriment in the *People*. At first the judge did not understand that 'have a go' meant a story in the news-paper rather than a physical attack.

How would they know that Spot did not have a cast-iron alibi? 'I will get Kye-Kye [Sid Kiki, the bookmaker] to find out,' said Hill. Russo had thought it over and then declined. Later he had heard of the slashing of Falco. When Spot was arrested Russo had both gone to the police and telephoned Billy Hill telling him what he had done. Why had he changed his mind? 'After all I do mix with crooked people and forever people would point at me and say: "That's the man that brought Spot down".'

The prosecution did what they could do discredit Russo, and another Glasgow hardman William Kennedy (who had been in Barlinnie with him) was called to say that Russo had told him he would make up a story. Then, surprisingly, the prosecution called both Hill and Dimes. Hill gave evidence denying Russo's allega-tion. Theatrically he asked permission to write down his address. Now he received some rough handling from Durand to which he stood his ground. No, he did not employ Fraser although he had met him in prison; nor was Bobby Warren one of his 'henchmen'. The reason he had taken so much interest in the trial of Fraser and Warren was that, 'In spite of the fact that I have proved quite conclusively that I was not involved in the attack on Comer, himself and his wife persist in stating I was there.' He knew nothing what-soever about the attack on 29 May. Did he know the people involved in the attack?

A: I know the parties who were accused of being there.
Q: You would not dream of telling a lie, would you?
A: Not about this case.
Durand: Are you the person who described himself as the King of Soho?
A: No.
Q: Have you ever described yourself as the King of Soho?

A: No.

Q: What title do you take for yourself if it is not a kingdom or dukedom?

A: Boss of the Underworld.

Durand: That is a modern democratic term.

Dimes followed him into the witness box to say he was upset about the seven-year sentences. He did not know Fraser very well, and neither Rossi nor Blythe were under his wing; they were very good friends whom he had known since his schooldays.

It was not often in those days that judges summed up for an acquittal, but it is clear that Mr Justice Streatfield did not like the prosecution's evidence. He warned the jury not to take Spot's claim that he had been framed lightly:

> You may start your inquiry with the strong suspicion that there may well be something in it . . . How would Comer know that these men were going to come out of the club? Do you think he's going to lie in wait to slash the little one when he can be caught by that big burly man Rice the next second.

Which rather overlooked that whoever was the slasher had a razor.

In those days, if a jury retired for more than two hours it was a long time. Generally the quicker they returned the more likely it would be for a conviction, but when the jury returned after only thirty minutes they acquitted Spot. Rita Comer was outside court and the pair wept and embraced. When he walked into the street the crowd, said to be several hundred strong, called, 'Good old Spotty'.

The *Daily Express* announced that it had taken the decision to start Rita Comer's story on the Monday of the following week. 'Should this woman be allowed to speak?' The *Express* took the view that she should. But when it came to it there was a note that a decision had been taken to postpone the series.[5] This was probably very

[5] *Daily Express*, 23 July 1956.

sensible from a legal point of view, since she still had to give evidence in the trial of Rossi and Blythe.

Billy Hill was not amongst the pack outside the court. After Spot's acquittal Hill, with a pink-shirted Franny Daniels in attendance, held something of a press conference at a Bloomsbury hotel where, to the background of a four-piece orchestra, he said that he was glad Spot had been acquitted 'Because I don't like to see anyone in trouble. I have been inside too long – 17 years out of 44 – to want him to go through what I have been through.'[6] He also gave an interview to reporter Anthony Brown in a cobbled street outside Holloway prison. Hill was very much in control: 'Write this down. Say I am glad Jack Spot got off', and he repeated the substance of his earlier interview adding, 'Jack Spot hates me. I do not hate Jack Spot. He has sworn that I am his enemy.'

Would he make peace with Spot? 'Make peace with that villain? Never. He should come and make peace with me. If I go to him he will believe that it's a sign of weakness. I am a powerful man,' he said, 'and I don't have to make peace with anyone.'[7] A little later he thought he was being made the scapegoat and would ask for the help of the British people.

Already the Director of Public Prosecutions, Sir Theobald Mathew had called for a report on the allegations of a frame-up. What would Hill do? He was quite sure:

> Print this. I'm staying right here. I've still got my passport, but I'm not going to use it. To run away would look as if I've something to worry about. I've done no wrong, no wrong at all.
>
> Perjury? I've nothing to fear. All this talk going on that I framed Jack Spot to get even for what his wife has been saying in court – her evidence sent two of my boys Warren and Fraser down for seven years apiece – and gave perjured evidence is nonsense.

[6] *Daily Express*, 19 July 1956.
[7] *Daily Mail*, 19 July 1956. There are numerous accounts of the series of trials. One of the more entertaining is by Lawrence Wilkinson, *Behind the Face of Crime*.

Albert Dimes was there to add his two pennyworth: 'Get this. I'm a bookmaker. I'm an ordinary man. Ever since that fight I was involved in with Jack Spot last year I've been called a gangster. Nonsense, Lies.'[8] The speculation continued for a month more, but perhaps wisely the Director thought enough was enough.[9]

Hill was also at pains to deny that he was behind a smart jewel snatch in Hatton Garden earlier that week. On 16 July the secretary of a diamond merchant, travelling in her employer's Rolls-Royce, had been held up in traffic when the door was opened and the jewel case snatched from beside her feet. All he would say was that had he been involved 'the sparklers' would have been out of the country in ninety minutes. Now the papers thought that 'London's criminal genius' was the man and Scotland Yard 'Knows who it is. It knows he's short of money.'[10] One newspaper was even talking of the genius of The Phantom behind the fight, prison escapes and the slashings. Who could he possibly be? There were no real prizes for guessing.[11]

Neither Dimes nor Hill had any time for Russo, of whom it is often said that he received and kept the £500 offered to be slashed. Dimes in particular thought he would miss an apple core if he gave it to Russo.

That weekend it was time to hear from Aggie Hill again. What was it like to be Mrs Billy Hill? Not too bad actually. 'At least nobody takes any liberties with you.' Aggie Hill met her husband at the age of 16 shortly after she had run away from home. He was 'one of the gentlest, kindest fellows you could meet'. Although she was separated from Hill she had a nice little flat in Euston and still kept in touch with him. Indeed, he had recently bought her a bedside tea-maker. When her poodle Chloe had died he had immediately bought her another to be called Chico. Wasn't she once friendly with Rita?

[8] *Daily Mail*, 19 July 1956.
[9] *Daily Sketch*, 20 August 1956.
[10] *Daily Express*, 17 July 1956. On 19 November 1956 Frederick Harmsworth received seven years and John Morley Kelly three years for their part in the theft. It was accepted that neither was the planner nor the actual snatcher. The jewels were never recovered. *The Times*, 20 November 1956.
[11] Tom Tullett, 'Search for the Phantom' in *Sunday Pictorial*, 21 July 1956.

Yes, she used to like her very much: 'I first met her some years ago and I was very good to her and to her babies – even though I say it myself. Not having any kids of my own, I really made a fuss of her little girls. Bought them presents and that sort of thing.' They hadn't had a row or anything: 'We just drifted apart. Certainly I would talk to her if I ran into her. But somehow I don't think we shall be meeting.'[12]

On any showing, this was one of the more shameful episodes of gangland behaviour in general and that of Hill in particular. It was justified by specious argument that Spot had grassed up Fraser and Co., and although he had back-tracked he had not prevented his wife Rita from doing the same. Worse, Bobby Warren and Battles Rossi had been nowhere near the attack. It was to be open season on him. There would not be another attack; instead he would be fitted up. And fitted up he had been.

If there had been any real thought in the DPP's mind about prosecuting Hill, Duncan Webb put a swift end to it. The journalist was not best pleased that he had been dragged into things, and that he had not been called as a witness to clear his name. He favoured neither Spot nor Hill, he wrote in his column the following week. He was an investigating journalist. Look how he was the only person who had dared to attack the Messinas. As for the current allegation:

> For some reason that still needs explaining, my name has been dragged through the mud of the slimy London gangsters in the Jack Spot trial. I was put forward as the man who was behind the scenes in murky conversations. Hints were dropped that I was a stooge of the thugs and that I could have been got as a false witness of some childish 'cutting-up' attack.

After all, hadn't he been the crime reporter who had 'done more than any other man to expose gangsterdom and vice in London'? The Director of Public Prosecutions had, however, been very sensible. Letting Victor Durand (who appeared for Spot) loose on him in

---

[12] *Woman's Sunday Mirror*, 22 July 1956.

cross-examination would have been a sure way to an even earlier acquittal.

Webb accepted that he had indeed had a meeting with Hill around the time when Russo was said to have been approached. However, Russo was not there. Or if he was, he was lurking behind a curtain and could not possibly have heard what was being discussed. The conversation had, in fact, been about the best way in which Hill could approach his Member of Parliament for advice on the rising tide of gossip about him. 'I am on nobody's side. I am on the side of fact – and justice,' he wrote, but the article contains references to Hill as 'the most audacious cracksman the country has ever known – who was a born leader of men' and 'a man of courage'. As for the cracksman bit, all things considered this was a bit hard on Eddie Chapman and the Scot Johnny Ramensky or, indeed, the Yorkshireman Albert Hattersley.

Webb's impartiality was clear when he wrote:

> He [Hill] had dozens of men in his pay. One of them was Jack Spot, a small-time East End thug who was given his share in several clubs.
>
> Spot wasn't content to live quietly on his earnings. He began acting the 'big boy'. He got himself a bodyguard.
>
> For months I watched this situation develop. I even warned Hill about the way things were going. He could not see that the aggressive loud-mouthed Spot was likely to become a menace.

Two years earlier Hill had told Webb of his retirement – this would be after the robbery in Lincoln's Inn Fields – and Webb had warned him of the trouble this would cause. Surely Hill should let Webb write his memoirs? 'It is something the public should know before the blow-up comes.' Hill had agreed. Now Webb added the tidbit that he had turned down Spot's approach to him to write his memoirs.

When Hill had decided to retire:

> At once the trouble started. Jack Spot set out to try to take Hill's

place as the Underworld 'boss' but the burglars and racecourse gangs would not take it from him. I was not prepared to come to terms with Spot as I had with Hill. I could stomach neither his boasting nor his lies. Yet I tried to keep the peace.[13]

And he provided his own solution to the impasse:

> I can see only one way out – for Hill and Spot to shake hands and part for good.
>   For Spot to escape out of London into the 'quiet life' he says he wants and for Hill to disappear quietly into his business backwater.

And Webb?

> That leaves me to get on with the job. And I will do that ruthlessly and without favour. If either of them creep back into the Underworld, now rapidly being broken up, they can be sure I will know about it. I shall find out the facts as usual and, as always, print them. Neither threats nor slander will stop me doing that – as the Messina brothers know to their cost.

The next week Webb wrote a touching story about the values of Soho's denizens helping each other in their misery, and then he went away for a time. That month, wearing his whiter hat, he and the *People* were in trouble over an article relating to Anthony Micalleff, charged with being concerned in the management of a brothel at the Astoria Hotel, 57 Queen's Gardens, Paddington. He had written 'Arrest this Beast' while Micalleff was already awaiting trial on another charge. Webb claimed he did not know that there was a charge in existence, but the court said that did not matter. He and the editor were fined £500 and the publishers, Odhams Press Ltd, £1,000.

The immediate aftermath of the trial so far as the Spot family was concerned was that on 22 July their children were christened at Our Lady of the Rosary, Marylebone Road, by Father Frederick Bentley.

---

[13] Duncan Webb, 'Jack Spot, Billy Hill and me' in *People*, 22 July 1955.

Spot had apparently agreed to this course if he was acquitted, and Father Bentley thought that this was the happiest moment of the whole sad affair.[14] Rita Comer had been under constant police watch at a cost of £12 a day, and of course this spilled over onto Comer provided he stayed with her. The guardian officers attended the service. Meanwhile he was putting a brave, if scarred, face on things, telling a reporter, 'I am not being driven out of town. Everyone knows where I live and that's where I shall be. We have no plans and I have nothing to fear.'[15]

Then in the October came the trial of Blythe and Rossi, along with a third man Ginger Dennis, with Spot and Rita once again giving evidence. They were rather unlucky. After three hours the jury were deadlocked and returned to court to say they had explored every avenue. The evidence was really such that either the accused would be found guilty of causing grievous bodily harm or they would be acquitted. Mr Justice Cassels sent the jury out again, saying they must make a decision one way or another. They did. Still on the indictment was a less serious count alleging unlawful wounding, and the jury found the trio guilty on this. 'Monstrous', said Khaki Roberts, appearing for them in the Court of Appeal. No one, but no one, neither prosecution nor judge had envisaged that this was unlawful wounding. 'We cannot cross-examine the jury,' said Lord Goddard. 'They may have said "we find these fellows guilty but considering the character of the prosecutor we are not gong to find them guilty except of the less serious offence".' Which was a some-what Jesuitical argument on His Lordship's part. Leave to appeal was refused.[16]

Billy Blythe did not live long. He died in prison within a year of his sentence. He had a duodenal ulcer and was in his cell at Walton jail, Liverpool, when it burst. His funeral on 24 February 1957, organised by Hill, took place at the Roman Catholic Church at Kensal

[14] *Daily Express*, 23 July 1966.
[15] *Sunday Dispatch*, 17 July 1956.
[16] *The Times*, 17 October 1957, 29 January 1957.

Green cemetery. In the cortege were twelve Rolls-Royces with £1,500 of flowers on display including a five-foot cross of roses from his wife. Over a thousand watched as the procession left his home in Myddleton Street. One woman commented,' If Billy had been given the money spent on his funeral he'd have gone straight.' Three white feathers attached to some of the wreaths fluttered. These were not the symbols of cowardice of the Boer and First World Wars; they were, a reporter was told, 'gongs' – symbols of his loyalty. The trenchant Robert Connor (writing as Cassandra) was not pleased with the goings-on, pointing out that Blythe had put twenty stitches into the face of Vibart. He thought that rats lived in New York; now the good people of Clerkenwell might take notice.[17]

The police continued to make inquiries into the slashing of Spot, and on 17 March 1957 the *Empire News* published an article headed, 'Yard Starts New Spot Trial Probe' in which their reporter wrongly said that Frank Fraser had been seen by the police in Lincoln prison. Fraser, interpreting this as saying he had broken the Underworld code of *omerta*, and also no doubt wanting a spell out of the confines of prison, brought a libel action against Kemsley Newspapers.

When this came to court on 31 May 1959, he was represented by the leading left-wing barrister John Platts-Mills who later defended Ronnie Kray. The basis of Fraser's claim was that the article implied he was trying to ginger up some false evidence against Comer. The action did not last long when it was heard in court. Fraser gave evidence that if he had spoken with a police officer his reputation would be damaged in the eyes of everyone he knew.

Helenus Milmo, who later became a judge but who was then appearing for the newspaper, cross-examined him:

Q: Do you seriously suggest that an honest, law-abiding citizen would think a whit the worse of you because you gave information to the police?
A: I do not know what would be in an honest person's mind.

[17] *Daily Express*, 26 February 1957; *Daily Mirror*, 26, 27 February 1957.

Q: I appreciate your difficulty.

Milmo suggested Spot had been cut up:

Q: . . . a pretty ugly business?
A: A pretty ugly man.

The action was doomed to failure. The test in law was what a right-thinking person would think, and the jury took a bare twenty-five minutes to return a verdict against Fraser. He had apparently been offered £25 to settle the case, but he wanted his day in court. Who paid the solicitors Bellamy Bestford & Co. and Platts-Mills and his junior in this hopeless case is not clear.[18]

There were not many more happy moments to come for Spot. Now, pursued by Duncan Webb, who lodged the petition, it was bankruptcy time. On 17 September 1956 the original bankruptcy hearing was adjourned 'to give him time to raise the money', said his new solicitor, Ellis Lincoln.[19]

It is incredible that Spot really made no attempt to pay his debt to Webb. It was almost as if it was, to make a pun, a blind spot. Parker believes, 'Spot couldn't have cared less about being made bankrupt. He thought it was a joke. It wasn't as if he was the chairman of ICI.' It did have certain disadvantages, however, such as the forfeiture of the lease of his flat in Hyde Park Mansions.

One aspect of the bankruptcy is that it shows the depth of the slump in Spot's fortunes that he was unable to raise the money. Perceived wisdom is that the acquittal in the Falco case saw the end of his business interests in the West and East Ends. It may be that this was something put about by Hill and the Italians but, on this occasion, perceived wisdom is wrong. Spot may not have been the force he once was, but he still had a considerable number of interests. For a start there was the 41 Club on the corner of Dean and

[18] *Empire News*, 17 March 1957; *The Times*, 2 June 1951; Frank Fraser, *Mad Frank*.
[19] *Daily Express*, 18 September 1956.

Greek Street, the home for some current and up-and-coming Soho faces including Ronnie and Johnny Olive. Rocky Fallon from the Midlands, thought by many to have been Rita Comer's nephew, manned the door. Stan Cullis, who as a young light-heavyweight had come down to London from Coventry, knew Fallon:

> Willie Fagin and me could get in because of Rocky. There was a bit of music, dancing and in another room there was a card game. Jack Spot was in charge. I became something of a regular and Rocky would sidle off and say, 'Look after the door.' I got paid £2 and tips. It was bad for my training; it closed at 1 a.m.[20]

Then there was the Jewish connection in Petticoat Lane. An East End face recalls that even after the trials:

> They couldn't give him money quick enough. It was all, 'Where's Spotty?' Spot would sit and someone would write figures in the book. It was all one pound notes and half quids. It was protection.[21]

There were also other interests such as the protection of hot-dog stalls in the West End.

In his bankruptcy examination Spot agreed that in December 1954 he received £3,200 for the *Sunday Chronicle* articles, the details in which he now accepted were exaggerated. In one of them he said he had 20 suits at £40 each; he was confused because of the beating. He did have a dozen shirts costing £98 between May 1953 and July 1954, which remained partly unpaid.[22]

He was right about that. Neville Davies, who worked for his father in his shop at the corner of the Edgware Road and Praed Street, remembers Spot and the others:

> It's odd how my father's shop was a magnet for so many villains

[20] Conversation with author.
[21] *Ibid*.
[22] *The Times*, 23 February 1957.

and some doubtful coppers such as Ted Greeno as well. You'd have them in at the same time. The coppers at one end of the counter and the villains at the other.

Spot used to have Sammy Lederman in tow. Lederman always seemed to be a wannabee villain, but was not much more than a gofer for Spot. Spot brought him and the American singer Billy Daniels into the shop and he became a regular customer. Always the same routine. Daniels would order a large quantity of white shirts and when told they were ready Lederman would come in to escort one of the staff plus a selection of ties to his regular suite at the Mayfair Hotel. Apparently he would pay from a heap of cash on a table plus a handsome tip. For reasons I don't recall now, my father guessed that the money came from Spot. The odd symbiosis of showbiz and the underworld once again.

I don't believe he ever bought suits from us. He and Charlie Taylor [a fraudsman with whom Billy Hill later went into partnership] had credit accounts which were fully honoured until the fateful moment. However, after his slashing and gradual decline he was also pretty broke. He stopped coming in and owed some money on his account. He stopped my father in Edgware Road one day, to apologise for his debt, saying he would try to settle it. Soon afterwards he decamped to Ireland and we wrote it off. However, sometime later his wife came in and said that she would do her best to clear the account by a weekly payment, which she did, before joining him in Dublin.[23]

The Comers were evicted from Hyde Park Mansions on 19 July 1957. Rita half-jokingly offered to let a reporter have her silver mink stole for £300. Spot, she said, had gone fishing with the girls in Ireland in Galway, and she was to join him in Dublin.[24]

On 4 September 1957 Spot went to Canada on the *Colombia*, travelling tourist class. He was seen off at Liverpool by Rita, and the story was that he was going to see his sick brother in Winnipeg. After Spot sailed, Rita went back to Dublin. However, it was a quick visit for both of them because he arrived back in England on 15 September. Information had been sent by Scotland Yard to the

[23] Letter to author.
[24] *Daily Mail*, 19 July 1957.

Canadian authorities and he was detained on landing. Even before
the boat docked Canadian immigration had announced that there
would be a full inquiry the moment he landed.[25] Spot claimed to
be an agent for a fruit and clothing firm in London, but a deportation order against him followed shortly. The suggestion was made
that he was planning to open a chain of illegal betting shops. On
his return he complained:

> With a false passport, a quick flight over, I would have been in
> the clear. But I play it straight and look what happens. I'm pushed
> around by a lot of immigration fellows. Lengthy criminal record?
> Who, me? Look, I've had a lot of minor charges laid against me
> but I've only done time for one offence.

He denied saying that he was going to see a sick brother. In fact he
was just visiting his sister-in-law, Sadie Molloy, in Toronto. The
abortive passage had cost him £20.[26]

In January 1958 Spot applied for his discharge from bankruptcy.
Paid or appearing *pro bono*, solicitor Ellis Lincoln, described – until
the paper corrected things the next day – as Lincoln Ellis, was there
to help out: 'He has no business to go into and he has no profession to which he can turn not having been trained in any particular line or trade.'

The reporter Duncan Webb wanted his pound of flesh and he
opposed the petition, saying that the defence to his original action
had been vexatious and he had not received a penny. There had also
been some difficulties over the ownership of furniture. At first Spot
had claimed that this belonged to Rita but later had changed his
mind. The Registrar did not think too harshly of it: 'Colmore [for
this was now his name] has been thoroughly muddled about the
ownership of the household furniture. On the whole I do not take
a very serious view of the matter.'

The discharge was granted but suspended for six months.[27]

[25] *Daily Telegraph*, 6 September 1957.
[26] *People*, 8, 16 September 1957; *Daily Express*, 16 September 1957.

After the hearing Rita spoke to the newspapers, telling them that she thought better days lay ahead: 'It has been two and a half years of hell, fighting for, and sticking to my husband who, though he was no saint in the past, is and has been a good man to me and our children and has now left his past life behind.'

She went on to say how they had been thwarted at every hand's turn. He had tried to set up a greengrocery stall with his brother on a poor pitch in Churton Street, Westminster, but his application for a licence had been turned down. She claimed that through the 'evil men who run the Underworld' Spot had been unable to get work even as a lorry driver or chauffeur. Now friends had offered to set them up in a coffee bar or restaurant. She had been working as a waitress for the past three months, trying to learn the business. 'We won't make a fortune, but maybe we'll find peace of mind . . . Seven years of marriage to my man have made me grow up quickly.' Incredibly she was still only twenty-eight. Given half a chance, Jack was determined to keep away from the Underworld.[28] When it came to it there was no restaurant and no coffee bar. Spot was finally discharged in the June and he and Rita opened the Highball Club in Lancaster Gate. In the meantime he had his portrait painted by Robert Thomas, a Bristol-born artist, with a view to it being exhibited at that summer's exhibition at the Royal Academy. Sadly it was rejected.

There is a tendency to think that crime in London is based in Soho and the West End, the East End and in South London, and that it stops at Marble Arch. This is principally because it has never been chronicled. There has long been a thriving West London crime scene with more than its share of families, feuds, drinking clubs, spielers, protection and organised prostitution. It is only that the players have not been so well known. Parker recalls, 'In the club I had in Inverness Terrace there'd be a poker game which ran for three days and nights and by the end the pot could be up to £28,000.'

[27] *The Times*, 17 January 1958
[28] *Daily Express*, 17 January 1958.

So when Spot and Rita Comer decided to open the Highball they were not only avoiding the stigma attached to them in Soho but going where the money was.

A silent partner was to be Mrs Kaszia Hinga. Spot proudly showed reporters around the club, which sported a tasteful cherry on a stick in a glass surrounded by other dancing cherries on sticks. Inside it was furnished with reproduction Louis XV furniture and a jukebox. 'We've not had any trouble here,' he said hubristically, 'and we aren't looking for it. We just want a peaceful club among our friends. We're limiting membership to our friends.'

There was a chain on the front door to keep out unwelcome visitors. At least, it was supposed to keep out unwelcome visitors and it did its work until the August when two men came into the club and hit a visiting seaman, Peter Edwards, over the head. They then ran to a parked van where a third man handed them crowbars, and they rushed back into the club and started to break it up. John Main of Islington and John and Benjamin Harris from Camberwell duly appeared in court charged with grievous bodily harm and assaulting two policemen.

A north London face was at the club:

> They wanted Spot to start a fight so they could nick him. Harris and Carter ran out of the club and I picked up a brick and hit Harris. I took Jack back into the club and I could hear screaming, 'You've just attacked me.' I shot up the stairs into the flat above when the police come.

The main charges went East with Peter Edwards. He had been in the Norwegian merchant navy, and Richard Du Cann for the prosecution told the court' . . . since this arrest he has gone back to sea and is, in the words of the song, on a slow boat to China'. Charges dismissed.

Ominously, in August 1958 Billy Hill denied the report that he was to take over the Stables Club in Lancaster Mews: 'Don't make me laugh. A club near Spot's place? Don't believe a word of it.'[29]

[29] *Daily Sketch*, 8 August 1958.

Hill was right. It was not a safe area and there was worse to come for Spot. Around 1.30 a.m. on 13 August the club was fired. Spot was still a sufficient headline for the *Daily Express* to print in their 4.30 a.m. 'Stop Press' that the police were investigating the matter. The next day Spot was the front-page headline – 'Jack Spot: Fire Bug Raid' – in the *Daily Mirror*. Admittedly it was the quiet season, and he shared top billing with 'Too Busy For Love' which told of the singer Connie Francis and a hitherto unknown Anne Bielby who had won a series of beauty contests. The police had no doubt it was arson. Furniture had been piled in the centre of the room and petrol was suspected as an accelerant. The job had been offered around the Underworld, but just who was actually behind the arson attack has long been a matter of speculation. Later Reg Kray would claim responsibility, but the better thought is that he was acting for Hill.[30]

Now, Spot had learned his lesson. 'I know who is responsible but I never complained to the police.' His daughters were sent to Torquay. Afterwards he was interviewed in one of the last issues of the dying weekly pictorial magazine *Illustrated*. He was pleased with his efforts at striking blows at Fascism. There was, he thought, a lot less anti-Semitism about than had been the case pre-war. He was perhaps even more pleased that the magazine's library had 352 cuttings about him, compared with the more modest 262 about Lord Goddard and the comparatively derisory 173 for Sophia Loren. He was a trifle disappointed about the rejection of his portrait: 'What a pity. It would have been better than being hung in Pentonville.' He was now completely reformed; his favourite drink of champagne and whisky had been replaced by non-alcoholic drink. He wished he had listened to Rita – voted by the Union of Post Office Workers as one of the three most beautiful women in the world – when she told him to get out of Soho. That day she was too ill to be interviewed properly but when asked whether Spot, if left alone by his enemies, could make good she replied,

[30] Reg Kray, *Villains We Have Known*, p. 39.

'Yes he could and soon.'[31] Later, however, he tried to brazen things out. Now he would open the Silver Slipper in Bayswater, a new club being financed by a big firm, within the fortnight. He never did.[32]

For the moment Jack Spot went with Rita to Ireland where he worked for a bookmaker, and this left a vacancy amongst the Jewish community in the East End which was partially filled by Harry Abrahams. The former East End hardman Mickey Bailey thought: 'He was the sort of successor to Spot as far as the Jews were concerned but he never used the power he could have. His father had fought as Joe Brahams in the thirties and 1940s. Harry would have been world champion if he'd ever been in the ring.'

Abrahams, who had worked on robberies with the Krays' self-styled lieutenant Albert Donaghue, was regarded as a quiet but hard man; a thief to start with, who subsequently acquired a reputation in the East End. His father had owned the Wentworth Club in Mile End around the corner from the Krays' billiard hall. Mickey Bailey worked with him:

> The work was bashing, debt collecting, putting someone in place: anything that Spotty was doing apart from the racing. He could have had everything. The difference was that where Spotty wasn't averse to cutting his own people, Harry would just give them a dig.
>
> Harry could hurt people and he wasn't afraid of anyone. He was offered financial gains beyond his dreams. He could have had what he wanted but he didn't have that ruthless streak to go and do it. Them Jews do love a Jewish villain.[33]

For a time Spot returned to the East End, living in Romford Street next to the street where he was born. Some time after the Highball incident Rita Comer left her husband for a period, living with another man in the Earl's Court area. It was not a success; he started beating

[31] Jack Aitken, 'Can a Gangster make Good?' in *Illustrated*, 6 September 1958. In the poll conducted in October 1956 the other two women were Queen Soraya of Iran and Drussila Demetriades, a Cypriot whose fiancé had been killed by terrorists.
[32] *People*, 26 October 1958.
[33] Conversation with the author.

her and she again turned to Nipper Read for informal advice, meeting him in a café below a block of flats. He advised her that she should make a complaint to the police, but she had had enough of those. She later returned to Spot.[34]

Meanwhile in the Underworld jokes circulated at Comer's expense: 'Billy Hill's the governor. Jack Spot's very cut up about it', and 'Did you know Spotty was born two days before the *Titanic* went down? Two fucking disasters within forty-eight hours'.[35]

---

[34] Conversation with the author.
[35] Joe Cannon, *Tough Guys Don't Cry*, p. 43.

17

The End of a Barrister

Patrick Marrinan's downfall began with his trip to Dublin to intervene in the Rossi-Blythe extradition, but he might still have saved
himself. It is difficult to know just how far he was being influenced
by Hill, but he does seem to have had a genuine sense of grievance about what happened there. He also believed that he had not
defended Bobby Warren as well as he might have done, and that
Warren was actually innocent. There was never any question as to
the guilt of Frank Fraser. In early October 1956, immediately after
their trial, Marrinan made a complaint against the police alleging
perjury in the case of Blythe, Rossi and Ginger Dennis. It was not
something the authorities would take lightly. Now the Establishment
hit back with a vengeance, and in turn on 17 October a complaint
was lodged against him over his alleged conduct at the Dublin
Bridewell. On 14 January 1957 Marrinan was summoned to meet
a committee of the Bar led by Sir Hartley Shawcross; on 8 February
he attended a second meeting. He does seem to have been genuinely
hard done by. Although he was told he need not say anything, he
chose to answer questions. What he did not realise was that he was
playing against a stacked deck. After the first twenty-four questions

Shawcross, for the first time disclosing his hand, said: 'I must tell you the reason I put these questions is that we have information of telephone conversations between you and Hill both before you went to Dublin and a further one in Dublin.'

Although he later claimed he had indeed known, Marrinan – like Fraser – cannot have realised that there had been a tap on Billy Hill's telephone. As a result, the conversations between him and Hill were recorded and were now going to be used against him. The Home Secretary David Lloyd George, later Lord Tenby, had authorised that the transcripts be sent to the Bar Council, a decision for which he was heavily criticised. That perennial thorn in the flesh of the authorities, Marcus Lipton, M.P., thought that for forwarding the tapes the Home Secretary himself should have been prosecuted under the Official Secrets Act.[1] The former Home Secretary Herbert Morrison thought Lloyd George should have asked himself, 'If I supply these records to the Bar Council where do I stop? Faced with this precedent where do my successors stop?'[2]

Disciplinary charges were preferred by the Bar Council that (1) he associated on terms of personal friendship and familiarity with Billy Hill and Albert Dimes and with Robert or Albert Rossi, persons who to his knowledge were of bad and disreputable character. . . . (3) without being instructed by a solicitor on 29 June 1956 he went to Dublin in order to give legal aid and advice to William Patrick Blythe and Robert or Albert Rossi in connection with a charge against them of wounding Jack Comer. . . . (3)(d) gave advice and assistance to Blythe and Rossi with a view to avoiding their identification at an identification parade; (4) at the Bridewell prison in Dublin attempted to obstruct an officer in the execution of his duties; (5) attempted to obstruct officers by saying to Blythe,

[1] *People*, 7 July 1957. It was Lipton who nearly a decade later would raise questions in the House of Commons about Sir Robert Boothby and the Kray Twins.
[2] Herbert Morrison, 'The phone talks I would tap' in *Empire News*, 30 June 1957. Lloyd George's other most challenged decision was not to grant a reprieve to Ruth Ellis, convicted two years previously of the murder of her former lover David Blakely. See Fenton Bresler, *Reprieve*.

'They are all outside and are going to nick you again. If I were you I should make a dive for it.'

Now Marrinan wrote to the Bar Council:

> Please do not believe that I would have any personal association with these horrible criminals. Necessity forced me to be caught up with them, particularly Hill. There is no profession that I love more than the law . . . Now I am making about £1,200 which is just enough to keep me and my family. After all these struggles I have been able to have my young children with me and I have been happy. Now this dreadful thing has come along accusing me of dishonour.

He knew he was up against it for he added: 'If it is within your power to recommend suspension rather than expulsion in the name of humanity I ask you to do so . . . my mind is in turmoil.'

It was no use. He was summoned to show why he should not be disbarred.

In the meantime there had been another problem with the temperamental Gypsy Hill. There had been a fight in the Miramar Club in Sussex Gardens on 12 January 1957 and, at the beginning of March, she was charged with wounding Arthur Ranns with intent to cause him grievous bodily harm. Patrick Marrinan was on hand to apply for bail, but he got absolutely nowhere with Detective Inspector I. Evans. One of the witnesses, a Mrs Woods, had apparently been approached and there were fears of intimidation:

> *Marrinan:* There are innumerable witnesses who say she had nothing to do with this (the fight)?
> *Evans:* I have not had that suggested to me.

Evans went on to say that a man named Wilson had been in charge at the club:

> *Marrinan:* Where does he live?
> *Evans:* He is in prison.

Gypsy Hill was remanded in custody for a week.

On 19 March Marrinan, in what would be one of his last appearances on behalf of Billy Hill and his friends, had rather better fortune. The evidence of the fight in the club was muddled in the extreme, and now witnesses had failed to identify her as the one who had caused the damage. 'That this woman was involved in the disturbance which led to the injury of this man is clear. It is not enough to say that she is *prima facie* guilty of inflicting less serious injuries upon Mr Ranns,' said the magistrate Geoffrey Raphael, declining to commit her for trial.[3]

For a time Marrinan thought of returning to Ireland, but he decided to stay and fight and the case for his expulsion began on 27 June 1957. Appearing for the Benchers was Mervyn Griffiths-Jones who would go on to become the Common Serjeant, the second most senior judge at the Old Bailey. He is perhaps best remembered for his comment to the jury in the Lady Chatterley obscenity trial, 'Is this the sort of book you would allow your maidservant to read?' Marrinan's fellow member of chambers, F. Ashe Lincoln, appeared for him. Disciplinary proceedings against members of the Bar were usually heard in private, but Marrinan wanted the case heard publicly and the Benchers agreed.

How had he come to meet Hill in the first place? It had come about when he was the junior to Khaki Roberts in the Dimes trial. A 'frail-looking' man had come to the consultation with leading counsel, and it was Hill.

Frank Fraser always claimed that Marrinan found himself in trouble because of his belief that the English legal system was unfair, and he is possibly right. 'I was quite sure Dimes was telling the truth,' Marrinan told the Benchers. He had thought Hill very shrewd.

In those days there was an arm's length to be kept between barristers and solicitors, let alone barristers and clients. To dine with solicitors was known as 'hugging the attorney'; even if that was not treated as harshly as it had been before the war, when it was almost a disbarring offence, it was still seriously frowned upon.

[3] *Paddington Mercury*, 22 March 1957.

As for barristers having any sort of personal relationship with a client, particularly in a criminal case, that was total anathema.

A number of things did for Marrinan, but a crucial one was the fact that he lived in the same block of flats in Barnes as Hill. With the post-war housing regulations Marrinan had been effectively homeless at the time. How had he found a flat in the very same block as Hill? Surely this was evidence of undue familiarity? Or perhaps it was absolute chance? Well, no it was not, but how had the conversation originated – with Khaki Roberts winding up the consultation, it was hardly a subject to be broached? The probability is that in the adjournments of the case against Dimes, Marrinan began to chat, professionally fatally, with Hill.

Questioned, Marrinan said:

> All these people who own bookmakers' businesses, clubs and such like have a terrific amount of influence in getting flats and such like. We as professional people are the last people to get one. Here is a man who has two clubs in the West End and a bookmaking business, and has the ways and means of getting things we have not.
>
> *Griffiths Jones:* You thought it proper, then, for you a counsel, to approach this man to get you a flat?
>
> *Marrinan:* The astonishing thing about this man is that he kept this matter in the forefront of his mind and eventually got me a flat.

It is difficult to believe that Marrinan had not known what he was doing. He was not exactly a criminal virgin himself. Was Hill acting completely altruistically or was he starting to spin a spider's web? He was always said to love children and Marrinan was separated from his family. It is hard, however, to believe that he did not have any personal benefit in mind. Robert Connor, 'Cassandra' in the *Daily Mirror*, admittedly never a fan of Hill, wrote,' Anybody who is affable and nice to Hill is making a great mistake.'[4]

---

[4] *Daily Mirror*, 1 July 1957.

Those who do good turns often find the recipients are not as grateful as perhaps they might be. Even before the hearing, Marrinan's wife Carmel had ill-repaid her benefactor, commenting, 'I do not wish to be unkind or uncharitable to him [Hill] but there are certain social conventions that must be observed.'[5]

Curiously, Lincoln accepted that the transcripts of the telephone calls could be read to the Benchers. In view of Marrinan's complaints that they were not accurate, it is difficult to understand his line of thinking. They included an alleged and particularly damaging telephone call from Marrinan in Dublin to Hill:

> *Marrinan:* This is a shocking thing that's happened. I was there. They did the two of them up.
> *Hill:* Did they?
> *Marrinan:* They did them up in the police station.
> *Hill:* Yes?
> *Marrinan:* I went in between them and they tried to push me out of the station.
> *Hill:* Go on!
> *Marrinan:* Shocking scene here.

When he gave evidence Marrinan did not accept that the transcripts were accurate:

> *Griffiths-Jones:* Do you imagine the machine somehow went off the rails and inserted that sentence?
> *Marrinan:* I know nothing about it but these conversations are not complete.

He wanted to hear the actual tapes but was told that they had been destroyed.

> *Marrinan:* Isn't that astonishing?

He had a genuine grievance. The machine might not have gone off the

[5] Carmel Marrinan as told to Gerald Byrne, 'Nightmare on a phone' in *Empire News*, 30 June 1957.

rails, but human hands might. It was possibly a very sophisticated form of the 'verbal'.

> *Griffiths-Jones:* It follows then that the three police officers put their heads together and invented this story.
> *Marrinan:* Yes, undoubtedly. I have not the slightest hesitation in saying that.

That kind of allegation was never going to do him any good, however true it might be. Here was a Hill man and, after his slashing by Blythe, Peter Vibart at least had every reason to dislike Hill men. In those days, however, the word of a senior police officer, let alone three of them, was sacrosanct.[6] Unfortunately Marrinan, who had nothing to back up his allegations, was also given to the flamboyant: 'I am a Catholic and I am prepared to give a very sacred oath.' And the reason he went to see Hill the night he left for Dublin? Hill was the treasurer of the defence fund. As if that was any defence to the allegations of impropriety against him. Marrinan simply had not covered his back. All he had had to do was get Hill to call the solicitor that night and receive instructions over the telephone.

At the end of the hearing on 4 July 1957 the Benchers found that Marrinan was not a witness of truth. They dismissed the charges of obstructing the police in Dublin, but found that he had associated with Hill. His conduct had been 'entirely inconsistent with the duties and proper behaviour of a member of the English Bar'.

Ashe Lincoln's plea – 'He was led away sometimes by emotion and passion in that he has permitted himself to do certain things which he has himself described as careless of his obligations to his profession. Mercy enables the profession that practises it' – was ignored. Marrinan was disbarred.[7]

---

[6] At the time there was a legal joke to which judges paid no attention. 'If one police officer gives evidence it might be true. If two police officers say the same thing it might not be true. If three say the same thing it cannot possibly be true.'
[7] *People*, 30 June 1957.

After the hearing Marrinan said he was going for a drink, but then he changed his mind and within three hours he was pictured writing his story for the *People*: 'I was a victim of the gang war. Without realising it I unwittingly became the defender of Hill's faction.'[8]

In fact, he put together a half-way decent defence for himself. Hill was a gang boss 'indeed, though he had long before given up'. Well, the previous year at any rate. Marrinan had really come into things after Hill was arrested on the basis of what the barrister saw as the vindictive account by Rita Comer. 'Quickly we were able to establish that Hill could have had nothing to do with the attack on Spot.' Now Marrinan was afraid 'Warren might be convicted by a perjurer. And I realised that Hill was the man in a position to get the evidence we needed. Faced with a defence of that kind I saw nothing wrong in discussing every angle of the defence with Hill. To be frank the verdict [of guilty against Warren] roused all my Irish fighting instincts. I was then quite prepared to help Hill all I could in defending men – criminals or not – who I felt were not getting a fair trial.'

Then at the end of the piece came a small encomium for Webb. 'It showed that, but for a newspaper man my client might have been found guilty on completely false evidence.' There followed in true *People* style next week's trailer:

> Still it has been an illuminating period of my life. It has given me a fascinating close-up of the criminal mind. I intend to tell you about that fraternity in due course to bring home to the public some disturbing facts about the Underworld in London.[9]

Marrinan was by now laying about him wildly. Hill was:

> A Cockney corner-boy whose every other word was a curse It is a frightful, horrifying thing for it to be put about that I am a

[8] *People*, 7 July 1957.
[9] *Ibid.*, 14, 21 July 1957.

personal friend of this man Hill because I happened to have telephone conversations with him. He is a notorious character. He got this notoriety through writing about himself in one of the papers and describing himself as a former King of the Underworld.

As for Jack Spot, 'I was told he was a scoundrel.' And Rita Comer? Well, she was, 'An iniquitous person who procured an old doddering clergyman twelve months previously to give false evidence about an attack on Comer . . .'

Carmel Marrinan was doing her bit too. To her the whole idea of the telephone tapping had been 'thoroughly un-English and despicable'.[10] From her husband's point of view it might have been better to wait for the appeal, but newspapers like a story to be hot.

Webb tried to put a gloss on matters to help an old comrade in distress. Marrinan had been drawn into things because he was a 'campaigner for justice'. He had taken 'such a personal dislike of Spot' that he set out 'determined to prove the innocence of those accused by him'. In fairness to him, Marrinan may actually have believed that he was acting on the side of the angels; he certainly maintained that was the position.

Unsurprisingly, Hill was less than sympathetic to his old friend: 'I ain't sorry for Pat, he had it coming. I've got the needle for him,' he told the *Daily Express*, and to the *Daily Mail* he added, 'So he says I'm a horrible criminal in a letter to Sir Hartley Shawcross. Ain't that the limit! The real laugh is that phone tapping . . . Pat talking away and him a lawyer too. And me . . . all I said was short sentences.'[11]

Marrinan's appeal was heard on 27 September, with five High Court judges sitting as Visitors to Lincoln's Inn. He had first requested that the appeal be heard in camera, but this was refused. Since he had originally asked that spectators be admitted, the judges were looking for consistency, and no doubt a little public humiliation.

[10] Carmel Marrinan, 'Billy Hill and my husband' in *Empire News*, 7 July 1957.
[11] *Daily Express, Daily Mail*, 4 July 1957.

Indeed, from that moment Marrinan must have realised what an uphill struggle he was going to have.

After the public were admitted he addressed the judges, beginning by saying that he hoped he had never been guilty of ungentlemanly conduct. Everything he had done had been to the ends of justice. He was not a friend of Hill and had nothing in common with him. His true friends were highly respected people – members of the aristocracy and the Services, artists and Members of Parliament. 'What a frightful, horrifying thing for it to be put about that I am a personal friend of that man Hill because I happened to have telephone conversations with him and met him in my flat on two occasions, once when he was leaving affidavits and once when he was discussing the case.' Marrinan was acting for Hill in the libel action he had brought against Spot and Rita. He had been round to Hill's flat only twice himself. 'I want the air cleared about this. I have never had any personal association with this man. He is a very notorious character.' With the benefit of the memoirs of people such as Frank Fraser, it is very clear that Marrinan was being less than open and that in fact, even then, everyone knew it.

He had, he repeated, taken such an interest in the Blythe-Rossi case because he felt he had let Warren down in the conduct of his trial. He had always tried to do his work honourably. 'Surely it can not be said that a barrister was to be disqualified from his profession for the rest of his life because of his enthusiasm about his work.'

As for the meeting with MacGarry and Dimes in the Soho club, he believed that the whole thing had been engineered as a scoop by MacGarry. And, in any event, what was wrong in his going to Dublin to make an affidavit or even give evidence if necessary? 'Was I not entitled to checkmate a scoundrel who was trying to get people arrested on false information?'

There was a good deal of toing and froing about who would give evidence. Marrinan said he wanted both MacGarry and Dimes. The judges had requested MacGarry to attend, but he had not come.

Dimes, said Marrinan, would only come if his evidence was heard in private.

Solicitor Brendan Quirke remembers as a young man hearing Marrinan plead for his professional life: 'It was very moving.' Half Marrinan's appeal was for pity and the other half a vigorous defence. The word 'bloody' had appeared on one of the telephone transcripts and this had been held to show undue familiarity. Marrinan could not accept this. Was it really fair, when a barrister was fighting to stay in his profession and fighting to support his family, seriously to suggest that it was evidence of familiarity for a barrister talking to a Cockney illiterate to use the word 'bloody'? Marrinan had looked the word up in a dictionary and there it was as a colloquialism, not even as slang. Much had been made of the fact that he had a flat in the same block as Hill; surely that was outside the scope of the inquiry. Besides, the flat was in a most respectable place where professionals and people from embassies lived. He was now beginning to regret writing the articles for the *People* and, as if this was exculpation, claimed he had not been paid for them. As for the pity:

> It is breaking my heart that I have to leave my friends just after I had settled down here and got my children into a convent right beside me in Barnes. But there it is. If I had never gone to Dublin at all I should have continued to practise for the rest of my natural life in this country.

Then he turned to trying to exclude the transcripts, and if he had any feeling for how the judicial winds blew he must have known he was facing a north-easterly.

> *Mr Justice Barry:* Surely you are not now addressing to this tribunal remarks concerning the acts of the Home Secretary in view of the statements by your counsel before the Benchers allowing admission, in your presence, of the intercepts and saying that the Benchers were wrong to consider the intercepts. It was a domestic proceeding. Do you suggest that we should not deal with them now?

And Marrinan, no doubt feeling the cold blast, said he would not press the matter. He moved on now to say how unfair it had been that when Sir Hartley Shawcross on behalf of the Bar Council had initially interviewed him before the disciplinary proceedings, it was not disclosed that the Council was in possession of the intercepts. And he was probably right. But there again bells should have been ringing as to just how they had all this knowledge. 'Why didn't they tell me about the intercepts?' he asked.

By then, however, MacGarry had arrived and this was a convenient moment for Mervyn Griffiths-Jones to interrupt to tell the Visitors the witness was now available. MacGarry had heard what Marrinan had said about him earlier and he was here to protect his reputation. Would Marrinan like him to be called? 'Very much, Sir.'

MacGarry started off by saying that he had no idea that Marrinan would make statements so far in excess of what had been said before the Benchers. When he was questioned by Marrinan he said that he thought the barrister was going to Dublin to intervene in a legal capacity, whatever that might mean. There had also been talk of MacGarry going to Dublin along with Marrinan. Who had paid for the taxi to see Hill? MacGarry accepted that he might well have done; it was the sort of thing reporters did. He remembered seeing Hill give Marrinan a series of banknotes. That was not something a reporter saw every day. According to MacGarry, his paper did not want him to go to Ireland but Marrinan had offered to pay his fare. He had refused, not wanting to accept a loan. Why, asked Griffiths-Jones, did Marrinan want MacGarry to go with him? Two reasons, was the damning answer. Company, and a word that was anathema to the legal profession at the time – publicity. However, he went on to say that Marrinan seemed to feel that by going he could give evidence that some form of gross injustice had been committed by perjury in this country and by the arrest of these men in Dublin.[12]

Almost the last chapter in that part of the slashing saga came

[12] *The Times*, 27 September 1957.

when Albert Dimes gave evidence that he had given Marrinan £20 to go to Ireland on behalf of Blythe and Rossi. Asked about his interest in the men, he replied, 'I would have been interested in anybody who got arrested over Spot and his wife – anybody, a stranger – because they tried to put me in prison.'[13]

Unsurprisingly Marrinan's appeal was rejected. However, he was not quite done for yet. He launched a libel action against the Home Secretary and Beaverbrook Newspapers which was settled in his favour, but an action against the police officers Peter Vibart and Tommy Butler, claiming they had conspired against him, failed at the first hurdle. Marrinan alleged that they had conspired to publish false statements against him, and these had been made in a report to the Director of Public Prosecutions; in evidence given at the trial of Fraser and Warren; and in the 1957 disciplinary hearing before the Benchers. The law was clear that there was absolute privilege regarding the report and evidence, but Marrinan argued that it was an antecedent agreement to injure him which mattered. It did not help him. On 25 July 1962 Mr Justice Salmon held that there was absolute privilege in regard to the report and to their evidence.

The truth is that the Bar was undoubtedly right to get rid of Marrinan but the methods used were not that attractive. The telephone tapping row simmered for some time. In June 1957 a small committee of Privy Councillors was set up under the chairmanship of Lord Birkett to inquire into safeguards and the disclosure of evidence obtained. In the autumn he published his report which included the note:

> The interference with the privacy of the ordinary law-abiding citizen or with his individual liberty is infinitesimal and only arises as the inevitable result of intercepting the communications of some wrongdoer. It has produced no harmful consequence.[14]

[13] *The Star*, 30 September 1957.
[14] *Report of the Committee of Privy Councillors appointed to inquire into the interception of Communications.* Cmd. 283 (October 1957).

The report laid down the authority and procedures to be used for the interception of communications. The most important of the rules was that telephone tapping by the police in England and Wales could only be undertaken by the Post Office with the authority of a warrant signed by the Home Secretary. Any information gathered was to be confined to the authority empowered and was not to be disclosed to private persons or parties such as the Bar Council. It was, however, far too late to help Marrinan.

He returned to Ireland and became a successful solicitor.

18

Aftermath

After the downfall of Jack Spot there was, of necessity, a certain amount of regrouping. The Twins were amongst the immediate beneficiaries from his slashing. John Pearson believes that with them behind him he could have regained control of London, albeit at a price. They had visited Comer in hospital, but he did not give his approval for any action. Whether this was due to Rita's influence is not clear; it may simply have been that he had lost heart. The Twins promptly went into a sulk and temporarily disappeared. Stories abounded: they were in prison; Billy Hill had paid them to go abroad; they were in the Bahamas; they were dead, laid out in the front room awaiting embalming. The rumours were wrong; it was simply a case of stepping back in order to jump higher.

Racecourse pitches were still allocated in the Central Club, the old Sabini hangout in Clerkenwell, and one evening they appeared to claim what they saw as their dues. Shots were fired and the Krays came away with a choice pitch.[1] The move marked the end of their apprenticeship. As the years went by they became more

---

[1] John Pearson, *The Profession of Violence*, pp. 91–2.

and more of a force to be reckoned with until, by the early 1960s, they effectively controlled the East End and the West End as well as having interests throughout London, with the exception of the Elephant and Castle area which remained in the hands of the Elephant Boys and the Richardsons. The Krays did not cross the water too well.

It is difficult to pinpoint the exact time of Hill's abdication as the Boss of Britain's Underworld. More, it was a gradual erosion of his power coupled with an increasing lack of interest. The Marrinan débâcle of 1957 really marked the end of Hill and Dimes as the top gangland figures. They suffered from the publicity provided by repeated court spectaculars. Times were also changing. Neither, in gangland terms, were they young men. Hill had quite sufficient money to enable him to take a back seat, and as for Dimes he was really only interested in bookmaking and racecourse pitches. What he craved for was a bookmaker's licence and the respectability which went with it.

Nevertheless over the years they both – as did Spot – made appearances in the papers, not always in totally favourable circumstances. It was clear that there were still a few shots left at least in Hill's locker, and the papers always found his activities good copy.

In the late 1950s Hill was involved with the club owner Harry Meadows. He played cards at the 21 Rooms and, on one occasion, sorted things out when Reg Kray and two other men were barred from entrance by the doormen. Kray and the others set about the bouncers, and for a time they feared there might be yet another charge of causing grievous bodily harm. Reg Kray went to see Hill, whom he knew protected the club, and asked for his help. Hill rang the club and said he had heard there had been trouble earlier; he had dealt with the problem personally and could give assurances that there would be no recurrence. He would be in the club the next night.

Instead of asking for a fee for this service, apparently he then gave the Krays £300 saying, 'Take that few quid, it would have cost me more to have arranged such a commotion to ensure my services are still necessary', and, according to Reg Kray, 'he smiled with a twinkle in his eyes'.[2]

Hill also played poker regularly at Crockfords – often in partnership with the noted fraudsman Charlie Taylor who, amongst other talents, was an expert in the dollar premium fraud. An adept card player with or without the edge, Hill nevertheless liked to have one and he expected Taylor to be able to manipulate the pack. In the early 1960s they found a particularly productive mark in Boyd Williamson, the heir to a Scottish cooperage firm. There are a number of accounts of how he was fleeced of every penny. Lilian Pizzichini, the granddaughter of Taylor, wrote that Hill had first met Williamson in Monte Carlo and had borrowed £500 from him with which to play roulette. The money was never repaid because Hill knew a mark when he saw one.[3] Over a short period of time Hill and Taylor cleaned him out of his fortune and then, when he had nothing left, bought him a ticket to Canada or Australia – the stories vary.

Eventually Williamson returned from the colonies divorced, friendless and an alcoholic. Taylor now put him behind the reception desk at the Leigham Court Hotel in Streatham, which under the Taylor ownership had something of a chequered history. It was a known meeting place for corrupt police officers and the criminal hierarchy of the neighbourhood, which included Taylor and the pornographer Jimmy Humphreys. The hotel was where, it was said, the plan was formed to have Humphreys framed for an attack on Peter 'Pooky' Garfath who was slashed in the lavatory in the Dauphine Club in Marylebone.[4]

In June 1959 Hill became (at least temporarily) an antique dealer, outbidding rivals for a chandelier at a sale of furnishings from the Bath Club. He had already purchased some sixteenth-century fire-

---

[2] Reg Kray, *Villains We Have Known*, pp. 15–16.
[3] Lilian Pizzichini, *Dead Men's Wages*, p. 198.
[4] Gilbert Kelland, *Crime in London*, pp. 167–8.

places and some marble pillars which were going to a man building a house in the Bahamas.[5] His involvement in the trade does not appear to have lasted long.

Hill was again in the news the next year saying he would make all the arrangements for the funeral of Selwyn Cooney, who had been shot in a fight on 7 February in the Pen Club in Duval Street, Stepney. The club had been given its name because it was said to have been purchased with the proceeds of a robbery from the Parker Pen Company.[6] Cooney, who came from a respectable family in Leeds, was also known as Jimmy Neill and Little Jimmy although he was over 6' tall and well built. He was at the time the manager of Aggie Hill's New Cabinet Club in Gerrard Street. The fight was ostensibly over who would pay for some minor car damage caused in an accident between Cooney and a girlfriend of Jimmy Nash, one of a number of brothers from North London who were seen by some as the new bosses of Soho. The girl, who was uninsured, promised to pay the requisite sum of the equivalent of £2.74p, but failed to do so. By chance Cooney later met her in a club in Notting Hill when she was with Ronnie Nash, another of the brothers. A quarrel broke out and one account has Cooney knocking Nash down. The next night Cooney was shot and killed in the club by – said the prosecution – Jimmy Nash, who was at the time the doorman of the Astor Club. The police officer Bert Wickstead, then a sergeant but later Commander, who towards the end of his career liked to be known as the Grey Fox and the Gangbuster, thought that the reality behind the quarrel was a question of who would become the Bosses of Soho in place of the increasingly weak Hill.

After a trial full of allegations of interference with witnesses and nobbling, Jimmy Nash was acquitted of his murder but, in a second

---

[5] *Daily Express*, 10 June 1959.
[6] Duval Street was the scene of the last recorded killing of Jack the Ripper, who murdered Mary Jane Kelly there in 1888. In the 1950s and 1960s clubs changed names with the same frequency as the owners changed their underwear. Within days of the incident the Pen Club became the Shamrock which, in turn, was raided and closed, after which it was reborn as Ricardo's.

trial, was convicted of grievous bodily harm and sentenced to five years. One of the witnesses was meant to have been Fay Sadler or Richardson, the girlfriend of Tommy Smithson, but she kept well out of the way. The police went to interview Hill to see what he could tell them about her whereabouts, but it was an abortive visit. Cups of tea were drunk and they left apparently none the wiser. Cooney's parents declined Hill's generous offer to pay for the obsequies, saying their son's funeral was not to be turned into a circus. Instead of the gangland turnout, he was cremated in a sparsely attended ceremony at the East End Road crematorium.[7] Fay Sadler resurfaced immediately after the trial.

In effect this case marked the end of the Nash family as serious contenders – if indeed they ever wished to be thought as such – for the title Bosses of London's Underworld. They certainly had some thoughts on the subject. Now Spot's and their protégés, the Krays, would really unfurl their wings.

In 1961 the names of both Hill and Dimes came up in the trial of the high-class conman Charles De Silva, then describing himself as a commission agent. Over the years De Silva swindled numerous people in one scheme after another. Just as the great American conman 'Count' Victor Lustig swindled Al Capone with his box which could apparently churn out real dollar notes, so De Silva swindled Billy Hill over a paint-buying scheme. De Silva simply bought the paint from Selfridges and relabelled it. Lustig confessed to his sins and Capone laughed. Hill was not so amused, and De Silva was given a beating. Hill seems to have been part of a scheme to defraud a Henry Smith, a Yorkshire chinchilla breeder, along with Reginald Power in the early months of 1961. This time De Silva, pretending to be a commission buyer for what was then the Ceylonese government, told Smith that his principals were prepared to spend an initial £100,000 to establish chinchilla farms in Ceylon. In addition, he persuaded Smith that the government was also

---

[7] For a full account of the fight and trial see Norman Lucas, *Britain's Gangland*; James Morton, *Gangland*; Bert Wickstead, *Gangbuster*. See also *People*, 1, 15 May 1960.

investing money in a series of ships; he could obtain them cheaply and sell them on to his employers at a profit. In Power's case it was a question of buying surplus cameras from the American forces in Germany and selling them in Switzerland. When the schemes unravelled De Silva told Power that Hill and Dimes had received £8,000 of the money. Power, who eventually went to the Atlantic Hotel in Hamburg where De Silva was beaten up by Hill, believed that the whole thing was part of an elaborate charade to prove to him that he had lost his money. In the subsequent trial De Silva received six years. Dimes was said to have received the £8,000. He was now on his way to quasi-respectability and obtained the services of the barrister Dai Tudor Price, later a High Court judge, to make a statement in open court denying his involvement in the scam.[8]

Hill received a rather more favourable mention in the press the next year when he was a guest at Crockfords gaming club. Afterwards, members who had parked nearby found invitations on their cars to another club, this time one with which Hill was associated. He was all innocence: 'I wonder who put them out?' he asked.[9]

By now Billy Hill was definitely away from the mainstream of criminal activity, although he never completely relinquished his interests. Quite who was man and who was master is open to doubt. 'He was shit scared of the Krays,' recalls one East London hardman, and there is a suggestion that Hill had more or less formally abdicated after the funeral of Tommy Smithson in July 1956.

Reg Kray concludes his chapter on Billy Hill: 'As a prelude to this story of my friend Billy Hill, I like to think that in some ways I have come close to emulating him; to be honest, I acknowledge that he stands alone and there will never be another Billy Hill.'[10]

---

[8] Ceylonese-born De Silva, described as looking like Omar Sharif, had been a long-time friend of Billy Hill. He was supposed to be the black sheep of a wealthy family and lived well off the art of the conman. He is one of the few examples of a Hill man who linked with the Krays, but at one time he was under their protection. He had been paying over a share of his profits to Charlie Mitchell. Later he took a drug overdose rather than face another substantial term of imprisonment.

[9] *Daily Express*, 1 March 1962.

[10] Reg Kray, *Villains We Have Known*, p. 16.

So far as the Krays are concerned they heap praise on Hill. Reg Kray tells the story of how on one occasion Hill telephoned Vallance Road and asked them to come over as quickly as possible. The Twins, Charlie and Willie Malone from the Watney Streeters drove to Moscow Road where Hill lived, taking guns with them. When they arrived he gave them £500 for their trouble. 'I was only testing you to see how fast you'd get over here, or if you'd blank the emergency.'

Abdicated or not, in the 1960s Hill's name could still be used to good effect. Brighton changed very soon after the Spot case. Sammy Bellson was another villain who was unable to resist the siren call of the newspapers and in 1957 he, along with the Chief Constable Charles Ridge, and two detectives, were charged with a variety of corruption charges. It was alleged that money had been paid to the police over a long period in Bellson's Burlesque Club. At the trial the detectives were convicted, as was Bellson who received three years. The Chief Constable was acquitted. After his sentence, Bellson left the town and returned to London.[11]

On the night of 15 September 1962, Harvey Leo Holford, the half-Belgian gun expert and owner of the Blue Gardenia Club in Brighton, shot and killed his 21-year-old wife Christine. She had five bullets in her body and one in her brain. Holford was found in his club cradling her in his arms. The self-styled 'King of Brighton' and the 'Errol Flynn of the South Coast', he had married Christine Hughes in defiance of her parents' wishes. They had met just before one Christmas at his club, which he described as 'the most luxurious on the South Coast'. In reality it was little more than a drinker for the numerous Underworld characters of the town. By August 1960 they were living together in a Regency-style terrace house in Queen Square, Brighton, over a number of clubs: the Whisky A Gogo on the ground floor, the Calypso on the first and on the second the Blue Gardenia. By November her parents' resistance to their relationship had been broken and they were married; she was then nineteen. Within six months the marriage was

---

[11] See James Morton, *Bent Coppers*, pp. 95–101.

effectively over. The Errol Flynn of the South Coast was no good in bed, said Christine to her friends.

In the summer of 1962 Christine began a series of relationships which included Vilasar Cresteff, a Swiss boy who had also worked at the Gardenia and with whom she went to Cannes and San Remo. She then travelled to Juan-les-Pins where she had an affair with a drummer from a rock band. From Juan it was back to Cannes where she met John Bloom, the then washing-machine tycoon, and his long-time friend and Conservative MP, Richard Reader Harris. She stayed with Bloom at his villa, the Petit Maison, and according to Holford she became obsessed with him and the money he then had. In a quarrel she told Holford that their daughter was not his. After beating her he cropped her hair, standard treatment for a 'loose' woman.

In the autumn Christine returned and on Friday 14 September 1962, she and Holford went to the Press Ball at the Town Hall in Hove, later looking in at the New Hove Albany Club. Back home, they went into the Blue Gardenia one floor down from their flat. It was the last time she was seen alive. The nanny was sent out to a coffee bar as, said Holford, he wanted a serious talk with his wife. When the nanny returned about 2.30 a.m. she found Christine's wig on the draining board covered in blood. On the stairs there was a cardboard carton also covered in blood. Terrified, the nanny went to bed where she presumably covered up her little head. It was, said Malcolm Morris QC, prosecuting, a clear case of capital murder.

Holford had a number of problems with his defence. The first was his possession of the gun. He had already been fined £15 for keeping one in his car. What was he doing with another gun handy and loaded?

The answer was that it was to protect him against Billy Hill and Albert Dimes. Holford had had an argument with a man named Gillett over the installation of a gambling game Legalite, a form of roulette, in the Blue Gardenia. According to a letter which Holford had written and deposited with a firm of Brighton solicitors – 'To

be opened in the event of my death, disappearance, or meeting with
any accident that would incapacitate me, or if these events should
happen to my wife' – Gillett had apparently hinted that he had
connections with Hill and Dimes who would deal with Holford. But
according to Frank Fraser, this was something approaching rubbish.
He had known Holford in Brighton and when he was on remand
went to see him in prison. Holford had put to him the possibility
of using Hill's name. Fraser had asked the great man:

> He said, 'By all means, if it's going to help him.' Albert didn't want
> it [his name used] because he'd just got his licence for betting
> shops and he thought it might harm him, although he wasn't too
> greatly against it. It stood Harvey in good stead because the judge
> pointed out how dangerous Bill and Albert were.[12]

But Holford overcame all his problems. There was sympathy for him
because while in Lewes prison, to which he had been transferred
from Brixton the night before his trial was due to begin on 4
December 1962, he threw himself from a balcony, fracturing his
skull. His fall was broken by a warder. 'The greatest stroke he could
have pulled', says Fraser. The newspapers were full of baby Karen
visiting him. It was reported that his 73-year-old Belgian-born
mother, Celeste Holford, had also visited him. 'Mama, hold my hand
– tightly', reported the *Daily Mirror*. And she did. And there was
more sympathy for him when Victor Durand, in one of his greatest
defences, coaxed the admission from Mrs Holford that she might
have encouraged him to take sexual liberties with her when he was
a child. By the end Morris, in his address to the jury, offered them
some help and Holford a lifeline: 'If you accept as the truth what
Holford says was said [about the paternity of Karen] then you will
think that was strong provocation.'

And strong provocation it turned out to be. His acquittal on the
murder charge on Friday 29 March 1963 was well received with the

[12] Frank Fraser, *Mad Frank*, p.131.

traditional cheers from women in the public gallery. The all-male jury found him guilty only of manslaughter, something with which the judge Mr Justice Streatfield, sentencing him to four years imprisonment, agreed:

> I fully recognise that there must be few men indeed who have been subjected to greater provocation than you were.
>
> At the same time I have to remember that in consequence a human life was forfeited and that human life was taken as a result of the prolonged firing of that gun.[13]

On 8 August of that year came the Great Train Robbery when something over £2 million was stolen – the most famous, if not the most successful, of all British robberies. It was inevitable that Hill's name should be in the frame, though for once in his life he was absolutely innocent. Interviewed in Cannes, he was adamant:

> There are veiled hints in the French newspapers and everyone is pointing me out as a hero in the sun.
>
> Look, I know nothing about it.
>
> So, all right, it wasn't a bad job. Perhaps slightly to be admired. But the boys who pulled it will be aggravated by the police a bit. I know nothing – except that it is nice here in the South of France and considerably better than jail.[14]

There are some, notably Frank Fraser, who believe that although he would have wanted the lion's share, if Hill had indeed been in charge of the operation things would have turned out better for the robbers. For a start he would not have allowed minor characters in the plot such as Billy Boal to have huge sums of money – the origin of which they could not hope to explain – in their hands.

---

[13] Holford was paroled on 2 October 1964. 'I am changing my name and going off in search of anonymity,' he told the *Daily Mirror*. In February 1974 under the name of Robert Keith Beaumont, but disclosing that he was indeed Holford, he stood as Independent candidate in the General Election for the constituency of Brighton Pavilion. He received 428 votes.

[14] *Daily Mirror*, 15 August 1963.

As the years went by, Hill took to spending more and more time in Tangier where Gypsy ran her club. After the Cornell murder in March 1966 the Twins went over to see Hill where he, now something of a local celebrity, had them driven around in his large white car. Reggie Kray, then with a blonde hostess from the Latin Quarter club in Wardour Street, even thought of opening a club there. Nothing came of the plan because they were effectively deported as undesirable aliens. However, none of the local police displeasure seems to have rubbed off on Hill.

Although he does not seem to have wanted Soho for himself, the now middle-aged 'Big Albert' Dimes, as Hill's right-hand man, almost certainly exerted a calming influence in the years following the fight with Spot. Questions of territory and ownership were referred to him for a solution. But as for ownership, 'He couldn't fight for fuck,' says one contemporary; while Albert Donaghue, later with the Kray firm, puts it more diplomatically. 'He didn't have the backing necessary,' he says. 'What he was, though, was King of the Point-to-Points.'[15]

Certainly Dimes was now in control of the best pitches at the tracks, and he remained so, granting the concessions and making sure that the odds chalked up suited him. 'If he had the favourite at say 7:4 and took a load on it, then he would wipe it to 6:4 and Bobby Warren or one of his men would walk down the line telling us it was the same price for the rest of us,' says Donaghue.

After Albert Dimes fell out with various hunt committees over the pitches, at a meeting in Clerkenwell's Central Club control of the point-to-points was then awarded to the Kray Twins. Their brother Charlie, along with the diminutive receiver Stan Davies, had the concession of erecting the stands for the bookies.

Dimes remained an almost unseen Godfather, keeping out of the public eye and surfacing on only rare but sometimes quite unfortunate occasions. In 1956, the year after the fight, he was awarded £666 for a back injury sustained in an accident when the cab in

---

[15] Conversation with author.

which he was travelling was involved in a collision with a van. He was, he said, working as a commission agent, earning about £10 a week. He was fortunate enough not to have paid tax since 1951. A little later in a separate case he agreed to pay National Insurance contribution arrears of £135.

In June that year he was named in the House of Commons by MP Anthony Greenwood, who called him a 'squalid, cowardly, small-time hoodlum'. Dimes admitted to a short stretch in Borstal in 1931 and a four-month sentence 'years ago', but surely that did not qualify him for Mr Greenwood's attack. So 'dapper in pebble-tweed jacket and clerical grey trousers' and accompanied by the press, off to the House of Commons he went. Greenwood was at lunch and Dimes remained in the lobby, only to be told that Greenwood would not see him. 'I don't want to associate with people like him,' said the MP. Dimes said that he had not gone in a bombastic or cheeky manner but, 'For the sake of my wife and two children who are feeling the repercussions of publicity given to unfounded allegations, I wanted MPs to clear my name of the mud that clings to it. I'm no gangster. Just a small bookmaker and professional gambler.'[16]

Dimes had this curious trait of getting himself into no-win situations. In January 1963 his name came up in the trial of a former apprentice jockey Lipman Leonard 'Darkie' Steward, who was charged with conspiracy to dope racehorses. This was probably the last of the great horse-doping trials of the era when William Roper as the supposed ringleader received three years. A pretty Swiss girl, Micheline Lugeon, who had worked as Roper's au pair, toured racing stables on the pretext of buying a horse and at twelve out of the twenty-one she visited, favourites were subsequently nobbled. She received twelve months imprisonment, the pain of which was no doubt lessened by her having previously sold her confession to a Sunday newspaper.

During the trial Steward said he had made £1,200 from book-makers and backers when Faultless Speech won the William Hill

[16] *Daily Sketch*, 23 June 1956.

Gold Cup at Redcar in 1959. After a good deal of prevarication he named Dimes as contributing £100 to the jockey's earnings. At the end of the trial Dimes had a barrister appear in court to express his innocence about horse doping. It cut no ice.

> *Judge:* What is his occupation?
> A: He is a bookmaker.
> *Judge:* I have heard what you said. Perhaps your client can assist the police. He will no doubt be able to help them in any way he can.[17]

There is no record that he did, since the likely truth of the story is that Dimes himself was behind the horse doping and it was possibly only thanks to Billy Howard that his name was merely mentioned in court and not added to the charge sheet. It was feared that with one of the co-conspirators, Eddie Smith (known as the Witch Doctor because of the potions he carried) possibly turning Queen's Evidence, Steward might just do the same. Apparently Howard arranged for Smith to be given a beating but did not specify the extent. On the eve of the trial Smith, then in Lewes prison, fell from the landing and died forty-two days later. From then on there was no question of Steward turning Queen's Evidence; he was too scared of a number of players, including the formidable Charlie Mitchell who had previously given him a beating. Before being sentenced Steward was given the opportunity to speak to the detective in the case but, shaking with fear, he would say nothing. He was sensible. On 30 July that year his conviction was quashed by the Court of Appeal on the grounds that inadmissible evidence had been allowed in the trial. However, he did not learn his lesson and was convicted of conspiracy to dope the horse Spare Filly before she ran at Kempton Park. He received another sentence of four years.[18]

Dimes last swam into public view in early 1968 when he was at

---

[17] *The Times*, 5, 9 January 1963; Michael Connor, *The Soho Don*, p. 67.
[18] Michael Connor, *The Soho Don*, p. 67; *The Times*, 31 July 1963, 9 February 1996; *Sporting Life*, 2, 3, 4, 5, 9 January 1963. It is possible that Smith was commemorated by the name of the Catford club Mr Smith and the Witchdoctor, where the Richardsons and the Hennesseys and Haywards had their shoot-out in March 1966.

the Tavistock Hotel in Bloomsbury to discuss money owed by a Max Fine to a 'Mr Corallo', described in a subsequent libel hearing as an 'American gangster'.[19] He also met Angelo Bruno of the Philadelphian family – of whom it was said he was the secret and trusted representative – when Bruno came to London between 27 November and 3 December 1966 as part of a gambling junket organised by a New York gaming club. Another of the card players on the trip was the celebrated Meyer Lanksy, now accepted as one of the great Mafia financiers. Dimes visited Bruno in Philadelphia the next year to discuss the installation of gaming machines in various clubs.[20]

Dimes certainly maintained interests with organised crime in America. As early as 1960 Corallo arranged for an associate named Bud Wilkins to move gaming machines into Britain. The operation was not entirely successful; some 420 machines were seized in New York. Corallo came to England in the summer of that year to form Machines Unlimited. It was to be a ground-laying operation. By 1965 Angelo Bruno owned 47 per cent of the Victoria Sporting Club in London.[21] Dimes had a small back office at the club.

In October 1964 Dimes gave an undercover FBI agent and lawyer Herbert Itkin £17,000 to be handed on to Tony Corallo, who had originally given Itkin Dimes' telephone number. He was still in touch with *mafiosi* three years later, for he was now dealing with Corallo's close friend Dick Kaminitsky (known as Dick Duke) about money owing to Corallo. Corallo was now trying to establish a line of credit to finance gaming machines in Britain, something he achieved the following year. Dimes' relationship with Bruno and Corallo became

[19] It was an entirely accurate description. For a short period of time head of the Lucchese Family, in 1987 Anthony 'Ducks' Corallo, who acquired his nickname through ducking sentences, received a sentence of 100 years in what was known as the Commission Case for a variety of offences including extortion, loan sharking and complicity in the killing of the Bonanno boss, Carmine Galente. He died in the federal prison at Springfield Missouri on 23 August 2000 at the age of eighty-seven.

[20] On 21 March 1980 Angelo Bruno left the Cous restaurant in Philadelphia and was shot behind the right ear in his car along with his bodyguard John Stanfa. Bruno died instantly. It was advanced that the reason for his murder was his refusal to enter into the lucrative narcotics trade. His death has led to a twenty-year power struggle between the rival clans in South Philadelphia.

[21] 'One Man's Family' in *Philadelphia Magazine*, September 1969.

public with the evidence of Itkin in the action brought by the directors of Photographic Equipment Ltd against the *Daily Mail* following an article 'West End Mafia faces attack by Sir Rasher'.[22] The company had earlier tried and failed to take over Butlins. The action against Associated Newspapers Ltd also failed. The jury found that the words were justified against three of the directors, and that they did not refer to the other five who had also sued. Dimes also went to America in 1968 and American couriers met him in London shortly before his death.[23] By then, he had acquired respectability, obtaining a licence to open a betting shop almost opposite Ronnie Scott's jazz club in Frith Street.

But now the face of the London Underworld had changed irrevocably.

[22] *Daily Mail*, 5 December 1968.
[23] *The Times*, 20 July 1971, 24 March 1972. Transcript of evidence *Associated Leisure v Associated Newspapers Ltd*. Testimony of Herbert Itkin; *Sports Illustrated*, 29 May 1972. For an account of the career of Herbert Itkin, described as a confidential informant for the FBI, see James Morton, *Gangland, The Lawyers*.

19

Graveyards

What happened to them all? Some faded away from the criminal scene; some even became respectable. Darby Sabini's son, who at the beginning of the war joined the RAF, was killed in action and Sabini never really recovered from the blow.[1] On 17 June 1943, Fred Sabini, who was said to be known as Darby, was convicted of receiving £383-worth of wine and silver which had been stolen by soldiers from the house of a retired Sussex magistrate living in Uckfield. The jury had rejected his defence that he believed that he was buying goods from an hotel which was being sold out. The Recorder, Gilbert Paull, passing sentence, told him in the time-honoured words judges love to use to receivers: 'It is men like you who lay temptation before soldiers. If there were none like you there would be no temptation to steal.' Sabini, who was said to have no previous convictions, received three years imprisonment. Whether the defendant was actually Darby or indeed his brother Fred, who by then also lived in Brighton, is not clear. It is likely that it was Fred because Darby had a conviction for assault at Brighton Magistrates'

[1] *The Times*, 2 November 1943.

Court back in 1929 when his fingerprints would have been taken.

Later Harry Sabini joined his brother in Brighton, and after the war Darby functioned as a small-time bookmaker with a pitch on the free course at Ascot – a danger to no one, certainly not the Whites who by then controlled the point-to-points, or to the up-and-coming Jack Spot and Billy Hill.

When Darby Sabini died in Hove in 1951, his family and friends were surprised that he apparently had so little money. Yet, so the story goes, the man who had been his clerk, Jimmy Napoletano, was stopped when leaving the country on his way to Italy with £36,000. Sabini's wife returned to live in Gray's Inn Road, Clerkenwell. Others of the family stayed on the South Coast.[2] The gang had not wholly disbanded. When the boxing and wrestling promoter George Callaghan was having some local difficulty at the Caledonian Road Baths in the late 1940s, he received a letter from Darby Sabini saying the boys would stand by him.[3]

Harry White died of throat cancer in early middle age. He was another to whom the years were not kind. He was now the god-father to the son of a former Flying Squad officer who recalls:

> At the time he was living in a council flat in the area of Copenhagen Street. Latterly, when he was not making a book more than half a dozen times a year and then only at point-to-points and small meetings, he was broke and developed the reputation of being a tapper, a mumper of free drinks, and something of a nuisance. My recollection is that David Hatter of the Premier barred him but an old barrow boy, the spiv with the hair-lip (the name has gone), persuaded him to relent.[4]

---

[2] Sabini also lives on in fiction and film as the Brighton gangleader Colleoni in Graham Greene's *Brighton Rock*. One of the key scenes in both book and film is the meeting between him and Pinky in the Brighton hotel, in which Pinky seeks to reach an accommodation of interests and instead is offered a job. The slashing of Pinky at the race meeting is based on the Lewes battle of 1936. Bryan Magee suggests that the name Pinky derives from the nickname Spinky given to Jimmy Spinks who received five years imprisonment following the battle. *Clouds of Glory*, pp. 145–6.

[3] Local History Section, Islington Library.

[4] Conversation with the author.

However, White had lost none of his cunning from the old days. A devout Catholic, while providing the betting on the Donkey Derby at the church fête he told his small son who was riding the favourite, 'If it looks like fucking winning, fall off.' His actress daughter went to Hollywood and was killed in a car accident while making the original of the film *Ocean's Eleven*. His son, also named Harry, became a senior and well-respected member of a well-known firm of bookmakers.

By now almost all of the players from the Croydon bullion robbery, the Airport robbery, the Eastcastle Street Post Office robbery – the Wood brothers amongst them – are dead. Many died through natural causes although in the Underworld a question surrounds the death of Charles Taylor, Billy Hill's partner in some of his later swindles. On 24 May 1978, while on trial over a currency fraud at the Old Bailey, he collapsed after court on the concourse at Waterloo station. Some said it was a heart attack possibly brought on by taking barbiturates. Others said, more darkly, that he had been murdered because of information he was about to give police officers.

Duncan Webb did not last long after the Spot trials. He was, as was the *People*, regularly in and out of the courts either as plaintiff or most usually as defendant. This was the kind of risk the paper took with Webb week in and week out, but overall those who threatened him and the paper with libel rarely succeeded.

Webb died in September 1958. He had suffered from high blood pressure for some time and, while in America researching a feature for the *People* on the continuing influence of organised crime on the New York waterfront, he suffered a severe heart attack and collapsed. He returned to England where he died in the Charing Cross Hospital.[5] He was, wrote Alan Hamilton, the 'greatest of all crime reporters'.[6] He left behind him Cynthia, the former wife of Donald Hume.

---

[5] For an account of Webb's tangles with the courts and the Spot case see his file. Nat. Arch. MEPO 3 3037.
[6] Alan Hamilton, 'They made their excuses and left' in *The Times*, 17 October 1981.

One who did not die from natural causes was the unpredictable and thoroughly dangerous Teddy Machin, who was shot and killed in the street on 23 May 1973. He had previously survived an unrelated attempt in 1971 while in bed at his home in Windsor Road, Forest Gate. The contract fee on that occasion was said to have been £500. He had then fled to Streatham where he worked for Charlie Taylor. At first his death was thought to herald another outbreak of warfare, but in fact it turned out to be a domestic incident. During his lifetime, as well as after his death, a number of gangland murders were attributed to him. Taylor's granddaughter Lilian Pizzichini described him as a 'rabid, fighting dog'.[7]

Moishe Goldstein aged with imprisonment. 'Moishe Blueball wasn't a bad grass after he came out. We'd meet him in the Cumberland Hotel in the late 1960s,' recalls former Flying Squad Detective John Rigbey.[8] Eventually he had a club in Green Dragon Yard in Aldgate in the 1960s. Parker remembers:

> They'd play 11/4 the field rummy. Moishe was known and so there was always people in the place. Eventually the Twins turned up and said they were taking over. Reggie hit Moishe and broke his jaw. He shouldn't have done that. That was a liberty. Moishe was an old man.

Schack fell out with Spot following his imprisonment because Spot could not or would not support his family during the period when he was away. After his release he bought an eel and pie shop near Canning Town which was run for him by his daughter. The other close friend of Spot, Hymie Rosen, took to drink and worked as a bookmaker's clerk sometimes for Gerry Parker. 'He didn't drink whilst he was working but he made up for it afterwards.' He died in the 1980s and was buried in Rainham. Spot attended the funeral.

---

[7] Lilian Pizzichini, *Dead Men's Wages*, p. 170. For an account of the murders rightly or wrongly attributed to Machin, see James Morton, *East End Gangland*.
[8] Goldstein is the informant in the story in James Morton's *Bent Coppers*, pp. 197–9.

In 1968 Billy Howard, dubbed the Soho Don, served a short sentence over allegations that he had been trying to extort money from a Streatham casino. Despite the fact that he was in poor health brought about, in part, by excessive drinking it was feared he might try to influence jurors and witnesses in the trials following the theft of bullion from Brinks-Mat in 1983. He died shortly afterwards in poor circumstances. Reggie Kray regarded the left-hander as one of the best street fighters in London: 'With a knife in his hand, Billy was particularly vicious.'[9]

Albert Dimes, who had been suffering from cancer, died at his home in Oakwood Avenue, Beckenham and was buried at St Edmund's Roman Catholic Church on 20 November 1971. His funeral was well attended by over 200 mourners, including the actor and gangland hanger-on Stanley Baker to whom Dimes had given technical advice for the film *Robbery*. The imprisoned Krays sent a £20 wreath with the inscription 'To a fine gentleman', a gesture which annoyed Dimes' friends on the grounds that it brought shame to the family. The wreath was destroyed. At the service the priest spoke of how proud Dimes had been that he could recite the Creed in Latin.[10]

There has been a story in the Underworld that on his deathbed Dimes said that the truth should be told about the shooting of 'Scotch' Jack Buggy at the Mount Street Bridge Club in Mayfair in May 1967. The case involved a number of old friends from the heyday of Hill and Spot. Buggy, an American who had come to Glasgow with the US forces and had remained, was a thoroughly difficult and obstreperous man over whose head Billy Hill had once broken a soda siphon in Al Burnett's Stork Room. In 1961 he had received nine years for shooting Robert Reeder outside the Pigalle, another of Burnett's clubs, in Swallow Street. Parker recalls him:

Jack Buggy was a sort of protection racketeer, an extraordinary fellow. He always walked about with his collar turned up. He was

[9] Reg Kray, *Villains We Have Known*, p.39.
[10] *Daily Telegraph*, 21 November 1971. For accounts of Baker's involvement in the Underworld, see Frank Fraser, *Mad Frank*, pp. 150–51.

a strutter, a bit like Tommy Smithson. He had a little moustache and he thought he looked like Clark Gable, and he did in a way. He was trying to show off to Billy Hill and he was used by him. He was a loner really.

It was thought that, at the time of his death, Buggy was trying to trace the whereabouts of money deposited with friends by the Great Train Robber Roy James. Buggy had been in prison with James and on his release went looking for James's missing money. Buggy disappeared on 12 May and his body was not found until the following month when, bound in bailing wire, it was found floating off the Sussex coast.

Frank Fraser maintains that the story of Dimes' deathbed request was untrue, but inquiries which had centred on the Mount Street Bridge Club (where a new carpet had been fitted immediately after Buggy's disappearance) were reopened. An Australian shoplifter, Donald Wardle, then serving nine years for blackmail, made a statement to the police and as a result Hill and Spot's old friend Franny Daniels was arrested. Along with Abraham Lewis who had been working in the club at the time of Buggy's death, he was charged with murder. Wardle gave evidence that he had been in the gaming room of the club when he heard three shots. Daniels came from another room and told him and the other players to go home. In November 1974 both men were acquitted.[11]

Dimes' death ended his unbroken forty years' involvement with Soho, its clubs and frequenters. But was Dimes the true Godfather of the Italians, or was there someone else standing behind and over him and even Hill? As the years have passed more and more people agree that when it came to it the Governor, if not of Hill but of the Italians, was the redoubtable Bert Marsh. A Soho denizen recalls: 'Bert ran a betting shop in Frith Street and had an off-licence in Old Compton Street and an interest in at least six books. He was a quiet

---

[11] For a full account of the case see Leonard Read, *Nipper Read, The Man Who Nicked the Krays*, pp. 121–4.

man, a very, very dapper man. He was the Guv'nor all right. He died back in Italy, a very rich man.'[12]

A former Flying Squad officer recalls:

He was something of a mystery. I met him in the early '60s in Clerkenwell when I was going out with an Italian girl. He was a very pleasant man, very courteous. People respected him, something I didn't understand then. I was later told that he was the Mafia's top man in this country and a man to be friends with.[13]

By the end things did not go well with Hill either. He took up with an African girl, Diana, who was determined to become a singer but who sadly had a history of mental problems. She had a son by the thief Johnny Dobbs and the boy was adored by Hill.[14] Unfortunately he could never bring himself to break completely with Gypsy with whom he had latterly been running a club in Surrey. For her part, Gypsy was not pleased with Diana and thought that she was being kept by Hill at the new house of his long-time friend Charlie Taylor. She would ring up demanding to speak to 'the tart' and threatening to come round with a knife. It was fortunate that the one time when she did so was when Taylor's grandmother had taken Diana out for the afternoon.[15]

It was not a relationship which could last and, after a number of unsuccessful attempts, Diana committed suicide. Hill ended being cared for by his old friend from Borstal, Percy Horne, at his flat in Moscow Road. Hill, a heavy smoker, died on New Year's Eve 1983. The last time he had visited Fraser in prison, he said that if he did not give up smoking the doctors had told him the longest he would

---

[12] Conversation with author.
[13] *Ibid.*
[14] Dobbs, a South London villain, had been with Jimmy Essex when a man died after a fight at a coffee stall. Dobbs received a year's imprisonment. Essex was charged with murder and convicted of manslaughter. He was one of the few people to be acquitted of a murder and charged a second time over a subsequent death. This followed a fight in Leeds prison, when he was again convicted of manslaughter and this time received ten years.
[15] Lilian Pizzichini, *Dead Man's Wages*, pp. 221–2.

last would be five years, but it would more likely be three. Fraser asked him if he could not give up smoking and Hill replied, 'I can't, Frank. I can't.'[16]

Hill is buried in an East End cemetery; ironically, his occupation on his death certificate is given as 'demolition'.[17] He left no will nor were any letters of administration taken out, but he is reputed to have left his substantial fortune which he had brought back from Switzerland with Gypsy, with instructions to bring up Diana's son. Over the years she has steadfastly refused to give any interviews. He also left a letter for Frank Fraser saying that he had given £50,000 to Dimes to look after for Fraser while he was in prison, but that Dimes had squandered it:

> I didn't believe it. He was always jealous of Albert and I think he wrote it to damage Albert's image in my eyes although Albert had been dead eleven years, as well as to excuse himself for not leaving me any money.[18]

Fraser thought Hill was 'like a very great snooker player':

> . . . thinking not of the next shot he's going to take but of four or five shots after that. He would put people in brackets. 'That Albert could be very useful to me, although I don't particularly like him and I'm a bit jealous. Nevertheless he's a good man and I'll keep him for a move or two ahead.' Bill had a great brain; there's no two ways about it.[19]

Two men who have lived into the twenty-first century are Bert Rossi and Frank Fraser – Rossi still maintaining that he had been wrongly identified by Spot and his wife. In 1965 he became involved in the case of Lilian Gold, a woman about town who was murdered in Clerkenwell. Rossi was charged with and

[16] Frank Fraser, *Mad Frank*, p. 225.
[17] *Mail on Sunday*, 22 January 1984.
[18] Frank Fraser, *Mad Frank*, p. 225.
[19] *Ibid.*, p. 226.

acquitted of the murder. 'Mad' Frank Fraser celebrated his 80th birthday on 13 December 2003. Those who knew him during his twenty years of imprisonment following convictions for an affray, his part in the so-called Torture Trial and the Parkhurst Riot would never have believed he would survive to see it. Instead, after his final release from prison he reinvented himself – writing a number of books, appearing in films, on television, in advertisements and in cabaret.

At the end of *Jack Spot: The Man of a Thousand Cuts*, the author Hank Janson suggests that Spot should change his name, find a small three-roomed flat in an unimportant town and get a job.

> Sure, what's so special about you anyway? Millions of other fellas have to take off their coats, roll up their sleeves and do an eight-hour stint. What's so special about you apart from our ability to cut folks a little?

Spot apparently ruminates on the possibility:

> I'm forty five now, I've got no craftsman's skill, no references and nothing to commend me. Yet I've got myself and my family to keep and my position is desperate. Maybe there's something in Hank Janson's suggestion after all.[20]

In fact he was still a figure for the newspapers to trot out from time to time for a sound bite. In January 1958 Spot went on record saying that the Mafia was in control of English crime, something which was promptly pooh-poohed by Bert Sparks. With hindsight we know Spot was substantially correct. Even then Arthur Helliwell had noted that two men had been sent to England by Frank Costello to intimidate a Midlands businessman into resigning from a company Costello wanted to control.[21]

On 6 February 1962 Spot was in the dock for the last time in

[20] Hank Janson, *Jack Spot: The Man of a Thousand Cuts*, pp. 188–9.
[21] *People*, 5 January 1958.

his life. He had been working at J. Lyons at Cadby Hall in West London, and had been dealing in meat stolen from the firm and selling it to local restaurants. He was fortunate; the matter was treated on the basis that the meat was for his own use rather than for resale, and he was fined £12 for the thirty shillingsworth of meat taken. He told Seymour Collins, the stipendiary magistrate at West London Court in Southcombe Street, 'I'm sorry this has happened. I lost my job because of it. I have to look for another.' He gave his name as John Colmore and his address as Romford Street, Whitechapel. He omitted to mention a furniture shop in the Gloucester Road in which he had an interest.[22]

The conviction proved only of minor embarrassment, for in March that year he was reported to be making an anti-crime film with producer Michael Goodman and actress Patricia Kilcarriff. They were going to Dublin to research locations for a documentary, *The Jack Spot Story*. 'All I've got now to show for my gangster days are 300 stitches and a marked face. The only people who know that there is nothing in crime in the long run are people like me,' he told reporters.

Spot's old friend Sammy Ross was said to be advising on the film, which was to show that crime did not pay: 'I have had something like thirty years' gaol and I have been mixed up with the biggest villainies of twenty years. Now I have quit. My children go to good schools. I have made fortunes and I've lost them and the whole business frankly hasn't been worth the candle.'[23] The film, if made, was never released.

Spot was not long out of a job but it is ironic that, as a man who spent so much time championing the Jewish cause, he more or less ended his working career in Thomas Walls' bacon-packing factory in the old Pears Soap buildings near Isleworth station. Colin Clegg, who was working there after University, remembers him well:

[22] *Daily Telegraph*, 7 February 1962.
[23] *Daily Express*, 5 March 1962.

It was a very mixed group including recent West Indian immigrants, Mauritian Chinese, Republican Irish, Poles, Latvians, Austrians displaced by the war, some local 'hard nuts' and small-time villains, ex-merchant seamen, a Glasgow 'stick man' on the run and a very well educated elderly gentleman who had sheep-farmed in Australia and for whom we had to cover the heavy work.[24]

Spot, known to the crew as The Professor, fitted effortlessly into this mixed bunch, taking people at face value:

He was always well dressed once out of the factory boiler suit. He definitely was not severely depressed, only at times did he look a little despairing as he described the many injustices that he felt he had suffered over the years; and even then showed less rancour than most do these days over some trivial traffic incident.

Although there was no attempt by him to dominate the group, Spot was not universally popular. Clegg recalls that a number treated him with disdain, as he kept up a steady patter and stream of his stories which most thought he was inventing. Certainly his name was invented. He was now Colmore, claiming that he had taken the name from a Birmingham road sign when he was in the Midlands avoiding heat in London.

Although he was always saying that one day we would know who he was, he had no 'side' to him at all. He kept up an endless stream of stories and banter. He had a self-mocking sense of humour. On ever getting any ideas with the women again, his favourite crack was that he would run it under the cold tap.

As we sat on the stairs awaiting a shift change, he frequently reminisced about sitting on the tenement stairs in his boyhood, and his favourite phrase was 'nobody loves you like your mother'. He gave nightly performances of market spiels with packets of

---

[24] Letter from Colin Clegg to the author, 27 August 2002. I am most grateful to Mr Clegg for the time and trouble he took to help with this chapter.

bacon, showing how to count notes to spot any double folded ones, and bookies' tic-tac. These were hilarious and top grade entertainment. Even if I was the only audience he still gave it the whole works.

Physically he was running down:

He was continually describing all his wounds in detail, taking the top half of his boiler suit down and pulling his shirt up to show the stab wounds in the chest and in the arm etc. Not an easy manoeuvre but this never stopped him. He was always claiming to have been built like a lion when he was younger, but the shift of fat from thighs and shoulders to the midriff seen in middle-aged men left no trace of his former physique, and he had shrunk to about 5'10" tall.

Clegg was impressed with the way he coped with the work:

We worked three weekly rotating eight-hour shifts 6.30 a.m. to 2.30 p.m.; 2.30 to 10 p.m. and 10.30 to 6 p.m. Overtime meant that you worked on over and above your eight-hour shift and/or worked shifts on your two days off each week. I can never remember him slacking, skiving, complaining of being tired or being off sick. I had the definite impression that despite himself he enjoyed being a member of the crew and definitely knew the value of friendship. I have worked with many, many people since who were much more two-faced and manipulative of their colleagues than he.

Spot may not have been depressed but, at the time, he was certainly a lonely man:

He always spoke highly of Rita and the children. Repeating time and again that he had not deserved her and that he never knew why she had stuck by him like she had. This was not the usual talk you hear down a place like that and was always quite touching. He was completely genuine over this, and all bombast fell away when he was on the topic.

On one occasion he invited Clegg and a young Asian worker back to his flat:

> I just felt uneasy about the prospect so we did not go. He was very hurt and upset with us when we met him on the shift. No trace or threat of violence, but genuinely hurt. I felt a bit rotten as I thought he was lonely and just wanted some company, but it was all forgotten before the shift was over. The overriding impression being that he wanted friendship and acceptance more than anything. Although I realise now he may have been planning to set up another meat scam or something.

In 1963 Spot appeared on television repeating his earlier claim that, 'Don't kid yourself that the evil of Mafia flourishes only in America. Every terrible thing that you've read about happening over there happens here – every day.' Once more he was flatly contradicted by Bert Sparks, but again there was a great deal of truth in what he said.[25]

Shortly after that came Sparks' own downfall. Persuaded to have his memoirs ghosted for the *People*, he fell foul of the highly intelligent safebreaker and prison escaper Alfie Hinds – 'a most dangerous criminal' said the Lord Chief Justice, Lord Goddard – whom he had put away following the Maples robbery in 1953. Almost certainly Hinds was on the robbery and almost certainly Sparks fitted him up with dust in his trouser turn-ups and a few verbals. Hinds continually protested his innocence and made two highly publicised escapes, followed by interviews one of which was given to Duncan Webb. In his memoirs Sparks wrote that Hinds had been out-thought by the police and should stop complaining and take his punishment like a man. Hinds sued for libel. This was at a time when, following the Challenor inquiry, the Metropolitan Police was at one of its periodic low ebbs. When Sparks, during his cross-examination, put his hands over his face a voice in the public gallery called, 'Watch out! He's doing a Challenor.' Despite a most unfavourable summing-up

[25] *On the Braden Beat*, 6 October 1963.

Hinds was awarded £1,300. The Court of Appeal, however, refused to quash his conviction.[26] The law was later changed so that it became impossible to challenge a criminal conviction by way of a subsequent civil action.

Even decades after the slashing, Spot's name was still held in contempt. At the club Parker had in Inverness Terrace, his manager-cum-partner wanted to bar the former gangleader:

> We rented it from a man French Lou. Everyone came to that club including Jack. He turned up just after we started but Mickey said he wasn't to come in again. He'd grassed. I said no, it was Rita, but Mickey said, 'Tell him not to come in.' I wouldn't have it, but when it came to it he only appeared a few times. And that was 20 years after the trouble.

By the 1980s, however, Parker was in touch with Spot once again:

> Once Jack returned from Ireland he started going again to the Lyons Corner House at Marble Arch. It was a bit of a comedown from the Cumberland Hotel but that was where I met him. I'd heard he would be there regularly and so I went with the intention of meeting him again.

By now Parker's wife, Shirley, had a fashion shop in Brook Street: 'He used to come to Shirley's shop. I think he was a bit afraid of her. He'd stand around outside and then he'd come in a bit like a sheep.'

Spot was still newsworthy and he was photographed and interviewed when, wearing a neat grey suit and matching trilby, he appeared at the Bruno-Witherspoon fight weigh-in complaining of a touch of arthritis. He was also seen at a charity show at the Elephant and Castle and obliged the newspapers with his favourite joke, 'I've had three hundred stitches. The doctors ran out of thread so I put them in touch with my tailor.'

He had a deep razor slash scar running down from the side of

---

[26] Alfred Hinds, *Contempt of Court*; James Morton, *Gangland*.

his lips over his chin. And he was carrying a rolled umbrella. He had been at the races and spoken with the Duke of Norfolk. 'He always held me responsible for solving the problems of welshing.'[27]

Spot declined to appear on the highly successful BBC series *Underworld*, but appeared on a rival programme produced by Martin Short. Parker wanted to try to get money for his memoirs. 'I used to say, "Don't talk to them. Phone me first." But if Jack heard the £ sign his ears used to go up.' It is doubtful if given the restrictions on paying criminals for interviews he received very much. It was about this time that Parker finally lost touch with him:

> One day I rang him at his flat in the North End Road and there was just an answer machine. I went round to the flat and there was no reply on the entry phone and a woman there said she thought Jack's daughters had swagged him away. The BBC had been on at him to make a programme or take part in one and it was driving him mad. I never saw him again. I never found out where he'd gone.

How did it all go so wrong for Spot? Back in 1956 he gave an interview to a reporter from the *Sunday Times* lamenting his fall. Declining to give his former colleague due credit, he commented:

> I made Billy Hill. He wrote to me when he was in jail, wanted me to help him . . . so I gave him some clothes and made him my right-hand man. Then he got over the top of me. If it wasn't for me he'd never have got there. I should have shot Billy Hill. I really should. I'd have got 10 years for it but it would have made me happy and I'd be out now – laughing.

Another reason is also advanced by Parker: 'He was mean. He wasn't a good paymaster. Billy Hill was good at that. There was money in it for everyone. As for Jack he'd say, "I've got £100, you can have £5." People who come out of the slums need money and Jack never really appreciated that fact.'

[27] *Daily Mirror*, 3 October 1984.

Reg Kray confirms Spot's meanness:

> In the early 1950s when I was around twenty-one, I travelled up
> to Manchester with Jack, accompanied by George and Jimmy
> Wood. Spot had arranged a rendezvous at the Grand Hotel with
> the boss of a pac-a-mac company and came away from the meeting
> four grand richer. On the return journey to London by train, he
> handed me twenty-five pounds. As a novice to the business, I
> accepted the paltry sum with indignation but held my tongue –
> I was learning.[28]

Later, in retirement, Spot would admit his principal mistake, one
made by others before and after him: 'The papers. All that "King of
the Underworld" thing. It was the worst day's work I ever did.
Nobody even knew me before that and then suddenly everyone's
trying to put one on me. That was my mistake, Nipper, publicity.'[29]

His biographer, the pulp writer Hank Janson, perceptively thought
there were other, more fundamental, reasons for Spot's downfall: '[It]
was *not* caused by authority, Spot's downfall was caused by his own
inordinate pride, a touch of persecution mania and an unwilling-
ness to admit he could be bested.'[30]

What did provincial criminals think of Spot and Hill? Albert
Hattersley, the Northern safebreaker who once blew the door off a
police station, thought Hill was, 'Likeable but full of tricks. He was
dodgy. He'd throw in a body now and again.' Hattersley never worked
for him: 'He had good information but whatever business he put
up it was wages only. He got the bulk of it.'

The crime reporter Michael Jacobson thought little of Spot: 'I
knew Spotty well and he was never more than just a thug. He had
no initiative of his own. He was never a gang leader. Hill was.'[31]

On the other hand, the columnist Cassandra of the *Daily Mirror*
did not like Hill, writing that 'anybody who is affable and nice to

[28] Reg Kray, *Villains We Have Known*, pp. 38–9.
[29] Leonard Read, *Nipper Read, The Man Who Nicked the Krays*, p. 57.
[30] Hank Janson, *Jack Spot*, p. 191.
[31] Conversation with author.

Hill is making a great mistake.' Jack (Spot) Comer would agree.[32]

When it came to it, the difference between Spot and Hill was that Hill was clever and Spot was not. He was naïve. '"Jack Schmock", I used to call him,' says Parker, 'and he'd laugh.' Most importantly, in the 1950s it was essential to have police protection. Hill did; Spot did not. Nipper Read was convinced that Hill was protected:

> I have no doubt that during his career Hill had some very senior officers in his pocket and I don't think Spotty did. That was the difference between them. I was involved in the inquiry from the beginning and I never heard any senior officer saying 'Poor old Jack, my friend Jack'. In my mind, at that time, anybody who achieved a superiority in the criminal world had useful friends in the police.[33]

Parker portrays Spot as essentially a man with simple tastes:

> Jack loved a joke, particularly a Jewish joke. He liked going to the pictures as he called them. He wanted to go and live in Brighton but he used to say that his card had been marked and his life wouldn't be worth living if he tried to. He wasn't a card player; he wasn't a drinker. None of us really drank. A lot of Jewish people don't. He liked being at home. He was a power man. He wanted to be called the King, the Governor. I think that where Jack came down was he had to be the Governor. It was like the bookmaker Manny King. He had a slogan, 'There's only one King and that's Manny King'. As far as Jack was concerned he had to be the King, and second best to Billy Hill wasn't good enough. That's what it all came down to.

Did any of them have any good points? Without doubt, Spot was devoted to Rita and the children. Hill loved children. Dimes seems to have been a good family man, as does Darby Sabini.

What, if any, legacy did Spot, Hill and the others leave? Legislation on telephone tapping was a direct result of the tap on Billy Hill's

[32] *Daily Mirror*, 1 July 1957.
[33] Leonard Read, *Nipper Read, The Man Who Nicked the Krays*, p. 56.

phone. Hill himself could genuinely be described – certainly in his later life – as a criminal mastermind. Given that he was the planner and financier of two major robberies in 1952 and 1954, and was never again in the courts as a defendant until his death twenty years later, he demonstrated that there was an entirely different and new way to plan and execute a robbery and was held up as an example of how to avoid trouble.

Just how much control Spot did exercise is debatable. He claimed to have united the gangs from as far apart as Upton Park and Aldgate in the East, Forest Hill and the Elephant and Castle in the South, through to Islington, Shepherd's Bush and Clerkenwell.

Possibly he never even aspired to 'running' Soho, which at the time was synonymous with the 'Underworld', although he had clubs there and took a cut of £200 a week from another. He may have held court in the Galahad Club off the Tottenham Court Road and in the Cumberland Hotel, but overall he was a family man with a beautiful wife. Perhaps, as has been said, he was too happily married to be a proper gangleader. Yet at his peak he maintained a style reminiscent of the American gangsters of the 1930s.

Spot, when it came to it, left little in the way of legacy although had the machinations which went on in 1955 occurred at the time of the Royal Commission on Gaming there might have been a much bigger lobby for a Tote monopoly. Although his claims on behalf of the Jewish population of the East End were mainly lies, he did raise anti-Semitism in the public profile.[34] He promoted himself as championing Jewish causes, but he generally eschewed them if they did not benefit him financially. Even the shopkeepers he protected against the Mosley marches – if he did – paid for the privilege. As Parker says: 'After the war Jack was getting a pound or two every week from the stalls in Oxford Street as well as Petticoat Lane. Nobody didn't pay. They felt they was protected. All they was protected was against themselves.'

[34] *The Times*, 22 June 1956.

After the Second World War the Jewish Club 43 was founded to deal with the new generation of Fascists. Protests were held outside Mosley meetings and Fascists were generally harried, but the great anti-Fascist Spot played no part. 'There wasn't any money in it for him,' says Parker.

Nipper Read, commenting on the Krays, thought:

> Their predecessors Billy Hill and Jack Spot avoided publicity until they were almost at the end of their reigns as Kings of the Underworld, and only when they courted it did they realise what a blessing it had been to keep out of the public eye. I well remember Jackie Spot, just before he had been so grievously assaulted by Frankie Fraser and the others, bemoaning his fate to me saying, 'Nipper, it's all down to the papers. Nobody knew nothing about us until then.'

Read was trying to obtain information on the Twins at the time:

> Jack was now living in West London in much reduced circumstances and knew nothing. He told me how he had tried to teach the Twins how to get plenty of money without doing all the violence but they wouldn't listen. I thought that was a bit rich bearing in mind his predilection for choppers and hammers.[35]

Rita Comer died at the age of sixty on 10 September 1988 at the Charing Cross Hospital; she had been suffering from cancer for some time. Jack Colmore – aka Spot, Comer, Comar, Comor, Comacho and possibly other names – died on 12 March 1995 at Nazareth House, Isleworth. The causes of his death were certified as a cerebrovascular accident and immobility. He left no will, nor were letters of administration taken out in his case either. As he had wanted, some of his ashes were later scattered in Israel.

Of them all, it may be that the trusted lieutenant Albert Dimes with his close links to the American Mafia and gambling was, in the long term, the most influential. The Home Secretary's fine words about

[35] Leonard Read, *Nipper Read, The Man Who Nicked the Krays*, p. 92.

there never being another Jack Spot turned out to be pretty hollow, although they may have applied to the racecourses. Changes in gaming legislation shifted power away from the racecourses and into the betting offices. For a time there were threats against smaller bookmakers, but it soon became a multi-million-pound operation. Despite those fine words, gangsters flourished in London in much the same way as they always had. The Krays came and went and in turn their mantles were assumed by others more shadowy but, in financial terms at least, much more successful than Spot if not Hill. Today's gangsters have metamorphosed into businessmen and crime into a multi-billion-pound industry. Now, as at the end of *Animal Farm*, it is difficult to distinguish the men from the pigs. Today's criminals do not give interviews nor appear too often at quasi-charity functions, but they are immensely rich and powerful. Hill, Spot, Dimes, Harry White, Billy Howard and Darby Sabini – who probably never travelled further than Doncaster in his life – would simply not recognise things.

Bibliography

Bebbington, W., *Rogues Go Racing* (n.d.) London, Good & Betts.

Bresler, F., *Reprieve* (1965) London, George G. Harrap & Co.

Browne, Douglas G., *Sir Travers Humphreys* (1953) London, Harrap.

Caminada, J., *Twenty-Five Years a Detective* (1983) Warrington, Prism Books.

Campbell, D., *The Underworld* (1994) London, BBC Books.

Cannon, E., *Gangster's Lady* (1993) London, Yellow Brick Press.

Cannon, J., *Tough Guys Don't Cry* (1983) London, Magnus Books.

Capstick, J., *Given in Evidence* (1960) London, John Long.

Cartwright, F.C., *G-Men of the G.P.O.* (1937) London, Sampson, Low & Co.

Chapman, E., *Free Agent* (1955) London, Allan Wingate.

Chibnall, S., *Law and Order News* (1977) London, Tavistock.

Chinn, C., *Better Betting with a Decent Fellow* (1991) Hemel Hempstead, Harvester Wheatsheaf.

Clarkson, W., *Hit 'em Hard* (2000) London, HarperCollins.

Connor, M., *The Soho Don* (2002) Edinburgh, Mainstream.

Darbyshire, N. and Hilliard, B., *The Flying Squad* (1993) London, Headline.

Docker, N., *Norah, The Autobiography of Lady Docker* (1959) London, W.H.Allen.

Donaldson, W., *Brewer's Rogues, Villains, Eccentrics* (2002) London, Cassell.

Fabian, F., *Fabian of the Yard* (1950) London, Naldrett Press.

—*London after Dark* (1954) London, Naldrett Press.

Fido, M., *The Krays – Unfinished Business* (1999) London, Carlton.

Ford, F., *King of Crooks* (n.d.) London, W.H.Allen.

Fraser, F. and Morton, J., *Mad Frank* (1994) London, Warner Books.

—*Mad Frank and Friends* (1999) London, Warner Books.

—*Mad Frank's Diary* (2001) London, Virgin Books.

—*Mad Frank's London* (2002) London, Virgin Books.

—*Mad Frank's Britain* (2003), London, Virgin Books.

Frost, J., *Flying Squad* (1948) London, Rockliff.

Goodman, D., *Villainy Unlimited* (1957) London, Elek Books.

Greeno, E., *War on the Underworld* (1960) London, John Long.

Hart, E.T., *Britain's Godfather* (1993) London, True Crime Library.

Hill, B., *Boss of Britain's Underworld* (1955) The Naldrett Press.

Hinds, A., *Contempt of Court* (1966) London, The Bodley Head.

Janson, H., *Jack Spot – Man of a Thousand Cuts* (1958) London, Alexander Moring.

Kelland, G., *Crime in London* (1986) London, The Bodley Head.

Kray, Reg., *Villains We Have Known* (1993) Leeds, NK. Publications.

Leach, J., *Sods I Have Cut on the Turf* (1961) London, Victor Gollancz.

Lee, J. and Smith, R., *Inside the Kray Family* (2001) London, Carlton Books.

Lewis, M., *Ted Kid Lewis* (1990) London, Robson.

Linnane, F., *London's Underworld* (2003) London, Robson Books.

Lucas, N., *Britain's Gangland* (1969) London, W.H.Allen.

McDonald, B., *Elephant Boys* (2000) Edinburgh, Mainstream.

Magee, B., *Clouds of Glory: a childhood in Hoxton* (2003) London, Jonathan Cape.

Montarron, M., *Histoire du Milieu* (1969) Paris, Librairie Plon.

Montgomery Hyde, H., *Norman Birkett* (1964) London, Hamish Hamilton.

Morton, J., *Gangland* (1992) London, Warner Books.

—*Bent Coppers* (1993) London, Warner Books.

—*A Calendar of Killing* (1997) London, Warner Books.

—*East End Gangland* (2001) London, Warner Books.

—*Gangland Today* (2003) London, Time Warner.

Murphy, R., *Smash and Grab* (1993) London, Faber and Faber.

Narborough, F., *Murder on my Mind* (1959) London, Allan Wingate.

O'Connor, J., *The Eleventh Commandment* (1976) St Peters Port, C.I., Seagull.

Owen, F., *The Eddie Chapman Story* (1953) London, Allan Wingate.

Parker, R., *Rough Justice* (1981) London, Fontana.

Pearson, J., *The Profession of Violence* (1972) London, Weidenfeld & Nicholson.

Pizzichini, L., *Dead Men's Wages* (2002) London, Picador.

Read, N. and Morton, J., *Nipper Read, The Man who nicked the Krays* (2002) London, Time Warner.

Samuel, R., *East End Underworld* (1981) London, Routledge & Kegan Paul.

Scott, P., *Gentleman Thief* (1995) London, HarperCollins.

Simpson, A.W.B., *In the Highest Degree Odious* (1992) Oxford, Oxford University Press.

Sparks, H., *Iron Man* (1964) London, John Long.

Sparks, R., *Burglar to the Nobility* (1961) London, Arthur Barker.

Spurling, M., *A Jewel Fell out of my Pocket* (1997) London, Little, Brown.

Thomas, D., *An Underworld at War* (2003) London, John Murray.

Thorp, A., *Calling Scotland Yard* (1954) London, Allan Wingate.

Tietjen, A., *Soho* (1956) London, Allan Wingate.

Walsh, P., *Gang War* (2003) Bury, Milo Books.

Ward, H. and Gray, T., (1974) London, Hodder & Stoughton.

Webb, D., *Line up for Crime* (1956) London, Frederick Muller.

Wickstead, B., *Gangbuster* (1985) London, Futura.

Wilkinson, L., *Behind the Face of Crime* (1957) London, Frederick Muller.

Selected articles etc.

Jack Aitken, 'Can a Gangster make Good?' in *Illustrated*, 6 September 1958.

Gerald Byrne, 'Frightened men all over Britain' in *Empire News*, 2 October 1955.

—'The Truth About Racing Gangs' in *Empire News*, 9 October 1955.

Chapman, E., 'Flamingo. . . . all the answers' in *Sunday Chronicle*, 18 July 1954 *et seq.*

Rita Comer, 'They call me a Gangster's Moll' in *Sunday Pictorial*, 11 December 1955.

Alan Hamilton, 'They made an excuse and stayed' in *The Times*, 17 October 1981.

A.W. Moss, 'The American Mobster who planned to take over London's Gangland' in *True Detective*, January 1996.

'One Man's Family' in *Philadelphia Magazine*, September 1969.

Pauline Peters, 'Jack Spot' in *Sunday Times Magazine*, 8 August 1965.

'Soho – Albert Dimes takes the lid off' in *People*, 2 October 1955.

'Spot – the Last Gangster' in *Sunday Chronicle*, 2 October 1955.

Jack Spot, 'My Life as a Gangster' in *Daily Sketch*, 31 September 1955 *et seq.*

Index

Abbott and Costello 169
Abnit, Sammy 97
Abrahams, Harry 242
Ackerman, Bill 7–8
Ackroyd, Thomas 33
Ady, Alfred Charles 164–5, 166
Ainsworth, William 110
Aldgate Fruit Exchange 83–4, 85
Aldgate Mob 26–7, 46
Alexandra Park 28
Ambridge, George Alfred 137
Ambrose, Frederick 46
Andrews, Allen 188
Andrews, Freddy 137–8, 141,
    149–50
Andrews, Rev. Basil Claude
    Hudson 186, 187, 189–202,
    215, 252
Anglo-American Fidelity 147
anti-Semitism 79, 80, 91, 92–3,
    104, 115, 132, 168–9, 241,
    290

Ascot racecourse internment camp
    21, 70, 87
Ashe, Jack 80
Associated Newspapers 272

Back, Patrick 135
Bailey, Mickey 7–8, 11, 242
Baker, Stanley 277
Ball, George ('Square Georgie') 17,
    76–7, 110, 141
Balmer, Herbert 160–61
Bannen, Ian 3
Bar Council 161, 245, 246, 255
Barry, Dave 126–7
Barry, Mr Justice 254
Batchelor, Meston 3
Beach, Norman 199
Beamish, Bill 145, 148, 149–50
Beaverbrook Newspapers 256
Bebbington, William 47
Beck, Det. Sgt Shirley 196
Beech, Albert 153

Belan, Johnny 123

Beland, William John 32

Belgian Johnny 123–4

Bell, Sgt James 220

Bellamy Bestford & Co. 235

Bellson, Sammy 162, 176, 179, 203, 215, 264

Bennett, Porky 66, 170

Benneyworth, Thomas 'Monkey' ('The Trimmer') 26, 41

Benstead, Billy 109, 110, 161–2

Bentley, Father Frederick 233

Beresford, Walter 23, 34–5

Berg, Jack 'Kid' 5

Bergmann, Eileen 133, 134

Bergmann, Richard 133

Bestford, E.J. 178

Bethnal Green Gang 47

Betting and Gaming Act (1960) 189

Beveridge, Det. Chief Supt 93–5, 209

Bielby, Anne 241

Bigland, Reuben ('Telephone Jack') 29

Birkett, Sir Norman KC 49, 256

Birnhak, Sol 9

Biron, Sir Chartres 10–11

Blackshirts *see* British Union of Fascists

Blitz, Barney *see* Emden, Buck

Bloom, John 265

Blueball, Moishe *see* Goldstein, Moishe

Blundell, R.H. 221

Blythe, William Patrick (Billy) 171–2, 173, 212, 218–20, 227, 228, 233–4, 244–6, 250, 253, 256

Boal, Billy 267

Boffa, Paul 32–3

Botolph's Club *see* Aldgate Fruit Exchange

Bottomley, Horatio 29

Bowater, Sir Frank 62

Bowen, Commander Basil 15–16

Brahams, Joe (father of Harry Abrahams) 242

Brett, Jim (aka Stevens), 32–3

Brindle, Eva (née Fraser) 176

Brindle, Jimmy 176

Brinks-Mat robbery 277

British Union of Fascists (BUF) 54–9

Brixton prison 50, 69, 179, 266

Broad Mob 26

Broadmoor 172, 173

Brown, Anthony 228

Brummagen Boys 23, 27–9, 31, 34, 35, 38, 88

Bruno, Angelo 271

Bruno–Witherspoon fight 286

Bryan, Harry 76–7

Buggy, 'Scotch' Jack 277–8

Buonacore, Sebastian (aka Vesta) 177, 181–2, 184

Burbridge, Inspector 49

Burge, Bella 22

Burgess, Guy 195

Burke, Shifty 112

Bushell, Ted 205

Butler, Tommy 219–20, 256

Camden Town Gang 17

Caminada, Jerome 20

Campbell, Sam 157

Cannon, Joe 208–12

    Tough Guys Don't Cry 208–9

Capocci, Harry 72, 74
Capone, Al 114, 207, 262
Capone, Ralph 'Bottles' 114
Capstick, Det. Chief Supt 12–13
Carbo, Frankie 114
Carbone, Paul 140
Cardozo, Carmen 26
Careless, Det. Sgt Charles Sidney
    131, 132–4, 173
Cariello, Niccolo (aka Joe Leon)
    72–3
Carlton Browne of the FO 3
Carney, Patrick 215–16
Carter, Johnny 119, 212
Caruana, George 126, 128
Carver, H. W. 56
Cassegrain, François 140
Cassels, J. D. KC 47, 233
Cerdan, Marcel 114–15, 169
Challenor Inquiry 285
Channel Islands 144
Chapman, Betty 149
Chapman, Eddie 119, 131, 141–5,
    147–50, 231
Charles, Mr Justice 16
Chatham, George 'Taters' 122–3,
    161
Chelmsford prison 77
Chester, Charlie 106
Cheyney, Peter 45
Christian, Linda 114, 169
Christiansen, Arthur 155
Church Commissioners 194
Civil Aviation Transport
    Organisation 44
Clark, Hubert Edward 164
Clerkson, Wensley 59, 60, 130
Clegg, Colin 282–5
'Clynes, Sam' 82–3

Cobden, Abraham 164
Cohen, Frank 10
Cohen, Harry 10, 30
Cohen, Jackie 10, 105–6
Cohen, Maurice (Moishe) (aka
    Major Collins) 10, 55
Cohen, Nat 5
Coleman, Neville 196
Collette, Joseph 72, 74
Collins, Jackie 125
Collins, Seymour 282
Colmore, John (Jacob) *see* Spot,
    Jack
Colonna, Jacques 140
Colonna, Jean 140
Comacho, Alexander 5, 6, 79
Comacho, Irving 5, 6
Comacho, John *see* Spot, Jack
Comacho, Piza 5, 6
Comacho, Rebecca 5
Comacho, Rifka 5, 7, 79
Combinatie 139, 141
Comer, John *see* Spot, Jack
Comer, John (son of Jack Spot) 9,
    61
Comer, Marion Margaret
    (daughter of Jack Spot) 102,
    168, 194
Comer, Rachelle Alexis (daughter
    of Jack Spot) 102, 136, 195
Comer, Rita (wife of Jack Spot)
    101–2, 105, 113, 168, 177,
    188, 194–6, 198–9, 201, 203,
    210, 211, 213–17, 222, 225,
    227–8, 230, 233, 236–43, 258,
    280, 284, 286, 289, 290: death
    291
Commissioner's Orders in Writing
    85

Communists: battle of Cable Street and 55, 56, 58–9; Stepney Borough party 55–6
Conley, Maurice 159
Connelly, Bert 72
Connor, Mrs P. 136
Connor, Robert ('Cassandra') 234, 248, 288–9
Constabulary Commissioners 20
Cook, Sidney 110
Cooney, Selwyn 261, 262
Cooper, Henry 48
Cooper, Mary (aka Kustanci) 166–7
Corallo, Anthony 'Ducks' 271
Cornell, George 268
Cornish, Chief Inspector Fred 222
Cortesi, Augustus 35–8
Cortesi, Enrico 23, 35–8
Cortesi, George 35–8
Cortesi, Paul 35–8
Cortesis 23, 36–7, 41
da Costa, Ettie 82
Costello, 'Uncle' Frank 141, 146, 281
Crane, Reginald 151, 153
Cresteff, Vilasar 265
Crews, Jean 156–7, 158
Critchley, Bobby 106
Crockfords gaming club 260, 263
Croydon Airport bullion robbery 43–5, 48, 50, 71, 275
Cullis, Stan 236
Curzon, Lady Cynthia 55
Curzon, Lord 55
Cussen, E.J.P. 180

Daily Express 38, 155–6, 207, 215, 218, 221, 223, 227, 241, 252

Daily Mail 189, 194, 198, 252, 272
Daily Mirror 113, 205, 241, 248, 266, 288
Daily Sketch 84, 112, 189–90, 191–2, 193, 194, 199, 207
Daily Worker 57
Daniels, Billy 105, 168–9, 237
Daniels, Franny 109–10, 141, 147, 218, 225, 228, 278
Darling, Mr Justice 25, 37–8
Dartmoor prison 78
Davies, J.A. 49
Davies, Neville, 236–7
Davies, Stan 268
Dawson, George 141
Dawson, Sgt 29
Day, Albie 66
Dean, Man Mountain 111
Defferary, John McCarthy 46
Delew, Jack 32
Demmy, Gus 81
Dennis, Ginger 244
De Silva, Charles 262–3
Diamond, Alice 14
Diamond, Bill 169–70
Dido, George 39
Dimes (aka Dimeo), Albert ('Italian Albert') 1–2, 64, 72–5, 89, 107, 169, 173–4, 206, 208–9, 218–19, 262, 263, 265–6, 268–72, 280, 289, 291–2: bookmakers' pitches, racing and 1–2, 203–4, 208, 222, 259, 268; fight with Spot and after 1–2, 39, 174–85, 187–8, 190, 191, 195, 199, 203, 225, 229, 247, 268; and attack on Spot 210–11; and Spot attack on

Falco 222–3, 225, 226–7; and
Patrick Marrinan 245, 247–8,
253–4, 256; end as top
gangland figure 259; and
Holford case 265–6; Krays and
268, 277; later years 268–9,
270–71; horse doping and
269–70; US connections
270–72, 291–2; death of 272,
277–8
Dimes, Victor 73
Dimmock, Phyllis 192
Distleman, 'Big Hubby' 73, 159,
196, 200
Distleman, 'Little Hubby' 73–4
Divall, ex Chief Det. Insp. Tom
10, 28, 34–5, 51, 52
Dobbs, Johnny 279
Docker, Lady Nora 205–6
Docker, Sir Bernard 205–6
Dodson, Recorder Sir Gerald 74–5,
78, 109, 138, 191
Donaghue, Albert 242, 268
Donoghue, Steve 29
Donovan, Mr Justice 213
Doralli, Louisa 36
Douglas, Archie 31
Dowling, Geoffrey 221
Downs, Walter 128
Drake, George 33–4
Droy, George and Trixie 32, 33
Du Cann, Richard 240
du Rose, Det. Insp. John 221
Dunlop, James 222
Durand, Victor QC 223, 224,
226–7, 231, 266

Eastcastle Street Great Mailbag
Robbery, 120–23, 152, 166, 175

East End Jews 26, 28
Eden Social Club 40–41
Edinburgh, Philip, Duke of 148
'Edgware Road Sam' 79, 80, 168
Edgware Road Teddy Boys 218
Edwards, Peter 240
Elephant & Castle Boys (aka
Elephant Gang) 26, 45, 71,
123, 204, 259
Elizabeth II, Queen 148
Ellul, Philip 128
Emden, Buck 39–40, 47
Emmanuel, Edward 30, 31, 38,
40–41, 50
Emmanuel, Philip 30
Empire News 234
Esmé 139
Evening News 39
Evening Standard 155

Fabian, Robert 168, 207
Falco, Tommy 61, 221, 222–5,
226, 235
Fallon, Rocky 236
Farmer, William 42
Fascism 54–61, 225, 241, 290–91:
see also British Union of
Fascists; Mosley, Oswald
Featherstonehaugh, Jesse 159
Fenton, Horace 47
Festival of Britain (1951) 119
Fine, Max 271
Fineberg, 'Fatty' 80
First World War 20, 21, 22, 23,
25, 29, 55, 234
Fish, Donald 109
Flamingo (ex *Fourth Lady*) 141,
145–6, 147–9
Flanagan, Mrs E. 136

Fleischer, 'Fair Hair' Eddie *see*
Fletcher, Eddie
Fleming, Peter 159
Fletcher, Eddie 72, 90
Flying Squad 19, 25, 38, 42, 109,
123, 132, 152, 276
Flynn, Paddy 44
Ford, Freddy 102–4
Ford, James 25, 30, 38, 42, 45
Forrest, Elliott 139–41
Forty Thieves (shoplifting gang)
13–14
Fox, Big Benny 106
Francis, Connie 241
Franks, Joseph 72
Fraser, Frank 17, 66, 75, 77,
88–9, 90, 107, 110, 119, 123,
125, 134, 145, 157–60, 162–3,
171–3, 176–7, 179, 184, 204,
206, 208–9, 210–11, 212–13,
215–7, 225–8, 230, 234–5,
244–5, 247, 253, 256, 266–7,
278–81, 291
Fratellanza Club 23, 28–9, 36,
37
Frater, Mark 47–8
Frenchies, the *see* Cortesis
Frett, Dido 212
Frygh, Matthew 33

Gale, Police Commissioner Sir
Philip 57, 58
gaming 2, 71–2, 81–2, 83–6, 88,
97–9, 100, 103–4, 127,
130–31, 168, 204, 236,
239–40, 259–60, 263, 271–2,
292: legislation 85, 290
Gaming Act (1960) 85
Garfath, Peter 'Pooky' 260

Gilbert, Fred (aka Clancy) 21, 27,
30, 31–2, 45
Gilbert, John 33
Ginicoli, Angelo (aka George
Thomas) 25
Glinski, Christopher 185–6,
199–201
Glyn-Jones, Mr Justice 180
Goddard, Lord Chief Justice 83,
213, 217, 233, 241, 285
Gold, Lilian 280–81
Goldstein, Moishe (Smokey) (aka
Blueball, Blueboy) 6, 7, 59, 62,
84, 110–11, 127, 136, 190,
195–6, 198, 276
Goller, Billy 89, 91–2
Goodman, Michael 282
Grade, Leslie 5
Grade, Lew 5
Gray, Danny 50
Great Train Robbery 267, 278
Green Goods swindle 102–3
Greeno, Chief Supt Edward 132,
143, 192, 194, 237
Greenwood, Anthony MP 269
Gregory, Recorder Sir Holam 63
greyhound racing 2, 42–3, 73, 80,
87–8, 89, 119, 160
Griffiths-Jones, Mervyn 247,
248–50, 255
Gross, Harry 99
Guerin, Eddie 14
Gyp, Jack 120

Hackney Gang 21, 45
Haigh, John George 157
Halkin, Hall 62
Hall, Gus 23
Hamilton, Alan 275

Hammersmith Boys 204
Handley, Harry/Henry *see* Sabini, 'Harryboy'
Hannam, Det. Supt 189
Harding, Arthur 88
Harding, Lawrence Edward 15–16
Hardy, G.L. 47
Harringay greyhound stadium 21, 87
Harris, Benjamin 240
Harris, George 22
Harris, Girchan 38
Harris, John 240
Harvey, Robert 27
Hattersley, Albert 19, 231, 288
Hayward family 107
Heath, Neville 200
Heathrow Airport Robbery 108–17, 122, 141, 152, 218, 275
Heilbron, Rose QC 180–83, 188
Helliwell, Arthur 112, 281
Hemming, William 133
Henderson, Edith 193
Henderson, Michael 141, 145
Henry, Divisional Det. Insp. John 49
Hesketh-Wright, Mildred 83
Hickey, William 207
Higgins, Det. Supt Robert 94–5
Highball Club 239–40
Hill, Aggie 96, 122, 124, 167–8, 170, 171, 208–9, 229–30, 261
Hill, Archie 104, 119, 223
Hill, Billy 2–3, 9–10, 12–19, 20, 29, 43, 87, 88, 96–101, 102, 104, 106–7, 112, 115, 132, 135–8, 146–7, 166–7, 170, 172, 188, 204, 210, 221, 224, 229, 234, 235, 241, 258, 262–3, 267, 274, 275, 277, 278, 287, 289, 292: memoirs, *Boss of Britain's Underworld* 2, 3, 9–10, 15, 68, 82, 93–4, 96, 97, 100, 118, 121, 122, 127, 135, 206–7, 231; and Spot 9–10, 12, 93–4, 100, 103–4, 106, 108, 124, 132, 146, 167, 179, 218, 228, 287, 289; childhood, early years 12–13, 14; first burglaries and arrests 14–18; Portland Borstal and birching 15–18; Frank Fraser and 17, 75, 77, 119, 280; smash-and-grab expertise, robberies, safebreaking 18–19, 75–8, 85–6, 104, 106–7; describes himself 18, 86, 150–51; racecourses and 24, 208; on the Sabinis 35, 43; Second World War crime 68, 75–8; Dartmoor 78; RAF 78; gaming 85–6, 94–5, 97, 100, 150, 260; and police 94–5, 118–19, 289; end of Whites 93–4, 96; Aggie Hill and 96, 122, 124, 167, 170, 171; parachute silk robbery 96–7; to S. Africa 97–100; and New Cabinet Club 100–101, 124; clubs, protection rackets 103–4, 106–7, 122, 150, 190, 240–41; anti-Semitism and 104; Heathrow Airport 'disaster' 108, 110; Eastcastle Street robbery and 120–23; debt collecting 124; to N. Africa 124, 138; contract killing and 124–5; slashes Tommy Smithson 127,

Hill, Billy – *cont'd*
129; and 'Gypsy' Riley 123–5, 136, 167–8, 170–71, 246–7, 268, 279–80; smuggling by 138–42, 145–6, 147, 150, 169; Lincoln's Inn robbery and 150–54, 231; and Duncan Webb 150, 153–4, 155, 157–9, 161–2, 190, 205, 218, 222–3, 230–32; and Patrick Marrinan 159–60, 161–3, 167, 218–20, 225–6, 244–57 *passim*, 259; in ascendance 167–8; unwanted in New Zealand, Australia and S. Africa 170–71; semi-retired 204; and Lady Docker 205–6; and attack on Spot 209–13, 217–19, 220; appearance 211, 217; and Spot's slashing of Tommy Falco 225–8, 229–30; the Krays and 258, 259–60, 263–4; abdication as Boss of Britain's Underworld 259, 263; antiques and 260–61; Selwyn Cooney and 261–2; Holford case and 265–6; Great Train Robbery, suspicion of 267; later years 268, 279–80; and Diana relationship 279–80; death 279–80; opinions on 288–90, 291; *see also* Dimes, Albert; Hill, Archie; Hill, Dolly; Hill, Maggie; Sabini, Darby; Spot, Jack
Hill, Dolly 14
Hill, Maggie ('Baby Face', Queen of the Forty Elephants) 12–13, 17
Hinds, Alfie 159, 217, 285–6
Hinga, Mrs Kaszia 240

Hogan, Terry 123
Holder, Eva 100
Holford, Celeste 265
Holford, Christine 264–5
Holford, Harvey Leo 264–7
Holford, Karen 266
Holloway prison 128, 196, 228
Horne, Percy 279
Horricky, Charlie 88
Howard, Billy (the Soho Don) 66, 104, 119, 176, 270, 277, 292
horse-doping 269–70
Hoxton Baths 22
Hoxton Mob 21, 24, 26, 45, 47
Hughes, Edward/Teddy ('Odd Legs') 3, 17, 77–8, 109, 122
Hume, Cynthia 157–8, 275: *see also* Webb, Cynthia
Hume, Donald 157–8, 275
Humez, Charles 115
Humphreys, Jimmy 260
Hunt, Jimmy 142–3
Hutton, Dick 105–6
Hyams, Alec 183
Hyams, Bertha 174, 182, 183
Hyams, Hyman 182–3
Hynes, James 82–3

Illustrated 241
Isaacs, David 52
Islington Mob 116
Italian faction 1–2, 173–4, 235, 278: *see also* Dimes, Albert; Marsh, Bert; Sabinis
Italian Mob *see* Sabinis
Itkin, Herbert 271–2

Jackson, Johnny 170
Jacob, Hyman 62

Jacobson, Michael 288
James, Roy 278
Janson, Hank 3, 281, 288
Jeacock, Thomas 90
Jewish Club 43 291
'JMD' (aka Beaumont, *Evening
    News*) 39
Jockey Club 31, 101, 131
Johnson, Francis 44
Johnstone, Nancy 44
Josephs, Sammy 100, 104, 108
Joynston Hicks, William 42

Kaminitsky, Dick (aka Dick Duke)
    271
Kankus, Solly (aka Solly the Turk)
    7, 8, 81
Kelland, Gilbert 85
Kelly, George 181
Kelly, Ray 170
Kemsley Newspapers 234
Kennedy, William 226
Kent, James 151
Kilcarriff, Patricia 282
Kimber, Billy 23–4, 26–8, 34–5
Kimberley, Fred 33, 34
King, Manny 289
King's Cross Gang 51
Kirby, Det. Insp. John 203
Kleintz, Harry 82–3
Kosky, Abe 79, 80, 83, 92, 112
Kray Twins 7, 72, 122, 171–2,
    173, 177, 242, 258–9, 262,
    263–4, 268, 277, 291, 292;
    Reggie 241, 259–60, 263–4,
    268, 276, 277, 288; Ronnie
    234
Kray, Charlie 264, 268
Kurasch, Hyman 102

Langham, George 30, 38
Lansky, Meyer 114, 271
Lawrence, Chick 2
Leach, Jack 51
Lederman, Sammy 72–3, 237
Lee, Chief Supt Robert 86, 121–2,
    151–2
Leon, Joe *see* Cariello, Niccolo
Lesnevich, Gus 115
Lever, Solomon 134
Levine, Jack (aka Maurice
    Fireman) 39
Levy, David 28–9, 88
Levy, Joe 21
Levy, John 151
Levy, Moses (Moey) 29, 87–8
Levy, R.F. QC 135
Lewes prison 142, 266, 270
Lewis, Abraham 278
Lewis, Ted 'Kid' 5, 62–4
Lincoln, Ellis 161, 235, 238
Lincoln, F. Ashe 161, 247, 249–50
Lincoln prison 234
Lincoln's Inn Fields bullion
    robbery 150–54, 231
Lipton, Marcus MP 245
Liverpool Cameo Murder case 181
'Liverpool Jack' 80
'Liverpool Mike' 168
Lloyd George, David 245
Locke, Joseph 106
Lockett, James 13
Loggerenberg, Dirk van 98–9
London Airport bullion robbery
    see Heathrow Airport Robbery
'London Alf' 80
Loren, Sophia 241
Luciano, Lucky 141
Lucy, Joe 67

Lugeon, Micheline 265
Lunies gang 23–4
Lustig, 'Count' Victor 262
Lyons, Patsy 212

McDermott, Bobby (King of the
    Barrowboys) 106, 212
McDonald, Brian 123, 175
MacDonough, Peter 195, 196,
    197–8
MacGarry, Frederick 218, 253–4,
    255
McGrath, Paddy 107
Maclean, Donald 195
MacMahon, Det. Insp. Philip
    219–20
MacMillan, John 109
Machin, Teddy 66, 91, 100, 104,
    108, 109, 114, 276
Mack, Thomas 25, 33, 48, 49, 73
Mafia 113–14, 141, 271, 279,
    285, 292
Maffia, Arthur 111
Maffia, Tony ('Magpie') 111
Mahon, Chief Supt Guy 152, 153
Main, John 240
Maidstone prison 46, 70
Malone, Willie 264
Mancini, Antonio 'Babe' 49, 65,
    69–70, 72–4
Mannings, Det. Chief Insp.
    200–201, 221–2, 225
Maples robbery (1953) 285
Margolis, Harry 32–3
Marks, Jack ('Milky') 80
Marlowe, Anthony QC 197
Marrinan, Patrick Aloysius
    159–63, 167, 179, 180,
    213–20, 259: downfall 244–57;

disbarred 250; appeal 252–6;
    see also Hill, Billy
Marrinan, Carmel 249, 252
Marsh, Bert (aka Papa Pasquale)
    21, 25, 45, 48–50, 71, 100,
    173, 174, 176–7, 179, 182,
    183–4, 208, 225, 278–9
Marshall Hall, Sir Edward KC 40
Maskelyne, Jasper 144
Mathew, Sir Theobald 228–30
Mathews, Valetta Mary 16
Maxim, Joey 115
Mazzardo, Silvio ('Shonk') 44
Meadows, Harry 259
Mella, Tony 119, 226
Mellor, J.L. 168
Mercado, Sid (aka Sid Kiki)
    224–5, 226
Messina brothers 69, 118, 128,
    158, 159, 230, 232
Metropolitan Police 189, 285
Micallef, Anthony 232
Milmo, Mr Justice Helenus 234–5
Mills, Freddie 97, 115
Mitchell, Charlie 270
Modernaires Club 167, 170
Molloy, Rita *see* Comer, Rita
Molloy, Sadie 238
Monte Columbo, Camillo 48, 50
Monte Columbo, Massimino 48–9
Monte Columbo, Nestor 48
Moore, George 31, 33, 39
Moran, Tommy 44, 58
Morocco, Sultan of 138, 147, 149
Morris, Malcolm QC 265–6
Morrison, Herbert 245
Morton, Annie 192
Mosley, Sir Oswald 54–9, 63, 168,
    290, 291

Mullins, Arthur 'Dodger' 47–8, 104
Murder Incorporated 82, 83, 114
Murnaghan, Mr Justice 219–20
Murphy, Patrick (Patsy) 116, 141, 148
Murphy, Robert 158, 160
Murtagh, Dennis 181
Muzziotti, Dominique 138–9, 140
Myrdle Street School 5

Napoletano, Jimmy 274
Nappi, Tony 176
Nash family 261–2
Nash, J. Robert
    Encyclopaedia of Organized Crime 83
Nash, Jimmy 261–2
Nash, Ronnie 261
Neill, Jimmy ('Little Jimmy') *see* Cooney, Selwyn
Neville, Arnold 97–9, 171
New Cabinet Club 100–101, 124, 167, 261
Newcastle Fred (bookmaker) 189
Newman, Thomas 88
Newman, Wassl 66
News of the World 133, 134
Noad-Johnston, Countess Thelma Madeleine (aka Black Maria, Black Orchid) 164–6
Noad-Johnston, Count J.E. 165
Norfolk, Duke of 115–16, 287
Nott-Bower, Sir John 189

O'Brien, John 44
O'Connor, James (Ginger) 137–8
Odhams Press Ltd 232
Official Secrets Act 245

Oliva, Jacques 140
Olive, Johnny 236
Olive, Ronnie 236
Orgen, 'Little Augie' 82, 83
Ormerod, Mr Justice 200–201
O'Rourke, Sgt Major Michael VC 39
Osmond, Frank Henry ('Taffy') 9
O'Sullivan, Tim 92
Owens, Sybil 192, 193

Paley, 'Nylon' Sid 139
Paolini, Antoine (aka 'Planche', 'The Board') 138–9, 140
Parker, Gerry 3–4, 7, 10, 59, 64–5, 66, 79, 81, 85, 104, 105–6, 111–12, 115, 123, 125–7, 132, 136, 146, 159, 176, 179, 201, 203, 235, 239–40, 276, 277–8, 286, 287, 289, 290–91
Parker, Shirley 286
Parkhurst prison 83: riot at 281
Paull, Recorder Gilbert 273
Payne, Prison Officer 50
Pearson, John 171–2, 258
    The Profession of Violence 171
People 112, 151, 153, 155, 157, 226, 232, 235, 251, 254, 275, 285
Perkoff, Bernie 177–8, 179, 195, 198
Peters, Morrie 53
Peter the Painter 79
Phillips, Al ('Aldgate Tiger') 114
Phillips, John Thomas 30, 38
Photographic Equipment Ltd 272
Pizzichini, Lilian 260, 276
Platts-Mills, John 234, 235

police 94–5, 285–6: bribery and corruption 104, 189, 260, 264; verbals 218–19, 285; *see also* Hill, Billy; Spot, Jack
Police and Criminal Evidence Act (1984) 218–19
Portland Borstal 15–17, 208
Powell, Dennis 142
Power, Reginald 262–3
Power, Tyrone 114, 169
Prevention of Crime Act (1953) 131
Prohibition 68
Prosecution of Offences Acts 156
prostitution 2, 69, 79–80, 103, 118, 128, 174, 232, 239

Quirke, Brendan 254

Racehorse Bookmakers and Backers Protection Association 30–33, 37
racecourses, point-to-points 1–2, 4, 43, 47, 73, 87–8, 208, 274: welshing 10, 115, 287; pitches, protection and violence 20–27, 36–9, 41–3, 47, 90–91, 93, 105, 169–70, 171, 184–5, 188–9, 203, 204, 208, 223, 238, 259, 274; Midland Beat 20; attendance 23; trotting 23, 27; Derby Day battle (1922) 29; during and after Second World War 87–8; *see also* Hill, Billy; Sabinis; Spot, Jack
Raczynski, Casimir 90
Rae, Norman 133
Raimo, Eddie 88
Ramensky, Johnny 231

Ramsay, Bobby 97, 98–9, 123, 147
Randall, Ginger 119, 207
Ranns, Arthur 246–7
Raphael, Geoffrey 247
Raphael, Monty 178
Ratcliffe, Owen 106–7
Read, Leonard ('Nipper') 122, 146–7, 169, 209, 211, 243, 288, 289, 291
Reader Harris, Richard MP 265
Reeder, Robert 277
Rees–Davies, Billy 199–200, 201
Regulation 18B 71, internment 21, 27, 69–71; Ascot racecourse camp 21, 70
Renucci, Julio 139
Reynolds, Jackie 66, 92, 104
Rice, Johnny 175, 217, 221, 222–5, 227
Rice, Sandy 27, 37
Richardson, Charlie 107, 201, 259
Richardson, Eddie 107, 201, 259
Richardson (aka Sadler), Fay 128–9, 262
Ridge, Chief Constable Charles 264
Rigbey, John (ex Flying Squad) 276
Riley, 'Gypsy' Phyllis May Blanche 123, 125, 167–8, 170–71, 246–7, 268, 279, 280
Rising Sun murder 192
Ritchie, John 216
Roberts, G.D. 'Khaki' 64, 180, 233, 247–8
Roche, Fred 72, 90
Roome, Alfred 110
Roper, William 269
Rosa, Jack 100

Rosa, Ray 212
Roseberry, Lord 116
Rosen, Hymie ('Little Hymie', 'Kid
   Rosen') 7–8, 84, 91, 114, 136,
   276
Ross, Sammy 109, 218, 282
Rossi, Bert 'Battles' 159, 212,
   218–20, 227–8, 230, 233,
   244–5, 253, 256, 280–81
Royal Commission on Gaming 290
Royal Variety Performance (1955)
   3
Russo, Victor ('Scarface Jock')
   104–5, 225–6, 229, 231

Sabini, Charles 21
Sabini, Charles snr 21, 22, 71
Sabini, Darby (Ullano) 12, 20–21,
   22, 27, 29, 30, 34–7, 39–41,
   51–3, 116, 155, 273–4, 289,
   292: first of gangland bosses
   20–21; early years 21–2; internment 21, 69–70; boxing,
   strong-arm man 22; appearance
   23; police and 25–6, 35, 37;
   arrest 27; racecourse protection
   see Sabinis; attacked by Cortesis
   36; describes himself 36; bankruptcy 51; sues for libel 51–2;
   moves to Brighton 52–3; death
   274
Sabini, Eliza (née Handley) 21, 22,
   71
Sabini, Frederick (aka Bob Wilson)
   21, 273
Sabini, George 22, 23, 33, 71
Sabini, Harry (Harryboy) 22–3,
   30, 34, 36, 39, 49, 51–2,
   274–5: internment 27, 69–71

Sabini, Harry jnr 275
Sabini, Joseph (aka Harry Lake)
   21–2, 23, 32, 33, 70
Sabinis ('the Italians', 'the Raddies')
   11, 20–53, 65, 69, 87, 116,
   177, 258, 274: racecourse
   crime, pitches and protection
   20–22, 24–31, 32–9, 41–2, 51;
   and the Cortesis 23, 35–8;
   Fratellanza Club and 23, 36,
   37; police and 25–6, 35, 37,
   38, 48; Derby Day battle 29;
   and Brummagen Boys 35; gang
   fighting 41–2; greyhound racing
   42–3; criminal protection and
   43, 72; and the Whites 42–3,
   47, 50–51, 274; and Croydon
   Airport robbery 43ff; end of
   Italian Mob 69–70
Sadler, Fay *see* Richardson, Fay
Sage, George 'Brummy' 27, 32–3,
   34
Sambridge, John 'Happy' 134
Samuels, Samuel 32, 48
Sands, ex-Chief Supt 84, 168
Schack, Bernard ('Codger', 'Sonny
   the Yank') 6, 7, 59, 62, 65,
   146, 190, 196–8, 276
Schenkman, Jacob 131
Scott, Ronnie 272
Scott, Sir Harold 168
Seaton, Reginald 162, 175, 178,
   180, 185, 199, 223, 224
Second World War 3, 21, 27,
   68–72, 139, 142, 144ff, 291: Hill
   and 68, 75; blackout 68–9, 75,
   87; black market 68–9, 75, 79,
   84; increased prostitution 69;
   deserters and 69; Spot and

Second World War – *cont'd*
71, 75, 78–81; robbery 75–6;
gaming 81–2; racing during 87;
petrol rationing 87
Setty, Stanley 157–8
Shackter, Bernard *see* Schack,
Bernard
Shaw, Sebag 180–81
Shawcross, Sir Hartley 244–5, 252,
255
Shepherd, William 52
Sherek, Henry 206
Short, Martin 287
Sibbett, Angus 134
Sidney Street, Siege of 102
Siegel, Bugsy 114
Silver, Mr 7–8, 9
Simmons, Nathaniel 'Itchky' 7,
62–3, 64–5
Simon, Sir John 57
Simpson, Mollie (later Comer)
60–61, 67
Sinclair, Det. Insp. 109
Skurry, Arthur 65, 66, 84, 91
Smart, Albert 14
Smith, Eddie ('Witch Doctor') 270
Smith, Henry 262–3
Smith, Joseph 26, 33
Smith, Rita 173
Smithson, Tommy (aka Mr Loser)
125–9, 262, 263
smuggling 137–50
Smythe, Mrs Barbara 199–200
Snoyman, Harry (aka Abe
Wiseman) 99
Solomon, Alfie 28, 29, 31, 39–41,
88
Solomon, Arthur 47
Solomon Harry (Henry) 29, 31

Solomons, Jack 4, 40, 63, 112,
113–15
Southern Cross 170, 171
South London Press 155
Sparkes, Reuben 'Brummy' 13
Sparks, Charlie 'Ruby' 18, 75
Sparks, Chief Supt Herbert 132,
178, 184, 192, 196, 200–201,
281, 285
Spinks, Jimmy 48
Spirito, François 140
Spot, Jack 1–3, 5–11, 20, 29, 42,
54–5, 59–63, 64–7, 71, 72, 87,
93, 102, 104–6, 112–13,
146–7, 155, 161, 170, 233,
252, 256, 259–60, 274, 276,
277–8, 280, 285–6, 292: fight
with Dimes and after 1–2, 39,
174–85, 187–8, 191, 194–6,
198–9, 203, 225, 229, 247,
268; appearance, dress 2, 5,
169, 236–7, 283–4, 286–7;
King of the Underworld 2, 54,
105, 288; and Billy Hill 2,
9–10, 12, 93–4, 100, 103–4,
106, 108, 124, 132, 146, 167,
179, 218, 228, 287, 289;
memoirs: *Jack Spot: The Man of
a Thousand Cuts* 3, 6, 12, 61,
110, 168–9, 281; early years,
school 5–11; jobs, first thefts
and convictions 6, 8–9, 60;
Merchant Navy 7; and protection rackets, clubs 8, 9, 61–2,
103–4, 106, 195, 225, 236,
290; racecourses, bookmaking
9, 24, 81, 87, 88–9, 90–91, 93,
105, 115, 169–70, 171–2,
173–4, 184–6, 203–4; Mollie

Simpson (later Comer) 9, 60–61, 66–7; 'Take a Pick' scam 10; welshing and 10, 287; describes himself 18, 60, 82, 282, 284; 'Champion of the Jews' legend, anti-Semitism and 54–5, 59, 61, 79–80, 91, 92–3, 115, 169, 225, 241, 282, 290–91; and Jimmy Wooder 62–3; crime during Second World War 71, 75, 78–81; in Royal Artillery 78–9; working in the North 79–81, 101–2, 105, 106, 115–16, 124, 168, 173; gaming and 81–5, 130–31, 168; police and 85, 118–19, 189, 289; crime post-war 87ff; and Rita Molloy (later Mrs Comer) 101–2, 105, 113, 168, 177, 188, 194–6, 198–9, 201, 203, 210, 211, 213–17, 222, 225, 227–8, 230, 233, 236–43, 258, 280, 284, 286, 289, 290; Heathrow Airport 'disaster' 108–9, 110, 111–12, 113, 122; and the Mob 113–14, 130; and Jack Solomons 114–15; debt-collecting 115, 124; and Darby Sabini 116; contract killing and 124–5; and Tommy Smithson slashing 127, 129; on the slide 130–36; and Duncan Webb 134–6, 155, 159, 190, 218, 225, 230, 231–2, 235, 238; in decline 167–8, 169–70, 171–4, 203; and Krays 171–2, 262, 268; is mean 208, 287–8; plans to shoot Hill and Dimes, and

repercussions 208–9, 209–18; is slashed 209–20, 233–5, 258, 286; and Tommy Falco slashing 221, 222–6, 235; bankruptcy 235–7, 238–9; deported from Canada 237–8; Highball Club and 239–41, 242; reformed life 241–2; downfall 258, 287–8; last court appearance 281–2; ends working career 282–5; opinions on 288–9, 290–91; death 291; *see also* Comacho, Alexander; Dimes, Albert; Hill, Billy

Stafford, Dennis 134
Steward, Lipman Leonard ('Darkie') 269–70
Streatfield, Mr Justice 223, 227, 267
'Stuttering Robo' 96
Sullivan, Alexander ('Sonny') 120, 122, 127, 131, 167
Sullivan, Dan 22
Sullivan, Frederick ('Slip') 122, 125–7, 166–7, 204
Sullivan, Michael 31
Sullivan, Mrs 166, 167
Sunday Chronicle 59, 61, 148, 168, 175, 188, 236
Sunday Dispatch 45, 61
Sunday Pictorial 194
Sunday Times 287
Sutton, Fred 22
Swaffer, Hannen 153, 206–7
Swan, Benny 92, 104
Swanland, Cecil 44–5
Swift, Lord Justice 34

Taylor, Charlie 237, 260, 275, 276, 279

Taylor, Louis 130–31
Taylor, William 103
Teddy, 'Odd Legs' *see* Hughes, Teddy
telephone tapping 290
Thomas, Christopher 128
Thomas, Peter Haig 100–101
Thomas, Robert 239
Thorp, Det. Insp. Arthur 73
Tietjen, Arthur 187
Tiger Lil 2
Tilly, John ('John the Tilter') 97
Times, The 28, 56–7, 159, 197;
    Index 190
Tomasso, Alexander *see* Rice,
    Sandy
Tomasso, Paul 37
Topical Times 51–2
Torture Trial 201, 281
Townie, Andrew 23
Townsend, Group Captain Peter
    195
Trinder, Tommy 3
Tulip (Maltese pimp) 123, 125
Turpin, Randolph 114–15, 169

Underworld (BBC TV) 287
Union of Post Office Workers 241
Upton Park Mob 65–6, 91, 92,
    100, 104, 108, 123

Vagrancy Act 10–11
Vaughan, John 51
Vibart, Peter 234, 250, 256
Vizard, Gertrude Adeline 192–4

Wadham, Herbert Gardner 156–7
Walcott, Jersey Joe 169
Walker, Billy 142
Walker, George 142

Wandsworth prison 100, 125
Ward, Robert 192
Ward, Simon 207
Wardle, Donald 278
Warren, Johnny 91, 92
Warren, Robert (Bobby) 204, 211,
    212–17, 226, 228, 230, 244,
    251, 253, 256
Watney Streeters 11, 264
Watts, Marthe Marie 69, 158–9
Webb, Cynthia (formerly Hume)
    157–8, 275
Webb, Thomas Duncan 3, 15, 93,
    114, 135–6, 150, 153–9
    passim, 190, 205–6, 217–18,
    225–6, 230–32, 238, 251–2,
    275, 285
Westbury, Billy 39
West End Boys 45
West, George (aka Dai Thomas)
    32–3, 45
White, Alf snr 29–34 *passim*, 42,
    46–7, 51, 87, 89, 90–94, 132
White, Alf jnr 46, 89
White, Carrie 46
White, Harry 50–51, 72, 89–90,
    91–3, 132, 180, 214, 223,
    274–5, 292
White, Johnny 89
White, William 46, 89
Whites 71, 87–94, 96, 119, 168,
    189, 274
Wicks, Jim 48
Wickstead, Commander Bert
    ('Gangbuster', 'Grey Fox') 122,
    261
Wilkins, Bert 48–50, 100
Wilkins, Bud 271
Williams, Sidney 214

Williamson, Boyd 260
Wilson, Clyde 178
Wirth, John 110
Wiseman, Abe 76
Wood, George (aka George Wallis)
    84, 91, 94, 108, 110, 122, 173,
    176, 190, 275, 288
Wood, James (Jimmy) 29, 31, 94,
    108, 110, 122, 176, 190,
    211–12, 275, 288

Wooder, Jimmy 47, 48, 49, 62–4,
    69, 91, 116
Workers' Circle Friendly Society
    134
Wyatt, Jock 77–8, 89

Yiddishers 35–6, 69, 72
de Yong, Moss 28
Young, George 177
Young, Ruby 192–3